RED TORY

How the Left and Right Have Broken Britain and How We Can Fix It

Phillip Blond

ff

faber and faber

First published in 2010
by Faber and Faber Limited
Bloomsbury House
74–77 Great Russell Street
London WC1B 3DA

Typeset by Donald Sommerville
Printed in England by CPI Mackays, Chatham

The right of Phillip Blond to be identified as author of this work
has been asserted in accordance with Section 77 of the Copyright,
Designs and Patents Act 1988

A CIP record for this book
is available from the British Library

ISBN 978–0–571–25167–4

10 9 8 7 6 5 4 3 2

Red Tory

Phillip Blond is a political thinker, writer and journalist. He was senior lecturer in theology and philosophy at the University of Cumbria until he left to take up a career in politics and public policy. He founded and now directs the think-tank ResPublica. He writes for the *Guardian*, *The Times*, *Financial Times*, the *Daily Mail*, the *Independent* and the *Sunday Times*. He appears regularly on the BBC.

by the same author

POST-SECULAR PHILOSOPHY (ED.)

To my Mother

For the Unfallen

Contents

Acknowledgements

I would like to thank several people without whom this book would not have been possible. Firstly the research staff at ResPublica who put together the briefings without which I would not have been able to complete the book. They are Adam Schoenborn, who worked on a number of aspects but particularly on the social crisis and democratic renewal chapters. Samuel Middleton, who, almost single-handed, put together the material for the prosperity chapter, and Sandra Gruescu who worked particularly on the family and its history. Secondly I would like to thank NESTA for their permission to republish a version of the 'Ownership State' paper that we published in September 2009 and I would like to repeat my thanks to all those who helped with that publication, particularly Simon Caulkin and John Seddon. Others who contributed to various aspects of the book were Michael Merrick, Emma Gordan, Dina Reznikova, Caroline McFarland and Kim Mandeng. I would also like to profoundly thank my agent Hannah Westland from RCW, and Kate Murray-Browne and Neil Belton from Faber and Faber, all of whom have persisted and positively encouraged the production and creation of what has now appeared. Finally my most consummate thanks and deepest debt go to John Milbank without whose time, dedication and sheer editorial enthusiasm this book would have not have appeared.

Thank you to you all.

Introduction

The problem

Something is seriously wrong with Britain. This is an intuition that everybody, whatever their politics, shares. But what is this malaise from which we suffer? We all know the symptoms: increasing fear, lack of trust and abundance of suspicion, long-term increase in violent crime, loneliness, recession, depression, private and public debt, family break-up, divorce, infidelity, bureaucratic and unresponsive public services, dirty hospitals, powerlessness, the rise of racism, excessive paperwork, longer and longer working hours, children who have no parents, concentrated and seemingly irremovable poverty, the permanence of inequality, teenagers with knives, teenagers being knifed, the decline of politeness, aggressive youths, the erosion of our civil liberties and the increase of obsessive surveillance, public authoritarianism, private libertarianism, general pointlessness, political cynicism and a pervading lack of daily joy.

This intuition is not just a private opinion held by a disgruntled few but a public discernment universally shared though seldom addressed. The inability of current politics to tackle these issues successfully requires serious reflection. Certainly all parties engage in ever more ferocious PR about measures to tackle violent youths, ineffective bureaucracies or dysfunctional families and their children. But none of the measures ever really amounts to much, nor do they seem to arrest the social trends that produce such dreadful outcomes. As a result we have a widening gap between the public and contemporary politics – and this has a number of dangerous consequences. It is not just that racist and fascist parties like the BNP grow and prosper in the face of widespread white working-class estrangement, nor is it the mere fact of declining participation in political elections. It is more serious and more ubiquitous than both. This gap between the politics of the elites and general mass disaffection reflects, and is caused by, a wholesale collapse of British culture, virtue and belief.

When I say that British culture has collapsed, we again, whatever our political beliefs, almost immediately recognise the truth of it. Our parents will tell us that things truly were better before: that children really were polite, that people really did know their neighbours, and that, yes, whole families really did stay together and form lasting bonds with their relations. In response, university lecturers in cultural studies departments will claim that everybody has always thought that things were better in the past and that we are consumed by false nostalgia and fake memories, and that if history is always conditional and constructed then truth and real achievement are social fictions produced by vested interests. Historically however, we now know that our elders (who for the most part are our betters) are right. Though some things were clearly worse (income levels and general health), many things were better in the past (familial security, human association and the percentage of carbon in the atmosphere). By denying their memories we are denying ourselves the recollection of a better and nobler recent history.

The loss of our culture is evinced in other ways. Perhaps it is best understood as the disappearance of British civil society. By civil society I connote everything that ordinary citizens do that is not reducible to the imposed activities of the central state or the compulsion and determination of the marketplace. So defined, it appears that we are now a flat society. By this I mean that there are only two powers in our country: the state and the marketplace. All other sources of independent autonomous power have been crushed. We no longer have, in any effective independent way, local government, churches, trade unions, cooperative societies, publicly funded educational institutions, civic organisations or locally organised groups that operate on the basis of more than single issues. Whatever these various institutions represent now, what they embodied in the past were means for ordinary people to exercise power. These associations helped to give form and direction to human beings; they allowed parents to craft their families and citizens to shape their communities. Nowadays, however, all such sources of independent power have been eroded; instead, these civil spaces have either vanished or become subject-domains of the centralised state or the monopolised market.

The state and the market have advanced from both left and right on virtually all the self-governing and independent domains that previously constituted civil society in Britain.

By finding civil society unbearably local, uneconomic or uneven, the market state was able to control and determine its character and so abolish genuine participation in society.[1] This uncritical alliance between the state and the market is highly peculiar. In a uniquely Anglo-American fashion, it was decided shortly after Mrs Thatcher's election in 1979 that the interests of the state and the market were synonymous. All her supporters agreed that to further the interests of the latter we had to restrict the activities of the former, but in order to extend the interests of the market, Thatcher had to increase the power of the state – a logic that was only compounded and increased by New Labour. Both market and state thus accrued power in the name of democracy, and effectively and progressively excluded ordinary citizens from economic and democratic participation. The market has become captured by producer interests along with the state, and, even though both political parties have offered an ideology that pretends that the reverse is true, there can be little doubt that the legacy of both, and of the last thirty years, has been economic and political exclusion for the many, and massive and monopolised enrichment for the few.

Why the governing elites in both Britain and America created this state of affairs and viewed the resulting market state as desirable requires explanation. That is to be found both in history and ideology, which I will come to a little later. Now, though, and perhaps for the first time in almost two generations, the financial meltdown of 2007/8 has given us an opportunity to see the game as it really is. We see that the crisis is due in no small part to the ideological and political complicity between Thatcher and Reagan over capital controls (or the need for abandoning them) and a naive market fundamentalism that allowed the banks to game the state and rig the market. Nor have many demurred (until now) from the continuing fervent advocacy of the market state by Clinton and Blair and Bush and Brown. Only now can we glimpse an alternative – one that can perhaps give us a truly free market and a properly participatory state, in which citizens feel valued.

Just about the only other country that has marshalled the state as rigorously as Britain and America to serve vested interests is communist China. And we can see the consequences of this insistent uniformity on our own high streets, as British towns – far from being expressions of region and locality – have become hideous homogeneous consumer zones that are indistinguishable from one another. Small businesses put off by high rents cannot get a foothold, as large retail concerns command via covert subsidy (in terms of business rates, transport infrastructure and low-taxed parking space) the economies of scale that their operations require and so dictate their presence and the shape of every high street and shopping centre. This impacts on the local economy as money is drained from the provinces to feed the corporate centre and we are all made into passive clients of a commerce that has no local distinction or allegiance. Smaller farmers, exhausted by the price-cutting demands of the large supermarkets, give up and surrender their fields to those who practise the pesticide monoculture that their land monopoly permits.

Even one trip abroad to France or Germany will show that this arrangement need not prevail. On the continent they still have what one can call a society and they still practise public expressions of a diverse culture. Partly this is because they long ago decided that the interests of the state and the market don't necessarily coincide. Traditionally they have seen the role of the state as that of protecting and sheltering the nation from the extremes of market monopolisation and fluctuation. Both Germany's federalist system and France's republican tradition have ensured that there is a healthy plurality of political power in the country and a balance between centre and periphery. This structural political complexity, combined with a view that the interest of the state differs from that of the marketplace, has ensured that civil society is both required and desired.

Such an active society of participating citizens has clear structural underpinnings. To quote Simon Jenkins, 'the lowest tier of government in France is the commune. It has an average population of 1,580. Germany's lowest tier is 4,925 ... The British average is 118,400.'[2] Though this example ignores English parishes, it does capture the scale of the accountability deficit. Little wonder then that British people are unable to control their own community, and that smaller units of political democracy have been progressively abolished by the central state for reasons of administrative ease, cost effectiveness and the desire for absolute control.

However, this present crisis is not just a matter of political structure, abstract theories, and debates about things that do not impinge on ordinary life. The crisis of civil society impacts upon us in the most intimate way. We are more isolated than at any other time in recorded history. We increasingly live alone and fail to have children, and when we do marry or cohabit it is for less time than at any stage since records began. The extended family has been destroyed and now the nuclear one is vanishing as well. The vast majority of us exercise little or no power within our own communities; we work within parameters established by others, according to agendas imposed from above. Most of us avoid voting at local elections, and little more than half manage to make it to the polls for national ones. We certainly don't join a church or political party; we probably don't know our neighbours; and we have fewer friends and social contacts than any British generation for which figures exist. The very idea of working with others to represent our collective interests or challenge some political decision is almost unthinkable. We would rather be stuck at home watching re-runs of *Friends* than making any.

The argument

British civil society, which is the source and well-spring of our culture, has been flattened by the unleashed authoritarianism of the state and the unrestricted freedom granted to the market. But something had to unleash the state and something had to give free rein to the market. In order for these powers to break all limits and moral restraints, our society had to collapse from within. A stronger civic culture would have permitted modernisation and technological development without sacrificing its social foundations. A more active and participatory civic culture would never have let the state destroy every alternative source of power. Other equally developed and indeed somewhat more advanced countries have not experienced a social collapse on anything like the British scale. Japan maintains traditional values – often against the demands of the market, precisely because its civic culture will accept nothing less. Similarly Germans tend only to buy a house in their native region in spite of being, if anything, more technologically advanced than us. The Spanish, even after the hideous train bombings sponsored by Al Qaeda, did not bring in any new oppressive laws, nor has Spain abandoned its hard-won liberties by retreating to its fascist past.

But in Britain we have achieved none of those things; listless and indifferent, we slide into a post-democratic culture of passive consumption and political acquiescence. Even the parliamentary expenses scandal, which seemed to implicate an entire political class in lazy corruption, has not sparked any new political formations. People seemed to favour smaller and more non-conventional parties in the UK county council elections of 2009, but nobody doubts that the major parties will dominate the general election in 2010 and things will, they fear, then proceed much as before. The future does not look much better than the immediate past: those aged 18–34 are more likely to choose a candidate in a *Big Brother* house eviction than they are to exercise their vote in a general election. In post-cultural Britain, only the market state and its vested interests rule, as we inactive and unhappy Britons pursue the only mass group activity left to us: the status competition of compulsive consumption.

The story

One cannot have a vibrant culture disseminated from the top down. If it is only the elites who are cultured we will have an oligarchy that calls itself civilised, while denying others a similar benefit; similarly, though one can have (and we do) a mass civilisation with a minority, or virtually non-existent culture, this is no reason to deny the existence of a higher kind of civilisation or the possibility of mass participation in it. Contrary to both extremes, a high mass culture has indeed existed in Britain; it was achieved by the working class and it has flourished at several times in our history. In calling for its resurrection I am being neither a-historical nor hopelessly romantic. What does seem to be a-historical and romantic is the belief that we can survive without a higher culture that is shared in by all and thereby enriched by all.

The British have always benefited from having a relatively organic culture. Our nation, despite its contested history, has – with the exception of the Civil War – never fatally divided over ideology. This is no small achievement: one reason why much of Europe fell into fascist or communist politics was because of this divide between the extremes of left and right. Mark Mazower's book *The Dark Continent* paints an unforgettable picture of societies tearing each other apart.[3] A separate and separated European elite despised and feared its mass peasant and proletarian populations. Right-wingers retreated into narrow nationalistic and racial hierarchies to defend the status quo, while the European left, increasingly trans-national, prophesied their downfall and called for the establishment of a new world order where nothing ancient would be preserved and all the old verities would be destroyed. Thus was Europe divided between two mutually exclusive traditions where each earnestly sought the destruction of its opposite.

Between these two extremes Britain managed to chart a more virtuous course. Any visit to an Oxbridge college where the names of the student dead from the world wars are inscribed on the walls will show you that the British elite died in almost as great a proportion as the poor, and any study of letters from the front written by the British 'Tommy' in WWI shows that many amongst the working classes died to defend a specifically British vision of a better world. Culturally speaking, the British have more often than not denied that the separation between the classes spoke of a more fundamental divide between them as men. Before the BBC was betrayed by John Birt and his ilk, there were giants like John Reith who, thank God, did not believe in choice but 'in equal access to things that are great' – a tradition that itself extends back to Tyndale's translation of the Bible and to Shakespeare, Marlowe and the other Elizabethan playwrights, all of whom spoke to both commoners and aristocrats. It was only with the advent of Restoration Comedy after Charles II's return that we began to get a modern art-form designed exclusively for the aristocrats and the court. And these writings could never stand against the genius of the poet-warrior Milton or his legacy as personified in Blake, Shelley, Coleridge or Keats. Our culture at its best has always spoken to all of us, and from the highest to the lowest it has always called us to a universal vision of a shared commonwealth.

And despite what some might think today, ordinary people used to have a very vivid cultural life indeed: Handel's musical legacy was largely sustained by them. Even before the Industrial Revolution people were not, as Marx and Engels supposed, living lives of 'rural idiocy' and mindless feudalism. There was a vibrant agrarian culture coupled with domestic production of finished goods in the market towns and cities. There really was a prosperous and relatively secure British peasantry – a class progressively destroyed by enclosure and its gradual acceleration in the Tudor period, further consolidation during the Civil War and the final acts of peasant dispossession during the Industrial Revolution.

Thanks to the conversion of parliamentary elites to the spurious logic of farm improvement via land dispossession, between 1750 and 1850 over 7.5 million acres of open fields and common land were lost to private enclosure, licensed through Parliament. The agrarian peasant class who had previously farmed this land were driven from it into the large and expanding cities. The working poor, deprived of security and livelihood, drifted to these large urban centres; there they formed the landless dispossessed mass that we now call the working class. Members of this newly created industrial proletariat were in a dire situation. Indigent and powerless, they relied on subsistence factory wages for survival. All the familial and social structures that had sustained them throughout the previous centuries had been erased; they either had to build them anew or succumb to the new economic order.

Yet these new industrial workers were a people whose intellectual and political qualities have been much maligned. When John Carey charts in his *The Intellectuals and the Masses* the all-too-typical story of intellectual and aristocratic distaste for mass proletarian culture, he himself falls into this paradigm, writing that 'the difference between the nineteenth-century mob and the twentieth-century mass is literacy'.[4] Leaving aside the fact that twentieth-century political achievements were the result of the activities and organisations begun by nineteenth-century workers, we also forget an earlier even more radical peasant history. The English had their revolution in the seventeenth century, well over a hundred years earlier than the rest of Europe, and this extraordinary event was coupled with levels of literacy that were not equalled until the beginning of the twentieth century. And if, at Putney Marshes in 1647, the Levellers had not lost to Cromwell's defence of the landowning class, who he claimed alone had a 'permanent interest' in the country, then the history of Britain would have been very different indeed. There never really was an illiterate working class mob. Always and everywhere one can find examples of cogent, intellectual and practical proletarian resistance. Mobs, such as they were, rarely acted spontaneously. Often they were the products of political organisation and design operating at the behest of radical factions to secure political advantage – a history that reveals the present state of working-class diffidence and powerlessness as a historical aberration.

Given that the collapse of our civic culture is most evident (though not necessarily most present) in the working-class sink estates that surround our cities, I have begun with working-class culture, but with what it was as opposed to what it became. E. P. Thompson commenced his celebrated work *The Making of the English Working Class* with an account of the inauguration of the London Corresponding Society in 1792. The society, a working-class association dedicated to extending the electoral franchise, consisted of weavers, shoemakers and tradesmen, who campaigned for electoral reform by writing to one another and engaging in public debate. Successful and widespread in the 1790s, the society and others like it were in the end viciously repressed by the British government and various of their members were indicted for high treason.

Partial victory seemed to be finally achieved with the Great Reform Act of 1832, which extended the franchise. Of course those who were wholly without property were among those still excluded; in response the Chartist movement campaigned vigorously for over twenty years for the enfranchisement of the poor and their access to political power.

Whilst it was the alliance with the Liberals in February 1858 that effectively ended the Chartist movement, working-class agitation and organisation continued apace. Throughout the nineteenth century, the workers formed friendly societies and social unions based on earlier agricultural bonds – they came together, and re-made communities and loyalties around their places of work and residence. They educated themselves and encouraged their children to do even better. Autonomous working-class social institutions arose and gave birth to health-insurance schemes, mutual-aid societies and the trade unions. Together such organisations began to better the lives of the working poor. Finally, of course, at the beginning of the twentieth century came the hope of political power with the formation and rise of the Labour Party, a party – ostensibly at least – dedicated to protecting the interests and needs of British working people.

Leaving aside the insurance schemes introduced in the early twentieth century by the Liberals under pressure from the Labour Party, and the various specific improvements in working conditions and working time, the welfare state has commonly been taken as the zenith of working-class achievement and aspiration. This longed-for measure came into being as a result of Clement Attlee's Labour administration elected, against all expectation, in 1945. While the aspiration for a universal system of care was right and necessary, and was indeed supported by all parties, its particular implementation and organisation has had a number of invidious consequences.

Perhaps the chief reason why the welfare state went astray was that the governing elite imposed a bureaucratic and centralised vision of the caring state upon a working class that wished for something far more radical, more mutual and more empowering. All working-class welfare organisations were sidelined by a universal entitlement, guaranteed by the state, based upon centralised assessments of need. Local requirements, organisation or practices were gradually ignored and rendered redundant. The welfare state, I believe, began the destruction of the independent life of the British working class.

This new configuration of state and citizen made the populace a supplicant citizenry dependent on the state rather than themselves, and it aborted indigenous traditions of working-class self-help, mutuality and social insurance. Rather than working with one another in order to change their situation or their locality, relying on the welfare state only to get them through a temporary rough patch, some working-class people increasingly became permanent passive recipients of centrally determined benefits. In this way, welfare ceased to function as a safety net through which people could not fall, becoming instead a ceiling through which the supplicant class – cut off from earlier working-class ambition and aspiration – could not break. This 'benefits culture' can be tied directly to the thwarting of working-class ambition by a middle-class elite who formed the machinery of the welfare state, partly indeed to alleviate poverty, but also to deprive the poor of their irritating habit of autonomous organisation.

Disempowered, with the structure of their lives increasingly formed around a centralised state which imposed its own solutions on them, working-class people had no way to influence the state that had been made in their name. This was particularly obvious in the 1960s when the welfare state began to destroy the extended family: the very institution that had kept the poor together during the poverty of the 1930s and the Blitz. Working-class parents were separated from their grown-up children when, under the impact of centrally based assessments, needy newcomers were housed at the expense of local people and their families. Bequeathing a legacy of racism and inner-city fragmentation, the welfare state shattered the vivid communal life of the urbanised white working class.

In addition, when in the 1960s fragments of the middle classes, some of them associated with the 'new left', preached personal pleasure as a means of public salvation, they had little idea what they were doing. While toxic to civilised middle-class life, this mixture was lethal to the working class. Some measure of sexual liberation was necessary, and could have led to a deepening of loyal relationships between men and women. But, in reality, it was contaminated by narcissism from the outset. For the working class this narcissism meant the dissolving of the social bonds that had kept the poorest together during the worst times of the 1930s – illegitimacy increased and family breakdown began in earnest.

In politics this new left is to be distinguished from the older more statist and more paternalist variant that had already lost power in the UK in the election of 1951. In addition the new left itself was torn between, on the one hand, an admirable concern with civil liberties and the ongoing debacle in Vietnam and, on the other, an increasing concern with identity politics, feelings of personal alienation and the subjective demands of an individualist and self-obsessed social class. This latter legacy increasingly disengaged the new left from the politics and needs of working-class people, as a politics of desire overwhelmed whatever was good and decent in its prior ethic. This license to express the self allowed the advocates of liberation in the late 1960s to embrace drugs and hedonism as if personal emancipation for bohemians would lead to the liberation of all.

The impact of this culture was first felt by working-class people in the breakdown of their families and consequently in their communities. And through the widespread imitation of this invidious and corrosive legacy, such a culture of self-indulgence has continued to flourish. The family is the first and the most intimate social institution that human beings have – it might vary by extension but nothing can challenge its decisive importance. But just look at what has happened to the British family: in 1964, 63,300 births were recorded outside marriage, only 7.3% of all births. In 2003 it was 257,225, over 41% of all those born. If present trends continue, soon the majority of UK children will be born out of wedlock, with all the pejorative consequences for the young that both sociology and statistics have amply elucidated. For example, each child born to unmarried parents has only a 38% chance of seeing out their childhood with both parents present. Marriage is clearly better for children: 70% of children of married parents can expect their mother and father to stay together during their childhood. But marriage is failing too: the number of divorces rose in 2008 to 167,000; in 1961 there were only 27,000 divorces granted. The picture isn't pretty – with family breakdown for many, the fundamental bedrock of civic life in Britain has been destroyed. It was some of the very people who thought themselves left-wing – the pleasure-seeking, mind-altering drug takers and sexual pioneers of the 1960s who instigated the fragmentation of the working-class family and sold the poor the poisonous idea of liberation through chemical and sexual experimentation.

In this way a segment of the left further opened the personal sphere to modern consumer capitalism. It began to commodify sexual relations; it was first to abandon the family for the delights of self-gratification. And it was a population shaped by the values of this left which the Conservatives spoke to so strongly in the person of Mrs Thatcher.

While the left had opened the personal sphere to capitalism, public culture was still formed by traditional practices and institutions. Mrs Thatcher, elected in 1979, instigated a much-needed modernisation of the British economy. Unfortunately, however, she threw the baby out with the bathwater by completely surrendering the entirety of British public life and its related values to the dictates of a neo-liberalism whose consequences she would not have supported and the operations of which she clearly did not understand. Instead of a popular capitalism with open and free markets, what we got instead was a capitalism captured by concentrations of capital and a market monopolised by vested interest and the dominance of the already wealthy. With the bottom half of the population progressively de-capitalised and subject to an ever-widening array of barriers to market entry, more and more people were unable to fulfil the promise of a capitalism for all. With no investment in, or transitional mechanisms for, those who were not yet ready to compete and prosper, whole traditions, regions and a generation or two were sacrificed to the demands of the neo-liberal market. If socialists laid waste to the private sphere, Mrs Thatcher completed the evisceration of British culture by allowing the same in the public realm. The clearly un-conservative idea that the market was the ultimate arbiter of value and the measure of all things ensured that civic life was ignored and that the interests of the state and the market were viewed as synonymous.

The neo-liberalism espoused by Mrs Thatcher was not quite the innovation it was commonly understood to be. Ted Heath's 1970 manifesto was more Thatcherite than anything ever published by the Iron Lady. Quite apart from the fact that the neo-liberals in the Conservative Party never forgave Heath for his corporatist U-turn of 1972, neo-liberal values were already established in the private lives and practices of the emergent British consumer class. In this sense Thatcher and the 1960s' left were already colluding in the reduction of all political questions to the neo-liberal maxims of freedom and economic liberalisation. The consequences of this collusion reached its apogee with John Major, under whom the nation embarked on a disastrous privatisation of the railways, while public services began to fail with the strain of under-provision and over-use.

When elected in May 1997, New Labour spoke to the public disquiet about the state of public services and the rise of a rootless mercantile materialism. Labour promised a renewed social contract, with increasing prosperity paying for a re-vivified welfare state. Some thirteen years on, the reality looks somewhat different. In truth, what New Labour offered was the worst of the left and the worst of the right. Concerning the left, statism of the most pernicious sort was embraced. Centralised standards were invented and imposed across a whole range of British public life. Sectors of the public realm largely untouched by Mrs Thatcher were now forced into competition that empowered managers rather than consumers. The health service, universities and schools were denied autonomy and given ever narrower remits. They were forced to operate with centralised benchmarks that pre-determined need outside of local consultation. The imposition of such targets distorted professional standards and further eroded the ethos that had previously underpinned public provision in Britain. Coupled with such centralising tendencies, the public sector was also at the same time subjected to the market. With internal health service markets imposed from above, school league tables enforced on a national scale and government interference with university admissions, the public sector was being alternately exposed to destabilising competition and rigid state control.

Much of the vaunted reputation and self-image of Blair and Brown lay in their claim to tackle social exclusion and poverty. Yet on their watch poverty has concentrated, inequality has increased and social mobility is worse than it was in the 1950s. Poverty doubled during Mrs Thatcher's premiership, a legacy which – despite much spin – New

Labour has barely dented. Inde... coefficient (the most widely accept... remained at 0.33, the same as when L...

Finally, and perhaps most worryingly, authoritarianism was (because of the terr... 11 September 2001 in New York and in Lond... 2007) allowed full rein. New Labour has either ... or removed (or attempted to remove) our most fundan... liberties. Habeas corpus has been suspended, mere suspic... of terrorist intent now merits permanent incarceration, and the government, in tacit compliance with foreign powers, has permitted extraordinary rendition, torture and extra-judicial police action.

Prior to the worldwide debt crisis of 2008, the truth is that, in spite of all the propaganda about endless economic growth and the awesome creativity of bankers and financiers, in the last thirty years (long before the global meltdown) the poor lost almost all of their savings and liquid capital, while they and the middle class have taken on unprecedented levels of personal debt. As official statistics demonstrate, the share of the non-propertied wealth enjoyed by the bottom 50% of the population fell from 12% in 1976 to just 1% in 2003 whereas, in the same period, the share enjoyed by the top 10% rose from 57% to 71%. Even when property is included, half the population still owns only 7% of the country's wealth. Clearly a bad asset situation has, for the worst-off, only become more invidious under the putative benefits of monopoly markets and debt-financed capitalism. Debt levels exploded under New Labour. When Blair came in 1997, the total debt held by individuals was £570 million. Just over ten years later it has leaped 165% to £1,512 billion.[5] This is an average increase of 10% for every year that New Labour has been in power. The debt problem is so fundamental to neo-liberalism that it extends also to the state, where our financial problems are so extreme and the global system of unregulated capitalism so murky that we don't even know, as a result of the banking assets that the Treasury has underwritten, how bad our public debt really is nor how long it will take to repay it.

The real outcome of the last thirty years of the left/right legacy is a state of disempowerment. Nowadays we have the worst of the left and the right combined in one philosophy: an authoritarian, illiberal, bureaucratic state coupled with an extreme ideology of markets and the unlimited sway of capital. Little wonder then that most Britons feel they cannot influence their locality let alone their region or nation. Passive and compliant, all we can do is shop – and after a while that doesn't make us particularly happy either.

It is not too much of an exaggeration to speak of a totalitarian culture developing in Britain. By this I do not just mean the repressive authoritarianism of New Labour with its ID cards, suspension of civil liberties and its crawling connivance with the extra-judicial policies of America under George Bush. I also mean the spineless duplicity embodied by David Blunkett's finest achievement as home secretary – the extradition of British citizens without an evidentiary hearing to the USA, or the European Arrest warrants which came into force in 2004 and which subject British citizens to the legal procedures of countries like Bulgaria – nations whose legal codes and procedures are so different, so corrupt and so open to abuse that no British citizen should be subject to them without a prior evidentiary hearing. And in Gordon Brown we had a Prime Minister who, for the sake of personal political authority, was willing to sacrifice habeas corpus for a statute that would have allowed forty-two days' detention without trial, a measure opposed by former intelligence chiefs, lawyers and the judiciary, and without any practical effect in the struggle to prevent terrorism. We imprison more people than any other country in Western Europe, and we have created the largest DNA database in the world, containing the genetic information of not only convicted criminals but over a million innocent citizens, 100,000 of whom are children. Then there is the notorious Investigatory Powers Act of 2000, a piece of legislation that has allowed nearly 800 government departments and public bodies to intercept our mail, tap our phones and look at our e-mails. Such is their insatiable curiosity, inevitable once the state is given licence to interfere in citizen's lives, that over a thousand requests to do just this are made every day. A culture of suspicion has developed that would be familiar to anyone who has seen *The Lives of Others*, the great film about the East German Stasi. In 2008 it emerged that Poole Borough Council had hired private investigators to spy for two weeks on the family of an infant school applicant whom they (wrongly) suspected of not living in the catchment area for the local school.

The alliance of the market and the state has produced a new oligarchy that spuriously claims to speak on behalf of the common rather than the vested interest. Ordinary concerns, be they local or simply less powerful than those of the state or large concentrations of money, are subject to a repressive consensus whereby whatever new vested interests or oligarchies demand becomes a de facto requirement for every aspect of our lives. We are all affected by the violence and public drunkenness that has followed the radical deregulation of pub opening hours and alcohol prices, which benefits only the large drinks manufacturers. Think also of the marketing that children are subjected to by our toy and clothing manufacturers; think of how television induces status competition between infants and presents children as sexually available. We fondly imagine that we differ in our private thoughts and opinions – but this is Solzhenitsyn's mechanism for imagining freedom whilst imprisoned in the Gulag.

However, even our minds are not free. In order to be truly liberated we have to be able to imagine an alternative to the prevailing order. This we manifestly cannot do at present. So colonised have we become by consumption, fantasies of glamour, and cynicism about the public good that we cannot envisage anything different from that which we currently experience. In order to create such an alternative one has to look both backwards and forwards. Backwards, because history tells us that things were different once and that what has happened need not have occurred. Forwards because with knowledge of an alternative past in a manner that isn't simply naive or idealistic, it is possible to envisage a better future that we all might inhabit.

Alternatives

So let me begin by looking backwards into my own past. In the 1980s I was left-wing. Growing up during Mrs Thatcher's premiership, I was appalled by the Conservatives. There was a reckless disregard for those who had become economically outmoded, a contempt for the poor, and a huge increase in the power and authority of the state. These Thatcherites seemed philistine; they had no appreciation for anything other than money and power. They despised the autonomy and power of anybody other than themselves and did everything they could to destroy all opposition. They abandoned perfectly decent businesses and looked with seeming pride on the doubling of poverty under their auspices.

But even then I had my doubts that anything good could be achieved by the state. It struck me that welfare was really only a form of very low wages and that it didn't seem particularly radical or transformative to agitate for small increases that would still be insufficient to meet human need. And that was all anybody really seemed to argue for – as if welfare could ever be the real solution to poverty. I hated Scargill, yet still sympathised with the miners as I thought that working-class communities shouldn't simply be abandoned to their fate once coal had become uneconomic to produce.

What I liked about socialism was its concern with social justice – the idea that our society should be ordered according to principles of equity, goodness and fairness. And it has to be said that many admirable policies came from the left: the refusal of racism, votes for women or the extension of voting to those without property. The left historically tended to position itself on the side of social justice. At that time it seemed to me that only the radical left-wing tradition believed in a society run for the good of all. I was also a republican, in the sense that I met seriously good people across all classes and cultures. I could never for the life of me understand why some despised those who differed from them by virtue of social class or race, or why, merely by accident of birth, the rich felt superior to the poor. The right just didn't seem to give a damn about poverty, social exclusion and powerlessness.

And I agreed with the ethical critique of unrestrained capitalism and believed in a life where values are not the creation of stimulated desire or human avarice. These values kept the environmental movement alive when all other idealisms seem to have died. The best parts of the left in the 1980s still tried to describe a good life based on real needs and authentic desires. It called for a communal and social responsibility for the earth and all those who lived in it. The left also remained internationalist and open to others: it opposed apartheid; it was concerned for the well-being of the Third World. I liked all these things and felt drawn to the radical political idealism that these attitudes conveyed.

But soon my leftish affiliation ended – and in a curious way. Many of my left-wing friends suddenly seemed to me to be right-wing. This dawned on me when I realised that, despite their rhetoric, all they really believed in was unlimited choice and unrestricted personal freedom. They seemed in important ways to have been stripped of integral values and to have embraced a rootless cultural relativism. They loved 'choice' but could never tell you what to choose or why. It was as if they preferred the act itself, rather than considering carefully the object of their volition to see whether it was good or not. They claimed to hate capitalism but appeared unable to explain what it was that they hated or what they would replace it with. The only people they decried were those who had more money than them, yet all they did was pursue more money and power. Their values seemed utterly at one with rootless capitalism, even as they criticised it. They seemed to delight in abortion, for example, and made a fetish out of the freedom to choose it, as if this were a real exercise of human freedom and unimpeded will, but they hated fox hunting because they thought it was cruel.

These people, I realised after a time, were really neo-liberals; not left-wing in the way I had understood it, but deeply and destructively right-wing. They despised religion precisely because it put a limit on freedom by suggesting what they should choose. In fact they hated anything which limited whatever impulse they might have. Pleasure and desire were self-validating: pornography, infidelity and drug use were no longer destructive social phenomena but under the right conditions became aesthetic forms of self-expression. Coupled with this private libertarianism, they assuaged their moral guilt by embracing the state as an ethical proxy. Privately liberal, publicly authoritarian, they were one of the constituencies that voted for New Labour.

Struck by the similarity between Blair and Thatcher, and convinced of the implicit concord between left and right,

I searched for more innovative solutions to our social and moral decline. I started to discover an interesting tradition of conservative and yet radical critiques of unrestrained capitalism, which seemed far more critical than anything I had read before. I discovered that conservatism has a more noble history than might be supposed. In the eighteenth century it was the Anglican Tory gentry who often defended the prosperity of the poor, their education and even their religious enthusiasm against the modish Whig aristocrats.[6] William Cobbett, Thomas Carlyle and John Ruskin, for example, were nineteenth-century critics of republican authoritarianism and statism as well as denouncers of a self-serving capitalism. As conservatives they vehemently hated the cultural consequences of industrialisation – the creation of a landless dispossessed mass forced to work at subsistence levels in factories for the benefit of others, and cut off from any cultural enrichment. They decried the loss of a settled and happy economy of the self-sufficient – and despised the slavish dependency now forced upon the poor. Economically they linked pauperisation with an original act of dispossession – variously the enclosures of common land in the eighteenth century, the Reformation or the rise of competition over custom. They argued for the restoration of the property rights of the landless, and called for the extension of self-sufficiency and autonomy through a distribution of capital and property to those rendered indigent by wage labour.

These requests are not without echo in Disraeli's one-nation conservatism or indeed Lord Randolph Churchill's campaign through the Primrose League for progressive Toryism in the 1880s. Both sought (albeit unsuccessfully) to ally the Tory party with the needs of the destitute and impoverished. Despite that, the potentiality and appeal of Randolph Churchill's Primrose League, which was founded in 1883, cannot be discounted. At one point in the 1890s it had over a million members (more than half of whom were women) and it outnumbered the entire membership of the trade unions. The Primrose League was named after the favourite flower of Disraeli – which formed the wreath that Queen Victoria sent to Disraeli's funeral. The blooms of the primrose were pinned to the lapel of every Tory MP in the House of Commons in celebration of the unveiling of Disraeli's statue and, lest we forget the original and deep appeal of such a conservatism, were worn by thousands on 19 April, the day of Disraeli's death, an anniversary celebration which became 'Primrose Day', which was popular for many years afterwards.

Yet all intellectual efforts by Tories to construct a political economy for the poor pale beside Hilaire Belloc's 1912 tour de force *The Servile State*.[7] In these pages he denounces both capitalism and socialism – both, he argues, institute master–slave relations and both rely on dispossession. The capitalist monopolises land, ownership and capital, thereby dispossessing the self-sufficient who are then forced to work for subsistence wages with no prospect of elevation. The socialist dispossesses the populace in the name of general ownership and a communal monopoly. From the perspective of the peasant or the worker both philosophies are exactly the same – both rely on dispossession, both deliver subsistence wages and both make the worker passive and dependent.

Belloc joined forces with G. K. Chesterton to form the Distributist League which campaigned for the restoration and distribution of property and assets to all. Since monopoly capitalism and socialism rely on the restriction and denial of ownership, the idea that they are opposed is delusory. Both tend to produce slavery in the form of the servile state. In essence Belloc accuses the then-embryonic welfare state of instituting a form of slavery in which the workers exchange their freedom and property for security and welfare. Their only true recourse to justice is to restore asset equity and make all men owners: 'If we do not restore the institution of property we cannot escape restoring the institution of slavery.' Though Belloc and Chesterton were radical liberals, their ideas were the decisive influence on Noel Skelton's shaping of the Tory idea of a property-owning democracy in the 1920s.

Looking back some ninety years it is hard not to see some merit in this position. The re-distributist egalitarian strategy of the postwar left has clearly failed. Welfare and punitive taxation have not saved the poor from their lot. Because they cannot imagine social justice being achieved except by the state, the left are condemned endlessly to repeat the cycle of disempowerment and dependency. Similarly, Tories have ignored or encouraged the monopolising and destructive tendencies of the market.

So we need to return to Skelton's distributist alternative. Anthony Eden's celebrated speech to the 1946 Conservative

Party conference already called for 'a nationwide property-owning democracy', as property is 'a right and a responsibility that must be shared as equitably as possible among all our citizens'. Backed by Winston Churchill, who argued that welfare should consist of both a floor and a ladder, the Tories conceived of – but were never able to make good on – the goal of an egalitarian distribution of private property. Together they signalled a participatory economics that is a far cry from that which dictates our lives today.

Of course Mrs Thatcher also spoke of a property-owning democracy – and sold off vast quantities of public housing stock to bring it about. I think she was right to do so. Crucially, however, this was a one-off sale – capital receipts could not be used to build new stock for distribution. Moreover, Mrs Thatcher was indifferent to the doubling of poverty that marked her premiership, a legacy of exclusion that New Labour, her bastard child, has barely addressed.

Mrs Thatcher's property-owning democracy soon degenerated into a monopoly speculation on residential asset values. And, with the real rate of wages only rising for those in the top half of society, ordinary people were encouraged to buy into the new order by borrowing ever more extreme multiples of their own incomes in order to finance a debt that they desperately hoped would become an asset. The argument for property ownership as a bastion of social stability and financial autonomy remained as strong as it ever was, but unfortunately the rising cost of homes and the increasing diminution of savings and capital meant that housing became the only asset that people could 'afford' and it became a subject of speculation which, in this country especially, goes through cycles of constant appreciation and collapse. As a consequence, people's greatest asset risks at one and the same time becoming their most dangerous and unstable debt.

An attempt to revive earlier and broader Tory ideas of egalitarianism is now under way, with renewed discussion of asset-based welfare and shared capital-ownership. Interestingly, the conservative financial journalist Samuel Brittan even advocates a basic income in conjunction with asset distribution – a combination that could incorporate everybody within a prospering society.

It is precisely this sort of political economy that I would argue needs to be incorporated in David Cameron's political philosophy. His surprise election as Conservative Party leader in December 2005 was the occasion of much cynicism. His PR background and easy cosmopolitanism, allied with his early attempts to rebrand Conservatism by 'hugging a hoodie' provoked widespread scorn and much sarcasm. Yet his forays to Norwegian fjords and the focus on a 'green conservatism' brought a new perspective to the Tory Party. However, it was the former Tory leader Iain Duncan Smith's report on the state of the nation, 'Breakdown Britain', in December 2006, that really refocused Conservatism around a new transformative agenda. The thesis of 'the broken society', the original insight of Dr Liam Fox (a former leadership contender), was then allied with Duncan Smith's landmark report to produce a nascent post-Thatcherite vision of Tory philosophy.

This new thinking is not of course uncontested, and it could go in different directions. Contemporary British conservatism still hovers between a reworked Thatcherism (using the language of progressive austerity) or a restored and yet to be radicalised one-nation Toryism. If he is not careful, Cameron risks presiding over the incoherence of a recapitulated free-market economics awkwardly allied with a compassionate and impotent version of socially concerned conservatism. One need only look at the rampant levels of inequality produced by George Bush's American variant of the same procrustean marriage.

Cameron's Conservatives badly need a political economy that can match the social analysis provided by Duncan Smith's 'Breakdown Britain'. George Osborne, the shadow chancellor, remains a convinced Thatcherite who nonetheless recognises the macro-economic errors of neo-liberalism; as such he is politically astute enough to recognise that the political and perhaps even the economic era of Thatcherism is over. His attention perhaps wholly absorbed by the deficit, he has however already spoken of the need for a new economic model. It is to be hoped that he has the opportunity and support to be able to craft it. If only the contemporary advocates of free-market economics could recognise that what we are seeing in our economy is rent-seeking capitalism exercising monopoly and the stranglehold of producers' interests over market mechanisms. What we have at present, after thirty years of letting the markets rip, would not be recognised even by the great liberal conservative economist Friedrich Hayek as a free economy –

it is Milton Friedman's bastard laissez-faire inversion of it, in which power and wealth flow upwards to the centralisers of capital, the new middle men who extract a form of rent (in the form of multiple modes of credit) from both consumers and producers, and who exercise such market power that they persuade people that monopoly is in their interest and that renting from them is cheaper and better than owning in its own right. The modern incarnations of left and right have thus, under the guise of the liberal market, strengthened the servile state. The state controls the majority through welfare and tax, while the super-rich, those not bound by nation or responsibility, exercise their lordly freedom and their wanton power. If we are to have real freedom and true liberty, the new conditions of serfdom must be recognised and challenged.

David Cameron has intuitions about conservative economic alternatives. He made an excellent speech at Rochdale in June 2008 in favour of conservative cooperatives. But he and the Conservatives he leads remain unsure how to generate a truly transformative political economy for the poor and indeed, since they are also so heavily indebted and in many cases proletarianised, the middle class as well. If the social vision of Cameron's Conservatives could be allied with a new political economy of shared assets, and a modernised mutualism coupled with genuinely free markets, then a just and transformative conservatism could yet emerge.

A revival of earlier versions of a conservatism for the poor, together with a restoration of the social and family structures that alone can truly empower the impoverished and disadvantaged, could lead to a transformation of British society for the better. And here we can find both an economic and a cultural solution to our contemporary crisis. A revived civic culture can only come about as a result of a shift in the British dispensation of power and money. And this will only happen when empowered families and communities start to chart a pattern for their lives that differs from that prescribed by the market state. This will require what might be called a politics of virtue. Such a politics does exist, nascent within a British tradition that has not yet fully surrendered to the forces that have surrounded it. There is a more radical conservative tradition, older and better than Thatcherism, more empowering than state socialism and more critical of the producer stranglehold of monopoly capitalism. It offers what the left and the right have still not delivered – a real political economy for the poor. It is essentially a conserving vision, for it seeks to preserve and extend human stability and create the conditions for human flourishing for all our people. What better name for it than Red Toryism? Red because it caters to the needs of the disadvantaged and believes in economic justice; Tory because it believes in virtue, tradition and the priority of the good. Let us begin to examine the case for such a philosophy, through an account and an analysis of the economic, social and democratic crises in which we are now mired.

PART I

The Mess We're in and How We Got There

1 The Economic Crisis

Global capitalism may be gradually recovering from the great crash of 2007/8. Nevertheless, if Britain is not facing a really prolonged recession, we are very lucky indeed. For it is clear that the financial meltdown and the crisis it has caused have revealed a profound vulnerability in the British economy, a fragility created by dependence on foreign capital flows and the financial sector, meaning that recovery will be a very fraught affair indeed. Britain has so far had the longest (six full quarters) and deepest recession on record. At the time of writing the UK is the last major economy to emerge from recession and even if we do get back to growth it will be fitful and incremental at best.

For, as a result of the recession and the collapse in tax revenues, and because Treasury spending plans were based on ridiculous assumptions about the longevity of Britain's asset bubbles, the country's national debt looks like doubling to some 80% of GDP within a couple of years. If present trends continue, it could even hit 100% of GDP by the middle of the next decade. The situation in the US is perhaps even worse, with unemployment in November 2009 surging past 10% for the first time in twenty-six years and 7.3 million American jobs lost since the recession began.[1] The hubris of this era was captured with unconscious irony by Gordon Brown in his Budget speech on 7 March 2001, when in praise of the new paradigm he declared, 'We will not return to boom and bust.' Now, after the crash, few can be found who are willing to boast about the Anglo-American economic miracle.

Interestingly, not only has neo-liberalism destroyed its own advocates, it has also eliminated their acolytes as well. All the countries which followed the dictates of market fundamentalism and allowed their markets to undergo asset inflation have either been bankrupted by it or come perilously close to this fate. Iceland is ruined. Ireland, were it not for the euro, would have suffered the same fate (because the ceiling provided by monetary union is also a floor), and the country is now saddled with toxic debts arising from its huge property bubble. Spain is economically dead in the water following the collapse of its housing sector and, trapped by the inflexibility of the European monetary system, cannot devalue its currency to allow it to grow again. Similar problems affect Portugal and Greece. These southern economies, with the bursting of their financial bubbles, will face ever more expensive and widening deficits. Their citizens face crippling wage deflation, collapsing incomes and high unemployment. If we Anglo-Americans, as the prime instigators and ideologues of wholly unregulated self-balancing markets, face a similar fate, then we should at least know why.

This meltdown has its origin, though not its final denouement, in the economic model supported on both sides of the Atlantic since the time of Ronald Reagan and Mrs Thatcher, and by their left-wing successors. The 'free-market' model, as conceived by the governing consensus of the last thirty years, finally and very visibly collapsed when Lehman Brothers was allowed to go bankrupt on 15 September 2008. Lehman was felled by the weight of about $60 billion in toxic bad debts. The failure of Lehman Brothers induced a global asset and value collapse of unprecedented proportions. Neo-liberalism fell with it.

Where did these bad debts come from?

One common understanding has it that the financial meltdown was caused by an extension of mortgaged residential housing to those economically undeserving of private property and personal assets and all the economic and social security they bring with them. This is the basis for the accusation that has been levelled at the various community housing schemes in North America licensed or backed by Freddie Mac and Fannie Mae: that in the name of social engineering, inappropriate people (in market terms) were given credit and therefore the responsibility of home ownership. Framed this way, it seems as if the collapse of the world's financial system lies with the attempt to extend property and assets to the poor. The standard narrative is that inappropriate lending was undertaken, albeit by unscrupulous brokers, and that the system itself is to be faulted only for lack of due systemic diligence.

The spurious nature of this argument is not eliminated by its perpetual repetition. The origin of the present crisis lies not in unwise lending to the poor but in a failure to secure the conditions for a widespread distribution of property. People's desire for security was exploited by propagating insecurity. There was an undue emphasis on mortgaged home ownership as the only secured form of property available to ordinary people, so that this form of asset acquisition became an unsustainable inflated burden for working families and ultimately, for many, a real financial catastrophe.

Residential housing became the base asset on which this entire crisis was played out. The Anglo-American paradigm, initiated by Thatcher and Reagan and sustained by Clinton and Blair, progressively removed all limits on capital movement and control. In essence a huge trans-atlantic monoculture of capital and investment was created, into which other nations opted to varying degrees. While creating huge opportunities for trade and investment and vastly increasing the amount of capital that could be deployed for profitable return, this system also reduced all national variations of the market and capital to itself. All capital, whether local, regional or national, became global. However, a worldwide system of capital requires not only a system of rates of exchange but also some form of security on which any subsequent credit can be based.

This need for a base asset was exacerbated by the fact that the nation states of the rising economies needed a secure income stream from their rising tax base, so they invested and secured their increased tax returns by purchasing the government debt of the developed nations. This in turn lowered the bond yield across the developed world and allowed these mature economies to deliver perversely low long-term interest rates to their own private sector. The deregulated capital systems of Britain and the United States positioned themselves to offer these low rates to their own citizens, and so the long credit-induced boom of the 1990s began in earnest.

True credit augmentation requires leverage – any expansion of credit needs a securing base. That base for Britain and America and many other nations (Ireland and Spain spring to mind) was residential housing. This was the asset that people most valued and would do their utmost to procure and, outside the basics of living, housing would be the spending priority that exceeded all others in importance and expense in any family budget. Through a growing bubble, more and more money was provided to finance more and more purchases, and house prices climbed accordingly, which in turn allowed a further increase of credit, and so on. This rise in asset value seemed inexorable, such that these high valuations themselves became the source of further valuation and further credit. Ability to pay or finance the debt no longer seemed necessary when so much equity was already in place.

All this had a staggering effect on house prices. According to American and British figures reaching back ten years from the end of the housing boom in 2007, house prices in America had climbed by 104.5% and in the UK the rise was even higher, with one index posting a 211% increase. Complementing this rise was a huge acceleration in the level of personal debt. Over the same ten-year period, since the summer of 1997, personal debt rose in America by 159%, jumping from $5,547 billion to $14,374 billion. The UK saw a similar rise in personal debt of 165.2% from £570 billion to £1,512 billion. Thus, in the name of acquiring an ever-increasing asset value, more and more people became heavily indebted in the hope of acquiring freedom from debt. All this in the age when ideologues on all sides told us that the problems of boom and bust had been solved, that inflation was permanently cured, that the world economy had entered a new paradigm – and that the only role for a government committed to growth and prosperity was that of extending the remit of the market and the reach of capital.

This is what happened, more or less, but how was such a huge 'bubble' allowed to develop and what explains its collapse? One explanation is at the level of the international economy.

The huge foreign exchange reserves and sovereign wealth funds in Asia needed a secure and stable home for their capital. It couldn't just sit there to be eroded by inflation – so its fund managers bought UK and US government gilts (the US and UK, as I've said, benefited thereby from artificially low interest rates). The huge capital influx gradually bid down the gilt yield on government paper to unprofitable levels. Managers therefore sought a higher return in equities, but this form of investment was hit by the stock market dot.com crash when that bubble burst on 10 March 2000 and over £5 trillion was wiped off technology shares. This collapse in equities produced a demand by fund managers for both return and security. Individuals themselves then switched into the housing market and the banks tracked this process by creating a new financial vehicle: so-called mortgage securitisation, the bundling of mortgage debts so that they could be sold on and used as a vehicle for speculation. Mortgage securitisation offered international capital both stability and high return.

The opening up of capital controls created a malign relationship between UK base rates and credit supply – the higher UK base rates rose to control credit supply, the more international capital flowed into London seeking a profitable return. Thus the lever used to depress price rises through interest rate rises had a perverse effect: it actually increased credit supply, and so the national government lost control over its own economy.

If housing was to be the foundation stone on which neo-liberal growth would sustain itself, this required a global economic system that progressively opened up credit to finance the asset boom. Though there were many different local providers of credit, these providers had to gain access to the capital provided by globalisation in order vastly to increase their ability to loan. A case in point is Freddie Mac and Fannie Mae, which in America acted as government sponsored enterprises to guarantee mortgage securities. When local providers of finance were able to get loans off their books, they were then able to loan again. Without this process, we could not have had the credit boom. It therefore makes sense of speak of a 'modal monopolisation of credit', which simply means that all home finance became increasingly reliant on one global system of provision.

The self-augmenting process of speculation was the other mechanism that allowed the bubble to develop. Once trade trades on itself, it becomes entirely abstracted from the real economy. Thus the real gains made on asset appreciation, for example investment in copper when there was a clear and increasing world demand for copper, become a speculation on the act of speculation as you anticipate a rise in copper prices and then take a further gamble on the extent and nature of that rise. Over time, when you have a continually appreciating asset, the acts of speculation begin to assume with ever greater certainty that the underlying value of that asset will remain as it is and that you can then use that asset as collateral to acquire ever larger amounts of the commodity. Eventually this means that the value of the trade itself is based on the historic exchange value of the tradable item. Exchange or nominal value supplants real value in the economy, and the underlying ability to finance or purchase that tradable commodity is no longer questioned. Companies cease to scrutinise these inflated values as a matter of due diligence. They are flying blind.

Then there was the securitisation of debt, aiding and intensifying both of the above processes. Previously, and especially in the US, non-systemic bank lending (that is to individuals and businesses rather than other banks) was often dangerous or vulnerable to default. If a bank over-invested in a town or a business sector and the economics of that locale or sector changed, then the bank could lose all its loans. Securitisation was presented as a pooling of that local risk and a diminution of exposure.

In the name of controlling risk the link between creditor and debtor was broken. Individual banks freed up their balance sheets (so as to extend more credit) by selling on their mortgage debt to merchant banks, who constructed a new bonded investment vehicle which mixed differently rated bonds (in order to hedge their bets) into one package for selling on as a securitised income stream to institutional investors — who in essence repeated the process and sold them on yet again. These 'securities' passed like a virus through the whole system so that virtually no AAA mortgage package (offering the highest possible credit rating) was without a link to a non-conforming or subprime loan. Strikingly, for a method that purported to guarantee the security of the financial system, none of its advocates ever explained how the financial system could in fact be secured by these dubious means. Thus there was no global clearing house for credit default options, and no provision for systemic failure in the securities packages that claimed to spread the risk across the whole system. Nor indeed was there any authority in reference to which overall leverage (the ratio of liabilities to assets) could be assessed and limited. What must be remembered is that these securities packages constituted a globally accessible asset base upon which the leverage of subsequent deal-making took place. If, as the *Financial Times* tells us, median leverage levels were at 35:1 (liabilities to assets) in the US and 45:1 in Europe, then we must assume that those who engaged in investment activity at those sorts of multiples never had any idea that asset values could fall as well as rise, and that some could even default. In the end banks and financial institutions were acutely vulnerable to any collapse in the underlying asset base on which so much of their security now rested.[2]

So much then for the 'what' and the 'how'. Now I would like to address the 'why' in the sense of the continuing relevance of a distributist critique of monopolised markets. So far the direct underwriting cost of the crisis in the UK is expected to exceed £1.5 trillion in terms of public taxpayer support for the British banking system, while in the US the estimate is well over $3 trillion – and both figures exclude the halving of the value of stock markets across the world and the underlying destruction of house prices and all the other costs associated with a general worldwide recession. In response to my critique of the global monopolisation of credit it might be said that modern capitalism has done more than any other comparable system to increase ownership; after all, if the aim is to produce a widely distributed system of private property and liberty, then shouldn't the capitalist system be supported and endorsed? Private ownership has never before been attained by almost three-quarters of the population in the developed world.

My critique, however, draws on the tradition of Catholic and Anglican social teaching and the work of the English distributists (as well as on some elements of the ordoliberal and Austrian school traditions), challenges the notion that the aim of contemporary capitalism is to deliver prosperity and property to all. On the contrary, it suggests that what we are spreading is a kind of indentured ownership via ever more extreme levels of credit and that it corresponds, in

48

part, to the analysis of servitude first offered by Chesterton and Belloc early in the twentieth century. For to own something on credit is not to own it at all, and since no security of tenure is available by rent, those who seek some sort of primary foundation or asset in the world have little choice but to buy into a form of ownership that ultimately converts its possessor into a debtor. And there is no 'outside' of the market, for to remain external to this economy is to be denied any access to security or prosperity.

From the 1980s onwards, the marketisation and globalisation of everything that could be traded gradually reduced the real purchasing power of skilled and unskilled wages. The further down the income scale you went, the more male wages tended to stagnate. As a result, women were forced (middle-class feminists often forget the economic nature of the compulsion involved), for the sake of household income, to enter the workforce. However, this was not enough, and men and women worked more and more hours to sustain their income levels. Though the poor benefited from the K-Mart effect – where cheap foreign production allowed the price of consumer durables to fall – this was still not enough to compensate for rising costs and declining wages, so each family took on more and more debt via the provision of both secured and unsecured lending. Little wonder then that the golden age for waged workers in the OECD was not in this recent allegedly great age of prosperity, but between 1945 and 1973, when they gained the greatest percentage share of GDP for their labour and enjoyed greater real purchasing power.

I outline all this in order to show how credit itself derives from an earlier form of dispossession – labour deprived of capital, ownership and security. The desperate drive to attain a stake in the world has for many culminated in a greater loss than they could ever have conceived possible. With over two million American homes facing foreclosure and over 300,000 Britons already in mortgage arrears, the misery will only intensify unless conditions ease.

This outcome, it is worth stressing again, has been achieved by governments of both left and right, and both state and market have allied to ensure the ultimate monopoly, a universal system of capital that drives wealth upwards and progressively denies the waged classes a purchasing power commensurate with their desire for self-sufficiency and security. That this demand was satisfied and then thwarted by credit is testimony to a capitalist logic of constant insecurity that in its turn generates calls for the servile condition to be re-established and freshly resourced, so as to contain the woes of the newly indigent.

Debt as the modern form of slavery: private debt

According to Office for National Statistics data, prior to the financial crash the household savings ratio (the proportion of household income which is saved) dropped to a fifty-year low of -1.1% in the first quarter of 2008, making the average Briton a net borrower for the first time since the fourth quarter of 1958.[3]

This was consistently down from the 1995 high of 10% and the postwar peak of 13.4% in the first quarter of 1984 and had been falling consistently from the end of 2005 when it was just under 6%. The long-term decline in savings requires both a cultural account of the attitude to debt and an economic account which explains the way an increased credit supply and asset bubbles encourage spending rather than saving

As it stands now, Britain is best characterised as a society that saves income after expenditure in order not to save but to finance debt. For all but the most affluent, Britain has become *a short-term society*, living hand-to-mouth, on income, and remaining incapable of using savings to generate assets. Instead, households have used debt to purchase assets, predominately housing, which has created the asset bubble economy which has rendered households so insecure. This trend towards consuming income rather than saving has occurred despite persistent growth in real income over the same period – between 1971 and 2007.[4]

And the overall increase in household debt explains where much of this excess is going. Nonetheless, any recent increase in savings is from a low base; there are many who do not save at all and they are the ones who most need to do so. According to Credit Action, TNS Omnibus found that, '32% of people made redundant would fail to meet their current living expenses in the first month, with one in six defaulting immediately'. And the remainder are no more secure: 'Less than half (43%) of working adults questioned had sufficient funds in place to survive more than three months.'[5]

That said, as in previous recessions, savings rates increased markedly during 2009, this time by threefold from the previous year, as people began to fear and readjust to a new economic climate. However, precautionary savings remain extremely low, both in historical terms and relative to other countries.

Even during the economic boom, the savings rate in the UK was consistently extremely low by international standards: it fell well beneath the EU and OECD averages. In fact the UK has had the lowest mean savings rate, as a proportion of GDP, of any OECD country in the twenty years leading up to the current recession.

The FSA's 2005 Financial Capability Survey found that half of all respondents had no savings.[6] In fact 35% of the population report never having saved from income.[7]

In addition the Association of British Insurers calculates that 9.6 million people in the UK are saving nothing for retirement, while an additional 3.8 million people in the UK are considered to be saving too little.[8]

The FSA has published research which indicates that an improvement in financial capability leads to an improvement in overall psychological well-being. The results of the research suggest that moving from low to average levels of financial capability increases psychological well-being by over 5%, and decreases anxiety and depression by 15%. The precision of such statistics is of course always open to question, but the positive trends and the relative scores are significant. For example, the research also concluded that the increase in life satisfaction from increased financial capability is twelve times greater than the impact of earning an extra £1,000 a year.

But the grim truth is that Britain faces a sustained period of deleveraging – according to a recent McKinsey Global Institute report, even after removing foreign lending by UK banks, the UK debt-to-GDP ratio remains higher than every country's except Japan's – and when one includes all domestic, private- and public-sector debt, total UK debt stands at around 469% of GDP.

Public debt

The trouble with much of the current debate about the public finances, the indebted state and private sector revival is that it is conducted in terms of a somewhat defunct economic model. Those on the left argue for the productive 'demand maintaining' role of public expenditure, while those on the right point out its essentially unproductive nature. For the left, high levels of public-sector debt and expenditure are, in the present situation, justifiable, as the real danger lies in the complete collapse of the labour market and a huge rise in unemployment that could force us back into recession. The right also fear a collapse in the private sector, but they worry about the state crowding out private-sector recovery with higher public debt, in turn leading to increased interest and tax burdens in the private sector.

In one sense both rationales have some justification. The right is correct that the public sector can break the private sector – an increasing public debt is unsustainable, as it needs higher taxes to finance it and the taxes levied on private businesses choke off private-sector recovery, which diminishes tax receipts and increases the deficit still further, which requires further tax rises and starts the cycle all over again. An unreformed state can gradually strangle the private sector, which alone can provide the tax receipts and revenue growth required for economic recovery. Increasing the tax take depresses the growth rate of the economy as a whole, with the standard GDP loss per tax dollar raised variously calculated at 30–50%.[9]

Similarly the left rightly argues that the issue is one of maintaining demand while the economy is frighteningly fragile. Knock out public expenditure too early in the economic cycle, they contend, and all the demand in the economy collapses and you have a huge jump in unemployment – which destroys both domestic consumption and investor confidence and plunges the economy back into an even deeper slump.

The key factor required for economic recovery is private-sector growth. Both left and right are cogent in arguing for it – but they have, it seems, diametrically opposed views on how to achieve it.

What the right often miss is that one key to providing private-sector growth is the public funding of infrastructure. If the state can provide the structural means to aid competitiveness – in transport, broadband capacity, education and the resulting development of high-end skills, for example – then public expenditure can aid private sector growth. But objectively – this is where Labour has so evidently failed – British infrastructure is in a terrible state. Even though we are the sixth-richest country in the world, we are rated 34th behind Namibia and Spain in terms of our infrastructure.[10] Insufficient investment in communications, utilities and transport is a key reason for low British productivity. Indeed Britain spends less on this area as a proportion of GDP than any other OECD country.[11] Our rail networks are decades behind those on the continent in terms of cost per mile for the user, easy inter-city access and comfort and convenience for the traveller. Our education is producing the fiction of ever greater internal success, while externally, in the real export-creating skills of languages, technical ability and industrial innovation, we are falling ever further behind.

In short, one might argue that, while we have improved the incomes of those dependent on the state for their wages (the GP contract springs to mind, as do the NHS consultants who have boosted their pay by more than 25% while working fewer hours), we have not generated enough national assets to make the growth in public expenditure a driver of private-sector growth and success. We have spent too much on the wrong things. We also seem to have got less for more: public-sector productivity has declined by 3.4% in the ten years since 1997, whereas the private sector over the same period has seen a rise of 27.9%. This productivity gap has produced a net loss to the public purse, if the public sector had mirrored the private-sector gain, of some £58 billion.[12] Any defence of the productive role of public expenditure has to address these issues and explain why we have failed to marshal the benefits of public expenditure for overall economic competitiveness.

Public spending rose from 36.3% of GDP in 1999–2000, to 47.5% of GDP in 2009–10. The figures of a massive growth in public expenditure are in part only so high because of a collapse in the level of GDP and the revenues that flow from it, from the middle of 2007 on. Nonetheless, the ongoing structural deficit is real – it comes from relying on the revenues generated from a bubble in asset prices and making that a norm which forms the governing baseline for all future state expenditure. It would have been better to assume, as Giles Wilkes has pointed out, a 2.5% long-term growth figure for the economy rather than the 3% the Treasury appears to have used.[13] Given that much of the ongoing deficit (some 25%) is caused by a collapse in revenues that began when the housing market stalled in the summer of 2007, then the criticism of the Labour Party is less that there has been an unplanned surge in expenditure than that they really believed their own propaganda: that a new economic paradigm with permanently low interest rates had been achieved, and that the time of boom and bust was over, so that growth figures and revenue streams from the good years could be safely incorporated into calculations of the ratio of debt to expenditure for the next.

But deficits are still real, and a false assumption on ongoing growth has left public expenditure worryingly exposed. Public spending is now approaching 50% of GDP and with the annual budget deficit likely to exceed £175 billion, the overall public debt could, if trends continue and nothing changes, hit nearly 100% of GDP by 2015.

If the benign interest-rate environment changes, as other countries begin to move out of recession, British debt may look increasingly unattractive. It would require a higher yield to sell it and thus our debt position would become increasingly expensive to maintain, and worsen the deficit still further.

We are not, however, in the 1980s, and few economists seriously think that we are facing a global inflationary problem. Thus the old right-wing agenda of restriction of the monetary supply is not applicable in current circumstances. The real risk is deflation, not inflation. Stimulating demand should be seen, even in a monetarist lexicon, as the right thing to do. The real fiscal decision lies in playing off unemployment against deficit reduction: cut too early and too soon and you risk kicking out the last prop holding up the British economy, producing another recession that increases the deficit still further. On the other hand, if nothing is done then the deficit continues to rise, and with it the cost and time of repayment and the risk of higher debt-servicing charges.

The key is to produce private-sector growth that generates the tax revenue to close the funding gap, while raising public-sector productivity so that we can do more with less. Britain has historically lagged behind the US, France and Germany in various productivity measures in the private sector, too. The key difference seems to be lack of capital investment in plant and machinery. However, that may be because the

UK is now a predominantly service-based economy that requires less capital investment. If so, then innovation in service delivery and in the service sector would deliver real productivity growth even though manufacture should also be revived, to obtain a more balanced economy.

It is here that the idea of a slimmed-down state and real increases in growth can start to gain traction. Since the earlier economic model was founded on an extreme individualism that requires the state to police the outcome, then the structural links between economically damaging self-interest and state bureaucracy become clear. An anarchic market, that has abandoned trust and eschewed any ethos of the public good, requires a huge state bureaucracy to monitor it and enforce contracts and compliance. The costs of this audit state is enormous.

Similarly, in the public sector, target-setting distorts outcomes, while budget-driven compliance substitutes false for true measures and erodes the quality of service, which in turn drives up failure rates and produces failure demand (the rise in demand on a service because of a failure to address the problem correctly in the first place – for example the need to see ten different people to get a benefit form filled in or many doctors to have an illness correctly diagnosed).

As Paul Lewis has pointed out in respect of the introduction of quasi-markets in the NHS during the 1980s, the NHS once employed around a thousand senior managers and overall administrative costs accounted for around 5% of the total budget. By 1995, the NHS employed 26,000 senior managers and administrative costs had more than doubled relative to the total NHS budget, absorbing about 12% of the total budget.[14] Any net gain in efficiency is absorbed by higher transaction costs, and there seems to be no real reason to assume that traditional contracting-out of services is really any different from this.

In place of the state increasing the costs of transactions through audit and compliance between two parties that are fundamentally suspicious of each other, we could instead begin to create a civil economy as an inherent aspect of civil society.[15] Such an economy serves society, it both demands and creates trust, and trust so conceived minimises and reduces the cost of compliance. If the cost of transactions falls then the regulatory burden on business is reduced and, if trust becomes the norm, more inter-group ventures are possible and so more business is engendered.

The state has too often been the agent of enforcement for an economy of individual suspicion. The radically conservative case for a slimmed-down state is not then what one initially suspects. It is not about the old contest between privatised individuals and a collectivised state. Properly conceived it represents the first sign of a new mutualism and a different sort of market. With less state you can have more society and with more society you can have a more productive economy. Now that our economy is in such a dire crisis we should abandon the logic that has led us to both state and market failure. We need instead what both these pseudo-alternatives have suppressed: the economy of a civil society.

2 The Democratic Crisis

A crisis of legitimacy

Democracy in the United Kingdom isn't working well. People have drifted, disillusioned and increasingly mistrustful, away from the rights and responsibilities of civic participation. In doing so, the public have become markedly dissatisfied, disaffected and distant from power.

Despite the government's much trumpeted localist agenda, over the past dozen years power and control have become increasingly concentrated in Westminster generally and in the government and Prime Minister's Office specifically. Local authorities and public services, long centralised and much constrained, suffered further indignity with remaining local decision-taking and variation suppressed through targets, statutory codes of practice and compliance-based auditing.

And, despite the government's putative commitment to electoral reform, abuses of this power and control continue with virtual immunity to electoral redress. It has taken the broadly opposed war in Iraq and the revelation of systematic corruption in the House of Commons to shift the public mood from apathy to anger. However, the public have found little effective outlet through which to channel this discontent and to force democratic accountability.

No surprise then that satisfaction with the political system has been rapidly declining. The proportion of people who are very or fairly satisfied with the way Parliament works has dropped from 34% in 1995 to 20% today, while over the same period the proportion who are very or fairly dissatisfied has grown from 31% to 66%.[1]

It goes almost without saying that the public's trust in politics today, both in political institutions and politicians themselves, is at an all-time low. Only 13% of people trust politicians, down 8 percentage points year-on-year following 2009's revelation of widespread exploitation of the expenses system by MPs.[2] This low level of trust places the political class at the bottom of the professions in the public regard.

However, attempts to restore the public's trust in Parliament is to get things backwards. The problem of democratic reform stems from a political class unwilling to trust the electorate, as well as its local representatives, to participate meaningfully or differently in decision-making.

Voting for change

Voting continues to constitute the sole form of engagement with the political system by the vast majority of citizens. Looking at other types of political expression over the past year, only 17% of people have presented their views to a local councillor or MP, only 6% have written a letter to an editor and only 1% have stood for public office.[3] Only 3% have donated money or paid a membership fee to a political party in the past year.[4] Ordinary people no longer see themselves as able to make effective and meaningful contributions towards the local or national interest. Only

32% agree with the statement: 'When people like me get involved in politics, they really can change the way that the country is run.'[5]

The civic middle in British public life – the self-organised associations such as unions, churches and activist organisations – has largely disappeared over the past thirty years, as fewer and fewer people join associative organisations, other than surrogate vertical ones, or sterile groups focussed around narrow obsessions. Yet not only has the civic middle historically acted as a balancing force between the public and the political, it has in the past provided alternative mechanisms for political participation.

The decline in varied and more involved forms of political participation is a trend which anyone concerned with having a robust and active civil society must seek to understand and reverse. Doing so will require a new civic culture of political association and participation, which will need to be matched (if not facilitated) by radical new forms of politics: devolving power, budgets and decisions to the lowest level possible; changing the architecture of institutions to encourage amateur involvement; extending indirect political participation by mechanisms such as easing and localising the selection and de-selection of candidates, and extending direct participation where constructive; facilitating and empowering self-organising associations in civil society; tapping into new technologies in order to inform the public, build networks and nudge participation.

Already the growing disaffection with politics has seen marginal and extremist parties begin to capture political ground, as people turn away from the mainstream of politics, or politics altogether. The most recent European parliamentary elections, which followed closely on the heels of the expenses scandal, saw a dire turnout in England (34.7%) and the election of two BNP candidates to Brussels.

While the insensitivity of Westminster's institutional structures to the public may ensure a certain continuity and shield against these more extreme forms of populism, this numbness has begun to spread from the political sphere right across society. Voter turnout has declined steadily over the past two decades, as even the cursory act of voting has been too much for the increasingly detached and bored citizen.

Those who do participate in elections often feel that their vote counts for very little – or, for a lucky few, a disproportionate amount. As it stands, 41% of people feel that they have little influence over local decision-making and a further 32% feel that they have no influence at all. Similarly, when it comes to national politics, 44% of people feel they have little influence over decision-making and a further 41% feel that they have no influence whatsoever.[6]

We have a fractured and disassociative citizenry that exercises little or no local power. In consequence it distrusts and repudiates national politics. So a renewal of the latter requires a revival of the former.

Disappearing mandates

Westminster works on a first-past-the-post system, where each MP is the single representative for a constituency. The thinning numbers of the public still looking to affect change through the ballot box are confronted with a system which often breeds further dissatisfaction, as well as complacency and even corruption in many of the elected officials that it fails to hold to account.

In the most recent general election in 2005, despite the issue of the Iraq War and the introduction of postal voting, only 61% of the electorate voted – a lower national turnout than in any of the fifteen other original EU member states. This was in fact a slight gain on 2001, which saw a historical low of 59% of the eligible public vote.[7] To give some context, modern voting levels peaked in 1950 at 83.9% and remained in the high 70s until dropping to 71.5% in 1997.[8]

Despite the slight increase in the proportion of the public voting in 2005, the proportion of the vote that Labour captured was 5 percentage points lower than in 2001, dropping to only 35.2% of the total vote.[9] This amounts to only 21.6% of eligible voters nationally supporting the party that went on to form the government. Although it took such a small proportion of the vote, Labour retained a 66-seat majority – capturing 55% of the total seats. This disparity between vote proportion and seat proportion has never been wider, leading the Electoral Reform Society to dub the 2005 general election 'the worst election ever'.[10]

The election was characterised by some genuinely scandalous deficiencies. In three constituencies, MPs were elected with less than 20% of their local electorate supporting them: George Galloway (Respect), Roger Godsiff (Labour) and Ann McKechin (Labour).[11] For the first time ever, fewer than 35% of MPs were elected by majorities of the electors in their own constituencies.[12] This historical anomaly represents not so much a fluke outcome as a honing of strategic campaigning, where political focus and resources shift to an increasingly limited number of 'swing voters' in marginal seats. So-called safe seats, where one candidate is highly unlikely to be defeated, are left effectively uncontested by all parties – weak candidates and few resources are put into contesting them. In the last election, the major parties were said to be concentrating predominantly on a field of some 800,000 voters who were not firmly resolved in favour of any particular party and happened to live in a marginal constituency.[13]

Besides the general democratic deficit that this strategic focus on an extremely limited subsection of the electorate engenders (the undecided 800,000 amounting to less than 2% of the eligible voting public), it also creates many related negative side-effects. Undecided voters are by no means a representative sample of the wider population. Furthermore, it has been widely noted that support for more extreme parties (such as the BNP) has grown precisely where the mainstream parties consider their vote safe and thus disengage from the electorate, diverting their resources to other fronts.

The problem of safe seats is neither a small nor a recent one: shockingly, half of all seats have not changed hands since 1970, and 29% have remained with the same party since 1945. This has also had a serious impact on voter turnout in these areas – in 2005, an average of 51.4% of people came out to vote in safe constituencies, whereas an average of 68.6% of people came out to vote in contested seats.[14]

While it is more difficult to get an overall picture of democratic involvement in local authority elections, which vary significantly between regions, turnout generally has been significantly lower than national rates, and election results have not proven particularly representative. Taking the most recent local elections in London as an example, the average vote share of parties running councils was 43%, with only five councils being won with a majority of votes cast. Minority voting support, however, often translated to large majorities in seats – in Newham, for example, 43% of the vote allowed Labour to capture 90% of seats.[15] Conversely, in six boroughs, the party which received the most votes did not win the most seats.

The three major parties have made specific pledges to address voter disenfranchisement and democratic deficit. This is not least the case with Labour, whose pledge to instigate electoral reform in 1997 and 2001 was repeated in the 2005 manifesto, which promised the public a referendum on 'the new electoral systems introduced for the devolved administrations, the European Parliament and the London Assembly'. Despite reneging on this proposal, Gordon Brown has recently called for a referendum on limited reform, in the form of the alternative vote system which would maintain the link between a constituency and its MP. The Liberal Democrats have called for the introduction of proportional representation through the single transferable vote system.

While the Conservatives have usually stood out against electoral reform as a matter of principle, they have sought to increase the power of Parliament over the central authority of the executive branch, and have suggested instead a radical devolution of power to local authorities.

In the end we need to balance the need for a more representative voting system with an equal need for strong government and the possibility of decisive leadership, rather than endless coalition. The lesson from the USA is that the legacy of 'checks and balances' is in reality a recipe for the preservation of vested interests and a guarantee of a perpetual stasis that cannot even deliver healthcare for its own citizens. If all proportional representation delivers is a dislocation between the MPs and those who elect them, then this would not be a desirable outcome. On the other hand the current system is palpably unfair, because a very small group of individuals and constituencies decisively turn the outcome of an election. What system would mediate between the two extremes? One might suggest the alternative vote system which would use the same constituency boundaries as now, so preserving the link of direct local representation. However, within each constituency under this system a majoritarian rule operates: each candidate is elected according to an order of preference of the voters. Whereas at present few candidates gain 50% of votes in the poll, in the alternative vote system, second and third preferences (the voter ranks candidates on the ballot paper) are also counted if in the first instance no candidate gets 50%. The strength of this system is that all MPs would have a solid support from the majority of their constituents, while the local link would be preserved. In addition the principle of first-past-the-post is sustained, thereby obviating the risk of perpetual compromise.

Yet however desirable, formal changes to the electoral system, or rebalancing the distribution of power within Parliament or between local and national politics, will not in itself be sufficient to re-invigorate political engagement. Parliamentary reform cannot be a substitute for political involvement: it must come as the result of renewed participation.

Quite how we achieve this is a matter of some debate. Clearly we need some measure of direct participation by voters in legislation. One measure we could adopt is the practice of indirect law creation which exists in some US states where a proposed measure is referred to the legislature after acquiring the requisite number of voters' signatures. Additional direct involvement by voters could be petitions to trigger a debate in parliament or to derogate powers for such decisions to the relevant constituencies – where if referenda were permitted the measure would go through. We might call this a local derogative power that would allow genuine democratic variation under a universal legislature.

However, the recovery of democracy is not just to do with Westminster. It also needs to be a bottom-up process. Governing authority should be derogated from the local council to areas, towns or even streets. This power could be two-fold: a power of budgetary devolution, whereby localities were able to appropriate for themselves the budget allocated to them in order to put it to better use, and the election of 'micro-mayors' who would have legislative 'push-up' and budgetary authority in that area.

There are powerful international examples of members of the general public and political class working within existing systems to innovate the public–political relationship. Most recently, the Obama presidential campaign in the US tapped into new technology in order to engage the public, using social networking platforms and peer-to-peer channels to build a broad and interconnected community of supporters. This garnered more than just votes. It facilitated the transmission of ideas in both directions and mobilised supporters to become directly involved in organised campaign work. This was especially effective at engaging young people in the political process.

A similar potential for political involvement exists in the British public. Tapping it will require innovative and inspirational as much as technical measures, and the crucial test of any new system will be whether it fosters a citizenry that is active, involved and desirous of associative relationships.

3 The Social Crisis

Besides the sudden crisis that has exposed Britain's economy and the creeping malaise that has eroded its democracy, another, more pernicious crisis has broken its society. Over years and decades, Britain has seen a piecemeal erosion of its social capital that has been far more costly – to our economy, to our public spending and ultimately to the quality of our lives – than the more immediate collapse of financial capital.

Social capital is a term that tries to express the value, both in terms of money and quality of life, that we derive from our reciprocal social relationships, through friendships, contacts, families, groups, neighbourliness, political membership, sports teams and churches. Despite a history dating back more than a century, the theory and concept of social capital were popularised by Robert Putnam's seminal 2000 work, *Bowling Alone*. In it, Putnam argues that: 'The core idea of social capital theory is that social networks have value. Just as a screwdriver (physical capital) or a college education (human capital) can increase productivity, so too can social contacts.'[1]

Indeed, some have gone so far as to argue that the underlying value of our social networks is significantly greater than that of the formal economy, even in monetary terms.[2] Furthermore, social capital is both a private and public good, as social connectedness improves not only the life of an individual connected to a community, but the life of the community as a whole.

The total stock of social capital that we individually and collectively hold has been declining steadily, as the everyday personal and social connections of Britons have withered. Civic participation of all varieties has fallen drastically since the 1960s. Trade union membership peaked in 1979 at over 13 million, and by 2006/7 had dropped to under 8 million.[3] The proportion of people who belong to a religion and attend a service with at least some degree of regularity has declined from 71% in 1970 to less than half that in 2005.[4] In 2005, only 1.3% of the electorate were registered members of political parties[5] and we have already considered the decline in voting at elections.

This anomie is not only civic but social: according to the Home Office Citizenship Survey 2003, fully a fifth of people have any contact with a friend or neighbour less than once a month. Fewer than half of Britons trust the people in their own neighbourhoods, and only 30% agree that 'most people can be trusted' – down from 60% in the 1950s and moving in the opposite direction from Sweden (68%) and Norway (74%).[6]

This social recession doesn't just rob increasingly isolated citizens of a rich, varied and socially meaningful life, it fundamentally affects the way that society functions, not least the relationship between individuals and the state. Gone is the Burkean ideal of a civic, religious, political or social middle to balance between the demands of individuals and the power accrued by the state in delivering them.

Closer to home, the extended family has all but disappeared from British life and now even family networks are disintegrating. The number of people living alone in Great Britain has increased from 3 million in 1971 to 7 million in 2005.[7] Year on year, the number of people who choose to marry has declined, from 415,000 in 1970 to 284,000 in 2007.[8] While divorce rates have stabilised, with 12 married persons per 1,000 getting divorced in 2006, this is offset by a low marriage rate and a steep rise in cohabiting partnerships, half of which break up before their first child's fifth birthday.[9] This has led to rises in the proportion of children born outside of marriage, increasing steadily from 37% in 1997 to 44% in 2007 (a rate which did not exceed 10% until the 1960s) and the proportion of children living in lone-parent families, which more than tripled between 1972 and 2006 to 24%.[10]

These are serious and unprecedented changes in what should be the most important and enduring relationships in our lives – relationships which shape our existence from childhood, giving us values and identity, guiding our decisions and forming our archetypes for further relationships; relationships which for previous generations would have extended through old age and infirmity.

While we can see and feel the effects of this social crisis all around us – our receding trust in others, the normalisation of antisocial behaviour, our fear of children in the streets, our political and civic disengagement, spiralling rates of drug and alcohol abuse, high levels of dependency on state income and personal debt – these signals have been easy to ignore, as they represent an insidious failure of social capital which is less easily measurable than other forms of capital.

One of the first public figures to call attention to this issue of social dysfunction in Britain was Iain Duncan Smith, the former Tory Party leader. Two years after visiting the massive Easterhouse estate in Glasgow in 2002, where he witnessed first-hand the particularly acute impact that these social failings have had on those living in the bottom 20% of society – the inter-generational transmission of poverty, the culture of lifelong worklessness, the greatly reduced life expectancy of those living one postal code away from the long-lived and prosperous – he and Tim Montgomerie founded the Centre for Social Justice (CSJ) along with Philippa Stroud, its current director.

The CSJ think-tank pioneered the term 'Broken Britain' to refer to the impact of this crisis on society, and particularly on its poorest and most vulnerable members. CSJ research has shown that social breakdown in the areas of worklessness and economic dependence, fractured families, substance addiction, debt and educational failure are particularly implicated in the transmission of poverty between generations, with the social environment playing a crucial role in child development, especially during the first three years of life.

The impact of social failure on children is particularly visible in terms of criminality. Tragically, risk factors cluster together in the lives of disadvantaged children, greatly increasing the likelihood that they will become offenders as teenagers or adults. Children growing up in dysfunctional households are less likely to develop the emotional, social and practical skills required to succeed at school or in society. It is all the more shocking, in light of this knowledge, how little has been done to address the root causes of social breakdown, especially for young people who are most vulnerable to its effects.

And yet, even as we can see and feel the effects of this social crisis all around us, we resign ourselves to our fate. Unlike our financial crisis, where we have been able to lay responsibility at the door of the bankers and politicians, this social failure has been all our own – a failure of individuals and communities to organise, connect, and support each other; hold the state to account; establish values and norms of reciprocity and pursue a common good. But as with our financial crisis, this social failure has been enabled by an unhinged liberalism that propagates both irresponsible economic individualism and extreme bureaucratic statism.

The Broken Britain thesis is crucial here because it establishes the critical link between the failure of social relationships and civic institutions on the one hand and the issue of socially just outcomes for the bottom 20% of society on the other. In establishing this link, it implicitly faults the middle-class set of liberal values shared widely by society and promoted across the political class, which have given social primacy to the individual and their right to choose. In promoting this radical social subjectivity, the political class have unwittingly given second-order status to our wider civic and social commitments, obedience to social norms, sexual responsibilities, levels of alcohol and drug consumption, and even the decision to work, reducing these fundamentally to individual choices in respect of which the state and society should try to remain neutral. As Margaret Thatcher illustrated with infamous brevity, the modern liberal consensus is without an adequate account of society.

Historically, relativistic value systems have been resisted by the working classes, for whom the mutualism of society, community and family has been more than a matter of convenience. While properly functioning networks of community support improve the lives of all members of society, for the poorest and most vulnerable members of society, relationships and norms of conduct and generalised reciprocity provide irreplaceable social safety nets.

Welfarism

The great tragedy of the modern British welfare state has been the corrosion of the long-standing social values held by the working class, and thereby the effective erosion of the mutualism these values enshrined. Norms around community, work, familial obligation and civic and economic participation have been replaced by expectation of, and dependency on, state provision. This tragedy has not been particularly ironic, as welfarist state policies have been designed precisely to shift the primary source of social support from the horizontal social safety nets of civil society to vertically delivered equivalents provided by the state alone.

It goes without saying that this has been underpinned by a noble ambition to secure an equal and consistent 'floor' of support for precisely the most vulnerable members of society. However, as Winston Churchill famously observed, a just society requires that every person have not only a floor beneath which their income cannot fall, but also a ladder available to allow them to raise themselves out of poverty. While the state has been able to ensure the former, it has not produced the latter. Behaviour that should facilitate routes out of poverty – work, saving and investing, entrepreneurship and coupling – has been rendered economically unappealing, risky or even irrational for the poorest members of society. At the same time, the types of association that have traditionally encouraged and facilitated this behaviour have all but been eliminated.

The pernicious outcomes of this situation are clearly visible in the stagnating rates of social mobility for benefit recipients and low earners, the widening gap between rich and poor, the persistence of child poverty and in-work poverty, and the emergence of inter-generational benefits lineages – dynasties of hopelessness. Coming to the end of twelve years of Labour government, the poorest half of society now own only 1% of non-property assets.

Perhaps the greatest challenge facing the modern state is how to ensure adequate support for its citizens without compromising (and, wherever possible, by cultivating and harnessing) horizontal social bonds and self-regulating communities.

The decline of the family

The most basic of these bonds is marriage and the most fundamental of these communities is the family. And of course it is children who are particularly vulnerable to failing social and familial relationships.

Children from lone-parent families – who today constitute nearly one quarter of all children – are 75% more likely to fail at school, 70% more likely to become drug addicts and 50% more likely to become alcohol-dependent. They constitute 70% of all young offenders. Girls from fatherless homes are an over-represented demographic in teen pregnancy statistics, while boys from fatherless families are typically over-represented in criminal gangs.

These outcomes are often the result of dysfunctional parenting. In Britain today, as many as 1.3 million children live with parental alcohol misuse at home and a further 350,000 children live with parental problem drug use.[11] Problem drug and alcohol use is not only a result of social and family breakdown, but also causes further personal disintegration, and is strongly linked to domestic violence, neglect and child abuse.

Neglect and abuse of children is especially connected to criminal activity later in life. Even poor nutrition at age three leads to more aggressive behaviour at age eight, more problems at age eleven, greater conduct disorder at age seventeen and aggressive antisocial behaviour in adults.[12]

Many at-risk children end up moving from non-functioning families into the woefully inadequate and over-stretched care system, a path which all too often ends in the criminal justice system. Some 27% of all prisoners have come from the former.[13] As things stand, despite custody being reserved for cases of last resort, there are over 2,000 children aged between fifteen and seventeen in prison rather than care in England and Wales – children so damaged and dangerous that apparently only jail can contain them.[14]

Recreational use and abuse

Nowhere has this failure to define and regulate socially acceptable limits to behaviour had more damaging effects than with regard to the use and abuse of drugs and alcohol. The social implications of these problems have become impossible to ignore, spilling out nightly onto the streets all over the country. The centres of many of our cities have become war zones late on Friday and Saturday nights, with shameless public drunkenness and the violence it causes. Over the past fifty years, the per capita consumption of alcohol has doubled. For women, consumption rates have doubled over the course of the past ten years, and for children they have doubled over the past fifteen.

Alcohol-related crime alone is estimated to cost the economy £7.3 billion per year, with alcohol being a factor in 45% of all violent crime.[15] This dangerous relationship with alcohol runs both ways – more than 50% of victims of assault have also been drinking.[16] Drugs and alcohol also contribute to the majority of homicides.[17]

The health costs of Britain's socially tolerated alcoholism are equally serious. Some 33,000 people die annually from alcohol-related causes. According to the Royal College of Physicians, the NHS spends up to an eighth of its total hospital expenditure on treating the effects of alcohol misuse.

Nor is the story any better for drug use. A report by the UK Drug Policy Commission claimed that the UK today 'has the worst drug problem in Europe', with the highest rate of problem drug use and the second-highest rate of drug-related deaths. The impact on society is devastating. Some 56% of all crime is committed by drug users;[18] 75% of crack and heroin users claim to commit crime in order to feed their voraciously expensive habit, which no impoverished person could possibly afford, and these are drugs widely used by those least able to fund the addiction they cause.[19]

Resuscitating society

So Britain today faces the fallout from twin crises – one economic and one social – which have jointly undermined confidence in both the market and the state, and revealed the absence of any social middle – any network of associations and shared responsibilities capable of mediating between the two. Reversing this trend and restoring social capital is a matter of individual will, but it also requires bold political leadership and a radical new localism that puts power in the hands of associative groups. It will require fostering, supporting and nudging new associations like communities of service users, as well as traditional and basic ones like families.

Despite widespread public acknowledgement of Britain's broken society, the power and value that horizontal social relationships can have in reversing its symptoms is only beginning to gain recognition. Many are sceptical that these trends can be reversed, seeing anomic individualism and norm-less social interactions as inevitable conditions of modernity. It is no great exaggeration to say that the future of British civil society, and the fate of its dispossessed poor, rests on our ability to create the civic middle.

One thing is certain: the public cannot be left for much longer with a choice between the tired statism of the left and an arid free-market alternative proposed by the right, two liberalisms whose shared hallmark has been complicity in the marginalisation of society itself.

Social class and the decline of the British family

However, in order to grasp the full scale of the social crisis, we have to examine the evidence which shows its disproportionate effect upon the working classes.

First of all, though, let me be still more specific about the decline of marriage and the family in general. There seem to be four changes in the way people behave in relationships:

- They are less likely to get married;
- People with children are less likely to live within a formal marriage than in the past;
- If people start a family they are far more likely to experience its breakdown than they were forty years ago;

- The negative outcomes for children when this happens are more pronounced in the UK than in most other developed countries.[20]

Marriage rates in England and Wales have fallen to their lowest level since records began in 1862.[21] In 2007, for every thousand men and women there were roughly 20 of them marrying. These figures have been declining for decades. As recently as the mid-1980s the general marriage rate was 48 for men and 40 for women. And although population is growing, the absolute number of marriages has been going down. Marriages fell to 231,450 in 2007, down from 239,450 in 2006.

One consequence of this downward trend is that fewer children live in families that have committed themselves to marriage.

As we have already seen, more and more children are living with lone parents or cohabiting couples. The proportion of dependent children in the UK living with married parents fell from almost three-quarters in 1997 to less than two-thirds in 2009. This is a drastic decline in general levels of commitment to our most important social and personal bond. During the same period, the proportion of dependent children living with cohabiting couples rose from 8% to 13%, and the proportion of dependent children living with lone-parent families rose from 22% to 23%. Though divorce rates are falling, men and women in their late twenties had the highest divorce rates of all age groups. All these figures are from the ONS, published in 2009, and they are startling. In 2007 there were 26 or so divorces per

1,000 married men and married women aged 25–29. One in five men and women divorcing in 2007 had a previous marriage ending in divorce. This proportion has doubled in a generation: in 1980 only one in ten men and women divorcing had a previous marriage ending in divorce.

The number of dependent children living in different family types is of course affected by the ways in which families form and break up. For many children, their family structure will alter over time, particularly when their parents start or end a partnership. In England and Wales, there were 136,000 children (defined as those aged sixteen or under) involved in divorce in 2005. This was lower than the peak of 176,000 in 1993, but nearly twice the 1970 figure of 71,000.

There is naturally a strong correlation between the number of divorces and the number of children under sixteen involved in divorce. Both figures rose markedly between 1970 and 1980. The overall number of divorces rose by 90,000 (from 58,000 to 148,000), while the number of children involved in divorce rose by 92,000. And this in a population in which the number of children fell from 12.3 million in 1970 to 11.1 million in 1980. Even though divorce is reducing, this is only because marriage as such is in decline and with it also the number of couples bringing up children together. In effect the recent decline in divorce is an accelerated increase in divorce.

However, the fall in marriage rates is somewhat surprising, given that the majority of men and women between 20 and 35 would, according to the polls, like to get married one day.[22] Clearly, people still have the aspiration to marry but somewhere along the way to the altar or the registrar something goes wrong. But not everyone diverts from the initial aspiration. Level of education (here seen as an indicator for social class) seems to influence the probability of someone getting married and of someone getting divorced. Studies have shown that divorce rates are strongly affected by levels of education.

There is evidence from the UK that the aspiration to marry is uniformly high across the social spectrum but that the financial and cultural barriers (including shifts in expectation concerning male responsibility) to marriage are harder to overcome in low-income communities. This makes marriage an issue of social justice. A greater concentration of lone parenthood here may not be an expression of diversity but, paradoxically, of reduced choice with inability to fulfil marital ambitions as another dimension of inequality. Many people suppose that emphasising marriage is a moralising approach. But given the marriage 'gap', it is important to support marriage and measures to prevent family breakdown (which will involve helping people make more durable partnerships from the outset) for reasons of social justice, not because of the rhetoric of 'middle-class morality'.

The 'marriage gap' is well documented in the USA but less so in the UK.[23] Professor John Ermisch points out that among women born in the 1970s, those with higher qualifications enter a first partnership later; are less likely to have their first child outside a live-in partnership; are less likely to have their first child in a cohabiting union; become mothers later; are less likely to dissolve a cohabiting union or marriage; and are less likely to become lone mothers.[24]

In other words, women with no or low educational levels are likely to enter a partnership earlier, are more likely to have a child outside a stable relationship (a cohabiting one at best), become a mother earlier and are more likely to break up with their partner and therefore become a lone parent.

The term family is, of course, very vague. Although there is an instinctive liberal distrust for it, we can start, for heuristic purposes, from the model of the male breadwinner family which was still central to the organisation of social and economic life in postwar Britain. From 1906 the government began to establish protectionist social policies that helped the individual battle sickness, unemployment, disability and retirement. After the Second World War, the state increasingly saw itself as a proxy parent, operating *in loco parentis*. When Britain after the war became a welfare state, it was assumed that the man's earnings would be sufficient to support a non-working wife and several children. This had the effect of reinforcing a gendered division of labour. Women were expected to take care of the home, raise the children and care for the husband who, as the primary breadwinner, was expected to work hard in order to provide for the family and the homestead.

The state subsidised large families, and the withdrawal of married women from work reduced pressure on the labour market. The introduction of shorter working hours also gave individuals more time for leisure and self-development. This had an adverse effect on gender relations within the family.

While the husband spent his free time on leisure, whether intellectual or sporting pursuits or merely the pub, all of a woman's time was expected to be spent on the needs of the husband, household and children and not on personal gratification. Financially this was a comfortable settlement for both sexes, but dissatisfaction with such a limited role began to rise among women as the social climate began to change.

'Starting in the late 1930s more men and many more women began marrying at earlier ages.' Several factors contributed to this custom. The First World War showed the brevity and fragility of human life and spawned a romantic inclination to do things fast because life is short. Sexual relations outside marriage or outside of traditional heterosexual practices were stigmatised by the moral atmosphere of the times and marriage was seen by men as a means towards lawful sexual gratification and by women as a means towards social and financial stability.

Between 1945 and 1970 it remained overwhelmingly normative for people to enter marriage. From then on, there was a precipitate fall, which can be attributed mainly to changes in sexual attitudes, the availability of contraceptives and to married women joining the workforce.

Even though Philip Larkin's idea that sex was invented in 1963 is a myth (as earlier statistics for the number of pregnant brides reveals) it was not until the 1960s that acceptable, effective and reasonably safe contraception became widely available for the first time. Fertility began to fall from the peak of a 2.94 total fertility rate in 1964, when there were 480,000 women taking the Pill, which had been introduced in 1961. It is estimated that the total fertility rate had fallen to 1.64 by 2001, the lowest point in recorded history. The result of the vast improvement in birth control was that sexual contacts between men and women no longer necessarily carried the uncontrollable and incalculable risks and major economic consequences of pregnancy.

It is no coincidence that the 'traditional' family and sexual morality began to alter in the second half of the 1960s at the same time as the system of prudential marriage finally broke down. In a kind of unrepeatable meeting of the older post-WWI sexual tide and the new post-1960s one, the average age at marriage reached its lowest point of 21.29 in 1966–70. But of course the new lack of sexual restraint was far more dramatically reflected in the increased sexual activities of young people outside marriage. These changes also followed a long period in which incomes and their purchasing power had risen relative to the retail price index. By the 1950s male working-class manual employees and managers were already earning over three times more than they had in the mid-1930s and most other occupational groups were earning over two and half times as much. Thus couples could more easily afford to set up their own homes and one of the key traditional constraints on sexual behaviour had largely ceased to operate.

The sixties also saw a great shift in attitudes towards marriage. Women no longer saw marriage as a necessary step towards child bearing. New legal measures gave women greater independence and control over their lives and bodies and shook the foundations of the traditional family to the core.

The Divorce Reform Act of 1969 greatly facilitated the process of divorce – it shifted the reasons allowing divorce from a fault-based premise (showing that one partner had been unfaithful, for example) to divorce on evidence that the marriage had irretrievably broken down.

Having removed some traditional constraints (and rightly in many cases), subsequent social policies did little to help the continuation of family tradition and high fertility in new ways. Unmarried or divorced, single mothers received very little or fragmented help from the state. Many have pointed out that the British government has adopted a hands-off approach, arguing that social issues are for the labour market partners rather than government to sort out. This approach has resulted in comparatively underdeveloped employment policies for parents, disparate responses by employers, and uneven distribution of arrangements to support working parents.

Marriage now offers little attraction to the 'Noughties' generation in Britain. Most couples are happy to cohabit without getting married. Divorces have become exceedingly simple affairs, especially after the 1994 Act that allowed couples to divorce after one year. Few divorcees seem to want to remarry. Weak family-orientated social policies and long working hours provide little incentive to have many children. All of this has resulted in very low fertility rates among the British population.

Another trend leading to low fertility over the past thirty years has been the increasing postponement of childbearing in marriage. The most conspicuous postponement occurred among men and women graduates who aimed to have families after they had sorted out their careers. Some researchers estimate that about a quarter of graduate women born in 1970 will remain childless.

The traditional radicalism of the family

Most historians and sociologists now agree that the nuclear family in the west predated the arrival of industrial capitalism as well as surviving that transition.[25] Moreover most now concur that the nuclear family is not some western invention but is as close as possible to an anthropological and human universal.[26] Indeed what now appears to be the case is that it is the composition of the extended family that varies with time and culture. It is not that any nuclear family was ever without an extension to it; rather it is what constitutes that extension that varies and differs across the ages. More shocking then is the general western crisis – particularly exemplified in the UK in ways that I have detailed. The decline of the traditional family is so extreme that Lawrence Stone wrote: 'There has been nothing like it in the last two thousand years and probably much longer.'[27]

Now some of the developments that have helped deepen the crisis might well be welcome, such as the demise of the sole male breadwinner and the mass employment of married women working outside the home. But we cannot hide from the compounded effect of all these consequences – there really is a crisis in the family and we are undergoing it and inflicting its most invidious consequences on our children. The factors behind this shift are both economic and cultural and, insofar as we fail to name this crisis and culturally resist the erosion of the family, then we allow the economic destruction of our familial life to proceed apace and unaddressed.

One would think that, given the destruction of the most important relationships that we have in our lives, that the tradition that purports to most value the social and relational would be first to issue a call to arms to defend the family and all the nurture, responsibility and mutuality that its structure implies. Yet the left has a long tradition of suspicion and hostility to the family – Marx and Engels both regarded the family as another site of exploitation, with the wife as the proletariat and the husband as the propertied owner. As Tristram Hunt has noted, Engels could see little difference between a street whore and an ordinary bourgeois wife who 'merely does not let her body out on a piece work as a wage worker, but sells it once and for all into slavery'.[28] Sometimes in addition the left has regarded marriage as a barrier to hedonism and an institution that prevented the fulfilment of sexual desire. Charles Fourier, an early nineteenth-century French utopian socialist, wished for every form of sexual variety as a liberation of human passion and even invented a card-indexing system for the facilitation of casual sex for the inhabitants of his communities or *Phalanstères*. For him marriage was an arbitrary imposition of an order on a culture that should enjoy no such fixity – he even suggested that children could choose their parents just as adults choose their partners. Likewise, as Hunt also notes, Robert Owen, the patriarch of New Lanark, identified the family with selfishness and resisted any attempt to have a family interest that could impede the will of the community.

Despite the overwhelming pro-family stance of the religiously influenced old Labour Party, ever since the 1960s left-wing hostility to familial bonds and modes of faithful reciprocity between men and women has revived.

But the family is a deeply radical and indeed feminist institution. It binds men to women and offers a cultural account of how they should behave towards one another. Instead, after the successful assault on the family by progressives, unmarried women have it worse three times over: they have to work externally, labour domestically, and look after their children entirely by themselves. Moreover, as we have seen above, the outcomes for their children are far worse than for those not so affected.

For the family offers the site of both sharing and nurture: it is where people learn to limit their desires and give to the greater good. It is the site of character formation and life orientation. In short, the family is a profoundly relational institution and, since it places individuals within a context of obligation and responsibility, it embodies the essence of mutuality. The fact that many now celebrate its destruction as somehow part of the liberation of women only testifies to the destruction of the chance for a real feminism founded on what most women want – marriage and children alongside creative work and social engagement.

Of course the crisis of the British working classes is in part a crisis of de-industrialisation, and of the removal of an entire ethos that gathered round industry. And yet a balanced view will not see that as the whole story. We do not need to choose between impersonal structural and personal ethical shifts: they are both involved and they both reinforce each other. The strength of the family allowed ordinary people to weather equally severe or worse traumas in the past: the Reformation and the Industrial Revolution. But today its collapse is part of what leaves working people less able to act for themselves to renew their future.

4 The Errors of the Right

Britain after the Second World War was a confused and confusing place. We had won the war. We had stood against fascism when every other European country had either succumbed or made a craven and corrupt peace. We had held the line and through sheer British romanticism we had somehow conjured up the idea that however logical peace with Hitler might be, or however necessary conceding Europe to Germany was if we were to save the Empire, we were not going to surrender or sue for peace. We were a great and good power, and what sustained us through the dark days of 1940 and 1941 and the many defeats was that belief and confidence in our nation, our historic legacy and each other. We won the Battle of Britain, thereby making eventual total victory along with our allies possible. Together we liberated Europe and freed the world from a great evil (even if the US and UK failed to deal with the evil of communism). All of this we did through an act of collective imagination, sheer bloody-minded persistence and, most crucially, the recognition of a common good that we were not prepared to betray.

And then, having won the war, we lost the peace. After a brief halcyon moment and the constitution of something like a shared state and a secure and more just society, we squandered the inheritance of Empire, resurrected the sectional interests and the economics of class and turned in and upon ourselves. As the fifties flowed into the sixties, we gradually became the sick man of Europe. Unable to innovate, trade and prosper, we fought each other for a greater share of a shrinking cake. Trapped in an economic death-spiral that culminated in the winter of discontent in 1978–79, the British turned to the most radical and charismatic European politician of the postwar era – Margaret Thatcher. She saw the stakes for what they were and fundamentally shifted direction – but by so doing a whole swathe of our population was abandoned to a life of permanent unemployment or temporary wages and astonishingly low rewards. As a nation we started to despise those we had abandoned and, to hide our shame, we blamed them for what we had done. But by the same token, the ultimately unsatisfactory postwar settlement was at least broken and Britain could begin to restructure. And to a certain extent we did: entrepreneurship and ownership were recognised as self-evident goods, but other equally self-evident goods such as service and vocation were denigrated and ridiculed as virtues of a bygone age. Notions of intrinsic worth and the behaviours that accompanied such values had – apparently – no place in Britain's new political economy.

The real financial fate of the next generation was being prepared, and it lay exclusively within the M25. Economically, Thatcher's Big Bang – her radical deregulation of the financial sector – removed all barriers to capital movements. This decisive move created a financial renaissance for the City of London. But, in the name of extending domestic investment, the Square Mile produced instead a centralised capitalism increasingly focused on international speculation and the capital inflows that this attracted. If the City did have a decisive impact on the real economy, it was in its financing and packaging of, and speculation in, the asset bubbles that grew so quickly under Blair and burst so spectacularly in 2007/8 under Brown. After his landslide victory in 1997, Blair made no attempt to rebalance the economy and direct the capital generated by the City to other parts of the nation. He bought into the myth of the City's financial genius. New Labour eulogised this vast centralisation of capital and celebrated the City as a taxation cash-cow. Rather than distribute investment capital and genuine economic growth, Blair and his Chancellor dispersed welfare and public expenditure instead. New Labour used the vast capital inflows to the City to create the tax revenue stream that they claimed would heal the rents in the social fabric that Mrs Thatcher created.

But the great debt/asset crisis of 2007/8 revealed that all the returns generated by the investment banks were made on the back of gaming the British state and its sovereign tax-paying base. The recession that the collapse of this model has created has put over a million in the UK out of work and saddled us with an unprecedented postwar public-sector debt – one that may well depress the rate of British economic growth for years to come.

How did Britain come to this? How did we allow the majority of our GDP growth over the last ten years to be in financial services, the public sector and housing, and very little else? How did we allow our economy to become so homogenous and unvariegated? In every other sphere of life lack of diversity is recognised as an inherent danger – did nobody in power notice what was happening as a result of their policies? And why did the rest of us let it happen?

To answer these questions we need to look briefly into economic and social history. Western Europe had an exceptionally successful period from the end of World War II to the late 1960s. In terms of GDP Western Europe grew more than twice as fast from 1950 to 1973 as it did at any time before or after this 'golden age'. Barry Eichengreen's brilliant study of the European economy argues convincingly that the unprecedented success of postwar Europe was due to the constitutional setting in which market forces were situated: 'It required a set of norms and conventions, some informal, others embodied in law, to coordinate the actions of social partners and solve a set of problems that decentralised markets could not.'[1] These continental institutions, from trade unions to employers' organisations to regional banks, directed capital lending, mobilised savings, financed investment and kept wages low enough to ensure relatively full employment, and adequate enough to ensure social peace. The continent was better placed for this due to its later economic development. The fact that Britain had industrialised first, though almost without the aid of the state, meant that, in order to catch up, the economies of mainland Europe had to involve the state and a full range of other economic actors to a far greater degree than in Britain. This created a tradition of coordination between the public and private sectors and the rise of a complex range of institutions all dedicated to the same end – economic modernisation and coordinated growth. So conceived, this set of organisations and consensual arrangements quickly recovered after the war and produced nearly a quarter century of growth.

There was a political side to this cooperative impulse too. So extreme was the cost of the war, that the Western European nations were determined to lock Germany into something greater than itself. Almost immediately, the integrationist imperative that existed on a national level became a supra-national phenomenon – with, for example, six major Western European nation states putting their own iron, steel and coal industries under multi-national control in the 1950s, just six years after the most extreme and bitter warfare between those very nations.

In this great European postwar narrative of economic success Britain was a poor relation as the UK economy increasingly failed to perform or deliver. Between 1950 and 1973 the average growth of GDP in the UK was only 2.5%, while the Western European average was 4.0% and Germany and Italy each averaged 5%.[2] These economies managed in this period to eliminate around 40% of the pre-WWII growth gap with the US. Indeed, if one measures GDP by hours worked as a percentage of American levels, by 1973 Britain averaged only 60% of US productivity, whereas Germany was at 79%, France at 74% and Italy at 78%. Even the productivity gain subsequently achieved during the Thatcher years has not been enough to compensate, as France by the same hourly measure in 2003 had a workforce that was more productive than the US by about 11%, while Germany and Italy were roughly equal, whereas the UK was still at 83% of US levels of productivity.[3] Legacies matter, and sometimes it can take decades for the consequences of certain structural patterns to become manifest. For instance, no other country in Western Europe had rates of non-residential investment as low as the UK did during the 1950s, and this is but one factor in explaining the structural inefficiency of the British postwar settlement. Another is the failure of our export markets – our total average annual export growth rate 1950–73 was only 6.9%, against an EU average of 12.2%, while Germany achieved a staggering 19.8% annual export growth.[4]

The British motor industry offers a sad cautionary tale that sums up many of these failings. The British Motor Corporation was formed from the merger of Austin and Morris in 1952 and had, by the early 1960s, nearly a quarter of the British car market, while in the mid-1960s about 40% of BMC's exports were going to the continent. In 1965 BMC made 846,000 vehicles (including the world-famous and iconic Mini), nearly twice the number it made in 1955. But the long-term lack of structural investment meant that production was highly labour-intensive, so that this output did not lead to a corresponding increase in productivity – and as Geoffrey Owen, former editor of the *Financial Times*, points out, 'Even in the good years profitability barely reached the level achieved in the mid 1950s.'[5] The company, after absorbing Jaguar, was eventually merged by the Labour government with Leyland in 1968 to create British Leyland.

The merger did not work. Managers were unable to create a new common purpose for the merged entity. Unable to decide between specialist cars or high-volume mass production, and unable to tackle sectional worker interests in the name of shared concerns, the new company produced cars that competed with each other and created product failure after product failure. Coupled with managerial incompetence was worker intransigence. Strikes were endemic in the corporation's factories, and the company made hard work less attractive by replacing an admittedly inefficient system of piece-work with a highly monitored production system that fixed pay and limited reward. In response, workers transferred their frustration to other areas of dispute, some of them in the name of ideological hostility to capitalism itself, producing fragmented wage bargaining and disputes over sectional responsibilities, which in turn led to ill-defined and badly executed work standards, all of which fed further the dysfunctional and hugely regressive autonomy of the shop stewards in the car factories.

The government stepped in once more and British Leyland was nationalised in 1975. But the nationalisation did not work, and by 1980 its share of the home market was just 18.2%. The company's exports had fallen by nearly 60% since 1970. It was now so far behind its competitors that it was unlikely to survive, and despite a revival in the 1980s with the Mini Metro the company was still less than the sum of its parts. After selling off its brands to foreign manufacturers, MG Rover (as it was now known) reached an ignominious end at the hands of the Phoenix Consortium, which bought the remnants of some of the greatest British companies for £10 in 2000. To add insult to injury the Phoenix Four, as they were known, acted with sublime self-interest and extracted £42 million for themselves in pay and pensions from the corpse of this great industry before the company finally collapsed in 2005 and the remaining brands were sold to the Chinese.

In 1960 the British Motor Corporation was one of the world's greatest car markers – with the exception of Volkswagen, it produced more cars than any other European company.[6] By the end of the century Britain was the only major European country not to have a serious domestic car company at all. We even sold the automobile division of Rolls Royce, makers of the engines that powered the Spitfire, to the Germans. The BMC/British Leyland/Rover story is perhaps Britain's most tragic and emblematic postwar industrial failure and it embodies everything that was wrong with the British postwar model.

Continental Europe prospered because it systematically organised and pooled interests that otherwise would have become conflictual in a form of coordinated capitalism, and established interdependent institutions that built on structures existing, in some cases, from before the war. Often it was the smaller states that were the most corporatist, perhaps because they were of the size that allow citizens to see their own interests in their neighbours or fellow inhabitants. Since continental Europe itself had seen such blood and carnage in the war, it is no surprise that all mainland states to a greater or lesser degree adopted quasi-corporatist models as a way of fostering common interest and suppressing conflict. They were helped in part because their educational and training resources were well fitted for the necessary work of modernisation. Emphasis on apprenticeship and training and vocational institutions created a technically adroit workforce that eschewed, for most of the postwar period, trade union militancy. Governments provided extensive employment protection and labour security. Welfare schemes, from holidays to sick pay, were introduced, as were systems of worker participation, with responsible union representatives sitting on most European supervisory boards so that they could verify that profits from their members' wage restraint were being invested in the business rather than extracted through share dividends.

In German steel companies after 1945, workers appointed half of all supervisory board members, and Germany's subsequent co-determination law of 1952 meant that similar measures were extended to the rest of industry. Austria and the Netherlands had similar arrangements, as did Norway with its planning councils and production committees. The strategy was reflected in macro-economic tax measures. The German government penalised dividend payments but rewarded investment with tax incentives. The Swedes followed suit. No institution was allowed to pursue its own exclusive interests. Banks were regionalised and encouraged to offer low interest rates for local investment. Meanwhile, wage restraint was successful in part because it led to higher benefits for workers. This social pact was secured by the development of centralised wage-bargaining – wage rounds had their levels set by a follow-the-leader policy in which wage rises for the nation were determined by lead industries which always accepted the broad wage ranges set by central government. Sky-high demands designed to cause crises, which were the norm in certain British industries, were unheard of. So well inculcated did this system become that the Swedes even fined firms which offered rises above the norm. The development of the common European economic area further facilitated growth as barriers fell and trade with neighbours increased.

This European investment-rich and export-led paradigm created what we can now see as the continental economic miracle. And while the corporatism pursued by mainland Europe delivered unprecedented rewards, Britain pursued instead a perverse form of what it failed properly to copy, adapt or achieve. Most importantly, the British state froze rather than overcoming conflict. A false Keynesian consensus financed a cosy and corrupt compromise between owners who were only interested in personal dividends and workers who shut themselves out from the boardroom and wanted nothing more than higher wages for work of less and less quality. This is all the more peculiar since Britain had just fought and won a war predicated on the very idea of a common interest that most actors in UK industry now denied. Each side of the capital–labour divide retreated to its comfort zone. British management was diffident, un-visionary and incompetent, preferring a quiet life rather than the testing demands of investment choices, product innovation and competition with foreign brands. Likewise labour unions refused anything that might threaten their perception of their own interests or compromise their narrow vision of the class struggle, and when the National Union of Mineworkers refused the Labour minister Manny Shinwell's twice-made offer in 1949 to join the board of the nationalised coal industry, that set the tone for the whole disastrous legacy of statist socialism and of union power divorced from responsibility. Labour, in this British industrial world, made demands on the state. And it was the statism imposed by Labour that left so many workers separated from real decision-making and control.

In a society founded on class, we Britons seemed incapable of truly escaping its legacy. The right blamed workers, the left blamed managers, and so both failed to see that the problem was a shared lack of social virtue. As the 1960s gathered steam we increasingly appeared to prefer confrontation and short-term gain over trust and cooperation. And the very fact that these words seem trivial or kitsch tells us how little we have learnt from those who did so much better than us in terms of prosperity. State welfarism separated the British working class from a new kind of industrial mutualism that was certainly at least thinkable during the post-1945 Labour government. Instead the state became a false broker, during the sixties and the seventies constantly mortgaging the future to bail out the present. And in freezing conflict rather than subsuming it under a newly articulated general interest, the postwar British settlement achieved by the state was always destined to break.

If the British left had sought another way at some point after 1945, then the left rather than the right might have been the agent of renewal, but given the dependence of the Labour Party on the unions that was already a forlorn hope by the late 1960s. Still there were moments when an alternative future could have been created. If, for example, Harold Wilson had read and fully absorbed Barbara Castle's 1969 white paper 'In Place of Strife', then he might have supported her against Jim Callaghan, the then Home Secretary – who sealed his own fate and that of the Labour movement by resisting Castle's attempt to suppress class sectarianism and create a new settlement with the trade unions. And of course all the dominant trends on the left were actually heading, despite themselves, headlong down the road towards a profoundly neo-liberal settlement. The new non-parliamentary left, with its emphasis on unilateral rights assertion for every conceivable variant of 'identity', and the repudiation of continuous virtue in the name of isolated 'values', was already busy destroying the earlier associative institutions of the working class. This it did by mostly ignoring working-class culture as it actually was, and creating a new language of rights and middle-class aspiration that then was subsequently sold to those lower down the pecking order as the only new form of progressive politics. These narrow values were in the sixties shaping a whole generation of middle-class people and creating the culture and the individuals that within a decade would consider themselves wholly deserving of exclusive economic advancement. Everywhere left bohemians were reversing the wisdom of ages in their claim for advancement, and the politics of personal intensity and individual privilege. Many, quite rightly, doubt the efficacy of this essentially middle-class culture, and make the point that the new left was a minority faction and that for the overwhelming majority of Britons continuity was what most marked this decade.[7] But for me this gets the transmission of social change wrong. When the masses are given no reason to believe what they have always held to be true, and when such beliefs are no longer practised or celebrated by crucial opinion-formers and community leaders, then a small group of counter-cultural activists can be surprisingly effective in removing some of the most important supports and mainstays of a stable and secured society.

Interestingly, however, the unexpected defeat of Harold Wilson's government in June 1970 was in large part a working-class repudiation of the Labour Party's and the left's whole economic and cultural approach. This Conservative victory was largely achieved by Enoch Powell's break with the British political consensus, but it was not his 'rivers of blood' speech that really drew these new votes. It was Powell's implicit appeal to an earlier non-statist society governed by duty, obligation and equal participation in free trade that captured working-class support much more than his warnings about the destruction of working-class communities through the opening up of housing lists to new migrants. Powellism brought millions of new working-class votes to the Conservative Party, which Edward Heath squandered through not creating a more radical settlement in line with the needs of this new and emboldened constituency.[8]

Even allowing for the difficult circumstances it inherited, the government of Edward Heath clearly failed. Growth fell sharply from 3.3% in the second half of 1970 to 0.3% in 1971 and unemployment surged to levels not seen since the start of the war. Facing both stagflation and industrial unrest around the recently enacted 1971 Industrial Relations Act, which attempted to clip the wings of the big unions, Heath with his Chancellor Antony Barber enacted a corporatist U-turn in 1972 that attempted to inflate demand so as to achieve, they hoped, a growth rate twice that attained in the past decade, and kick-start Britain's economy out of its problems. Barber raised personal allowances and reduced purchase tax. He also increased government borrowing. The 'Barber boom' took off and then just as promptly, given the intrinsic weakness of the British economy, collapsed. Inflation rose from 7% in 1972 to 24% in 1975, exacerbated of course by the 1973 OPEC ambush when the rentier oil states hiked the price of the one commodity they controlled. Government borrowing exploded. Barber was forced to introduce deflationary measures in December 1973, and after a miner's strike and the advent of Arthur Scargill, and the introduction of a three-day week, the Conservatives ended up losing the election of February 1974 to a minority Labour government led once more by Harold Wilson.

All of which exposed, to those influenced by the new pro-market think-tanks such as the Institute of Economic Affairs and a group of radicalised Tory MPs around Keith

Joseph, the fundamental failure of demand-driven Keynesian economics. These neo-liberal Tories never really forgave Heath for his failure of nerve and the U-turn of 1972. For them the true alternative to the ruling orthodoxy – a radical neo-liberalism – became etched ever more deeply in their minds.

The country knew it had to change, yet it did not know which way to go – a situation illustrated by the two general elections held in 1974. Both elections, however, due to the withdrawal of the Ulster Unionist MPs from the Conservative Party whip over the 1973 Sunningdale Agreement, which offered power sharing in Northern Ireland, ended with Labour narrowly in control. The first resulted in a minority government, the second in a tiny majority of some three MPs. Despite this wafer-thin support of the status quo, the Labour government continued to believe that the problems of the British economy could only be solved by more government ownership and control. The National Enterprise Board was created in 1975 and became an instrument of arbitrary nationalisation or intervention, propping up now almost-forgotten companies that had already failed such as British Leyland, Ferranti and Alfred Herbert. Once again, it missed an opportunity. If it had done things differently – radically restructured British industry and labour relations, or encouraged serious innovation – then something might have changed, but the maintenance of the existing order continued to capture all its energy and effort. Harold Wilson's resignation in March 1976 led to James Callaghan facing down Michael Foot and winning the party plebiscite.

Callaghan assumed leadership of an increasingly unstable government, and became Prime Minister when the Labour Party had already lost its majority. He struggled through the Lib–Lab pact – a woefully pragmatic alliance with the Liberal Party – with a sanguine and almost admirable disregard for the consequences of permanent inaction. Callaghan represented the status quo at its most conservative and uncreative. If he had called an election in September 1978 there is every likelihood that Labour would have won it. Instead – not unlike Gordon Brown in autumn 2008 – he delayed when he could have won and set himself up to become the victim of circumstances long prepared by British postwar history. And circumstance did not let him down. The winter of discontent of 1978–79 was one of the worst-ever periods of strikes in the country's history. The TUC 'day of action' on 22 January 1979 was the most disruptive day of British labour unrest since the 1926 General Strike. Bodies remained unburied, rubbish was not collected, and in parts of the country the ambulance crews even refused to attend 999 calls. No wonder Jim Callaghan lost. And he lost to Europe's most radical postwar politician. The status quo was about to be upended.

Margaret Thatcher

Mrs Thatcher – Churchill excepted – remains the most decisive and important British leader of the twentieth century. The first woman to be Prime Minister, she set the terms of political debate for the next three decades, and in many ways still does. She kicked down the whole rotten infrastructure of the British postwar settlement and replaced that paradigm with a new politics and a new economic and social model, a resolution to do things differently.

For a country that was increasingly riven by class-based politics and the dominance of sectarian interests, she brought an end to the bankrupt politics of the workers' state and the eroding and debilitating compromises that industry had made with organised labour. Her election in 1979 seemed to offer a new settlement such that even some of the organised working class, hankering after a different place in the order of things, voted for her – so exhausted were they by the preceding winter of discontent and the gutless pragmatism of the Callaghan era.

Britain now seems unthinkable without Mrs Thatcher – and in private conversation most left-wing thinkers think that, given the situation in the late 1970s, her ascendancy, or something very much like it, was inevitable. In 1979 Callaghan lost, but what did he lose to? Even now informed opinion remains divided. Was Mrs Thatcher a true conservative, or was she a new and radical kind of liberal? Did she rescue the British economy or did she condemn whole groups of people and whole areas of the country to permanent poverty and exclusion? Both narratives could be true of course. The apocryphal prayer of St Francis that Mrs Thatcher intoned on the day of her victory and just before she stepped into No 10, retains its purchase on the contemporary mind – its first line 'Where there is discord, may we bring harmony ...' is mirrored by its last: 'Where there is despair may we bring hope.' Even her closest allies and greatest advocates would have difficulty in claiming that Mrs Thatcher realised those aspirations.

Eschewing the Keynesian consensus and its commitment to full employment, Mrs Thatcher claimed that the wage demands of labour were one of the major causes of inflation and the source of industrial unrest. As a consequence she moved to eliminate the role and position of labour in the macro-economic framework of the country. The Pay Comparability Commission was abolished; legal immunities for the trade unions were removed, as were restrictions on the hiring and firing of temporary workers. But wage inflation continued to rise, by 20% in 1980 and 15% in the first half of 1981. Higher interest rates (they rose by four percentage points between 1979 and 1981) led to rapid appreciation of sterling – putting further pressure on the industrial base and export-driven industries.[9] With the real effective exchange rate rising by some 25%, an unavoidable recession ensued. Within a year GDP fell by 5% and unemployment hit 10.4% by the second quarter of 1981. The need to deflate without forcing industry to its knees led to an abandonment of simplistic monetarist strategy, and monetary policy was loosened. Tax rises were now used to depress inflationary demand, the linking of income tax brackets to inflation was abandoned in 1981 and tax revenues rose while the crunch continued.

However, the abandonment of one form of monetarism did not lead to the rejection of the idea that an increase in money supply caused inflation. Hence the adoption of the medium-term financial strategy, which targeted M3 money supply, the preferred measure of the amount of cash in the economy. This, however, proved equally ineffective since M3 had risen since 1982 whilst inflation had fallen. The money supply seemed to have little or nothing to do with inflation, hence Chancellor Nigel Lawson's final dismissal of that approach in 1985 and his attempt to control inflation through the exchange rate.

But monetarism as an ideology seemed to be at a complete remove from the real economic situation and that was taking its own course. Monetarism was, as Sir Ian Gilmour, one of Thatcher's 'wet' Conservative opponents, called it, the 'uncontrollable in pursuit of the undefinable'. The pound slid from a high of $1.91 against the dollar at the end of 1981 to $1.10 at the beginning of 1985, largely because of the continuing weakness of the British economy. It was this devaluation more than anything else that gradually restored our competitiveness in world markets. However, what the recession and the rise in unemployment did permit was the effective destruction of a perverse culture of inefficiency and over-manning, allowing genuine efficiencies to be achieved in parts of British industry. But the benefits of the growth that resulted were unevenly distributed and quite staccato in impact. By 1983 British GDP was still 4% below what it was in 1979. And even though, according to most economic indicators, the economy started to recover in 1984, it was only beneficial for some, and unemployment hit 3.2 million by the middle of that year. Meanwhile, the destruction of the export base in the first recession, and the sucking in of imports, was causing a balance of payments deficit, and interest rates were jacked up to 12% which itself then threatened to derail the recovery via a sudden downturn. At the party conference that October Mrs Thatcher insisted that Keynes would have agreed with her and that capital investment could not be delivered by government expenditure. The markets disagreed and the pound fell further and interest rates had to be raised even higher.

Unemployment continued to divide the nation, and the great miner's strike of 1984, which dragged on into 1985, polarised opinion and the country still further. These social strains caused severe internal political problems (now almost forgotten) for the seeming ascendancy of Thatcherism in the Conservative Party, and though Chancellor Lawson had cheerfully claimed that Britain could get along with double-digit unemployment, by 1985 Tories were losing council seats and the shires and counties that they controlled. Previously loyal Thatcherites voiced deep dissatisfaction with 'the government's unimaginative laissez-faire attitude to the greatest social problem of our time'.[10] Increasing the sense of social crisis, the autumn of 1985 saw a repetition of the infamous riots of 1981, when there were further disturbances in Toxteth, Brixton and Tottenham, where a policeman lost his life to a vicious machete attack. As a consequence Thatcher's poll ratings by 1986 had steadily dwindled, such that they were barely higher than in the depths of her unpopularity in 1981.[11]

Finally in October 1986 unemployment began to fall. And in a development the full implications of which were not fully grasped until two decades later, this year also saw an epochal change in financial deregulation. In the so-called Big Bang of 27 October 1986, the City of London was almost fully deregulated and controls on international capital were abandoned.[12] From this point on, aided by a fall in the oil price that pushed sterling 16% lower in the year, Lawson was able to drive a boom which was driven by tax cuts and aided by a massive increase in credit supply that shot asset prices and consumer demand to ever higher levels. New bank lending trebled and in 1986–7 the number of new mortgages taken out doubled in a single year. In a fantastic inversion of monetarism, it was another Barber boom, but without the regulatory mechanisms to control the money supply – they had been junked in the Big Bang. Britain's popular capitalism had received from Lawson its decisive asset-bubble shape and it had nothing to do with sound money.

This state-engineered boom allowed the Conservatives to win the 1987 General Election, but the bust followed soon after. The stock market crash in October 1987 led to immediate interest-rate cuts. Lawson further intensified the up-cycle by assuming it was the new norm and in 1988 he pumped a further £4.2 billion into the economy. House prices in London rose 15% in just three months. But, unaided by national exports, the deficit soared as cash-rich consumers pulled in imports. Lawson was forced to raise interest rates to choke back the very demand he had created, so that by September of that year interest rates had reached 12% and by September of the next year 15%.

Thatcher privately and later publicly despaired that her 'monetarist' Chancellor was now using interest rates not to control inflation but as part of a strategy to reach a targeted exchange rate with the deutschmark. In one sense Lawson was right. The British economy was better managed through exchange-rate competitiveness rather than by money supply, not least because, since the Big Bang, it was impossible to control the amount of capital that flowed into the UK. But Thatcher's instinct about the loss of economic sovereignty this implied, given the relative distinction between the UK and mainland European economies, and the importance therefore of monetary autonomy, was also well placed. In any case, when in office Lawson ran monetary policy and much like Gordon Brown after him he believed he had bucked the economic trends and escaped from the sterling and balance of payments crises that bedevilled the 1960s and 70s.

But hubris stalks all such illusions, and the miracle Chancellor in 1987 who promised zero inflation and a new economic paradigm was, by 1989, presiding over inflation of nearly 10% and interest rates being raised in the vain hope of containing demand and prices. This, coupled with ongoing weakness in exports and the pricking of the housing bubble, meant that in Britain the prolonged recession of the early nineties saw unemployment rising back to 3 million in 1993.

I tell this story in this somewhat prosaic and factual manner because memory has falsified our recent past. We tend to look back on Thatcher's economic legacy from the perspective of the last economic golden age, those ten years before the crash of 2007 when everything was always going up – house prices, shares, profits. From this viewpoint we forget that the Thatcher governments were less revolutionary and more ordinary in their economic management than we suppose – there were no economic miracles, and we had two debilitating recessions and those who lost out lost out permanently and, it now seems, generationally. The children of workers who lost their jobs in the 1980s are in very bad shape. Moreover, the sense that the underfunding of institutional infrastructure was tearing apart the social fabric and undermining the basis of not just working-class but also middle-class life was palpable. Thatcherism itself progressively lost all public legitimacy when this general intuition was personalised for people by a series of public disasters – from the sinking of the *Herald of Free Enterprise* in 1987, to the King's Cross fire of the same year and the Clapham Rail disaster in 1988, the Hillsborough tragedy and sinking of the Thames cruiser the *Marchioness* in 1989. All these tragedies seemed to stem from a loss of human regard and care, which in the public mind was related to a lack of state regulation and investment.

But leaving aside the ideological ardour that normally characterises such discussions, let us try to reach some conclusions and assess the real legacy of Thatcherism.

It has to be recognised that the entire postwar British economic settlement was rotten. It may well have been, as Correlli Barnett has so brilliantly argued in his 'Pride and Fall' series, that Britain had over-extended itself in its Empire, and that in the twentieth century we had an innate anti-technical bias in our educational system, producing an ill-educated, ill-trained and poorly motivated workforce.[13] Unable in the first half of the twentieth century to create and train the nation for industrial success, after the Second World War we squandered the opportunity to remake ourselves by seeking a vaunted new Jerusalem in the welfare state. And in exchange for this illusion we surrendered the resources to remake our industrial and economic base. But for me what was squandered was not so much the resources that went into the welfare state, as the genuine industrial and investment opportunity that the undoubted need for a new social settlement offered. For, if we had had a different kind of welfare state, one that was more mutual and reciprocal, we could have used this to re-engage and even re-unite capital and labour and so to inculcate in our own particular manner the processes that proved so successful in postwar Europe. We could have localised welfare and tied it to a different regional settlement and thereby brought in the workers and allied them with the type of public capital that could have secured them and their families in exchange for new demarcations and practices at work. Instead of a universal income-based welfare policy, we could have crafted a new mutualism, that in exchange for minimising wage claims made the proletariat asset owners in the businesses in which they spent their working lives. As such they could have ensured that profit was directed not towards the share dividend but to deep structural investment.

None of this happened and as a result, as we have seen, after the war continental Europe grew, while Britain slowly died. And Mrs Thatcher grasped this. In a way she despised both sides of the postwar bargain. She was as contemptuous of the old ruling elite as she was of its organised working class; she loved her nation but despised many of its institutions, and though she was indifferent to the fate of too many of its people, she was determined to remake it and cared not for what got in her way. As already indicated, her economic record is – if one reads it objectively – fairly ordinary, with two extreme cycles of boom and bust with a couple of very good years in between. Indeed national output per head averaged about 2% growth per year over the Thatcher decade, lower, as Simon Jenkins has pointed out, than in the despised era of Wilson and Heath.[14] But this is to read the country from its median average and the story of course is that hardly anybody occupied this mean. Thatcher's legacy was one of sharp divisions – with very real winners and very real losers.

The real winners were the new expanded middle class in south-eastern England. They were the ones who took up and made real the ideology of small business start-ups. By virtue of necessity or ambition, millions started their own businesses. By 1989 there were 3 million self-employed people, then forming some 11% of the workforce. Catering to a new service economy, the young and newly entrepreneurial created – from the Body Shop to Amstrad – the new tastes and products that defined the 1980s.

Even if you still worked for someone else, the benefits of a job seemed evident enough. Real wages rose by 20% between 1983 and 1987 which, when coupled with the new credit facilities, created an unprecedented boost for consumption and expenditure – much of which was fed into housing and personal debt, so that overall household indebtedness increased by 250% between 1982 and 1989.

Thatcher's attempt to modernise and indeed globalise did not just concern individual entrepreneurs. The elimination of the worst factories and the laying off of the most unskilled workers actually meant that labour productivity in manufacturing rose – by 18% between the end of 1980 and the beginning of 1983 – and this gain seems to have become a long-term achievement, with output per worker in manufacturing rising by 50% between 1979 and 1988. Yes, it was a more reduced base but that base became much more competitive.[15] And of course inflation, which was the yardstick by which Thatcher had asked to be judged, had been beaten. It fell from 22% at the end of Thatcher's first year, and although it picked up from 4% in the mid-1980s to over 10% in 1990, the average rate between 1983 and 1993 was, as Hutton notes, just over 5% – a massive improvement on the 9% average of the previous 25 years.[16] This put British inflation closer to the average of other industrialised countries, though it has to be pointed out that this was a time when inflation fell worldwide, and only in 1984 and 1995 was the British rate lower than its G7 counterparts.[17] Perhaps then her greatest legacy was the defeat of one half of the British disease: union militancy. This was done through democratisation – and who can object to that – and also mass unemployment, at a terribly high social cost. But it was done. Also she created what is a necessary condition for economic advancement – the sense of entrepreneurship and flexibility. Neither of these genuine virtues was culturally present or indeed available to the masses in the UK before Thatcherism, but no economist now thinks that a successful modern economy can function without them. In part this was achieved through the lure of tax-based incentives. The state, it was claimed, would take less of what you earned and finally make work pay.

Another of the central objectives of Thatcherism was to reduce the direct burden of taxation. Her governments ensured that the UK had the most lightly taxed incomes in Europe and a new base line that, as one writer puts it, confirmed for New Labour 'that a political party could not thrive in the United Kingdom if saddled with the reputation for "taxing and spending"'.[18] (These moves didn't reduce the amount of tax paid – by the end of 1996 taxation both direct and indirect accounted for 37.2% of a taxpayer's income, whereas in 1979 it had only been 31.3%.)

Finally, of course, there was the sale of council housing. When discussing Thatcher's legacy it is impossible not to mention what is perhaps the most progressive part of it, the controversial right-to-buy policy introduced by the 1980 Housing Act. At the time this policy served the dual purpose of spreading home ownership – seen as a critical element of the individual's economic self-sufficiency – and diminishing the responsibilities of the local authorities. The scheme was hugely popular, with 100,000 houses being sold annually at its mid-80s peak.[19] It managed to transform a whole class of local authority tenants into independent home owners and gave many of them the first genuine economic autonomy they had ever experienced. Evidently it was progressive – it was an asset sold at less than it was worth to many of the poorest in the land. As such it was the one truly distributist element of Thatcherism and gained her substantial working-class popularity. The great shame was that this was a one-off – councils were prevented from using the proceeds to build more housing stock – and so another need, that of secure low-priced rented accommodation, was not answered in poorer areas. Coupled with the rise in house prices, this has created a long-term housing crisis. Conservatives have singularly failed to learn the lesson that publicly supported assets can, with widespread support, be transferred from the public sector to those at the bottom of society. Why they have not examined the ongoing black hole of housing benefit in this regard is beyond me. If, for instance, all long-term payment of housing benefit had to involve an equity stake for both renter and government, then over time the benefit bill could be lessened by state equity in what it was financing. The truly transformative goal of creating a society of owners was glimpsed by Mrs Thatcher but never achieved.

When it seemed that the country was destined to be little more than a fading tourist destination floating alongside a more prosperous and rapidly advancing Europe, Mrs Thatcher aligned a part of the country – its dynamic financial sector – to a genuinely global economic future. She destroyed one aspect of what had inhibited and constrained British economic growth and development, and she created the economic form that would dictate for better or worse the shape and character of the next thirty years.

Yet it is also true that Britain became a much more unequal society under Thatcher. The tax cuts for the better-off brought real economic benefits, and general consumption increased sharply, but the real incomes of the poorest 10% declined by 18%, while those of the richest 10% increased by 61%.[20] Inequality doubled during her era and that has remained a permanent feature of our socio-economic landscape ever since. In the course of the 1980s private debt levels also doubled – from £57 for every £100 of disposable income per household in 1980, to £114 in 1990.[21] A large amount of this debt was from buying houses, with mortgage debt increasing six-fold from £52 billion in 1980 to £294 billion in 1990. This led to house prices more than doubling over the same period.[22] From 1979 to 1990 there was no year when bank and building society lending did not grow by at least 15%, reaching a peak of 24% in 1988.[23] So, while there was a rise in income levels, there was a still higher rise in levels of debt. Our present personal and public debt crisis has its clear origin in the Thatcher decade.

Writing in 1995 and from the perspective of a lost economic base, Will Hutton paints a dark picture of Britain. He points to massive unemployment and decaying industrial cities, describing the country as an 'inveterate consumer', but not of the products of an indigenous industry.[24] In place of past glories, the City of London has become 'a byword for speculation, inefficiency and cheating'.[25] Of course Hutton's claims, if they were made now, would have had an entirely different reception. As it was, the City took off and provided a seemingly permanent series of boosts for the economy, year after year, apparently able to defy gravity.

It was, ironically, the success of the New Labour years that really cemented Thatcher's reputation as the economic miracle worker – it was after all not until 1999 that Britain rose to the very top of the OECD ranking for economic freedom (in terms of absence of regulation) and it was New Labour that really reaped the benefit.

The greatest failing of Thatcherism and its New Labour offspring is to be found in its failure to constitute a free, diverse and propertied society. My reservations about Mrs Thatcher are somewhat different from those of the left, though I think that no British leader can or should abandon parts of the country or attack her own people. My real doubts about the legacy of Thatcherism are conservative misgivings. First, it is not clear to me that in attempting to liberate society from the state she did anything but build up the state and make it more central, powerful and pernicious. And second, she created an authoritarian state precisely because she was not a conservative but a liberal.

In order to clarify these remarks let me take a detour via the work of F. A. Hayek. Hayek was in many ways the true intellectual influence behind Thatcherism – his critique of socialist planning and the economic and political dangers that it represented resonate to this day, and captured the imagination of many of those on the right. Simply put, Hayek opposed the rationalistic constructivism of state planning – he ridiculed the synoptic illusion that any one figure or planner of social justice could ever be in a position to know and best calculate the outcome of decisions. And it should be added that he applied this consideration also to the individual economic actor, thereby breaking with both classical economics and rebuking neo-liberalism in advance. The individual also cannot guarantee the rationality of his decisions in market terms; he cannot be a good utilitarian calculator. For Hayek, what equally disrupted all state socialism and all liberal utilitarianisms were the inherent limits of human knowledge – the attempt to move outside such partial understanding and enforce an abstract and false universality on an unknowable and plural future space was the essence of totalitarianism. The hyper-rationalism of state socialism, which thought it could plan for the good of all, was coupled with the static and uniform collectivity that was the socialist vision of the planned society. So a false collectivism – based on the demotion of individuality – was being advanced by a theory of knowledge that claimed it was possible to know what was good for this illusory totality. Hayek's theory of knowledge therefore claims that, given the nature of human knowing, it is not possible to plan the good and form an ideal type into which a putative collective would fit. Society is, by contrast, a spontaneous order that naturally results from a multitude of finite beings making their own way in the world. The interaction of free individuals is the foundation of the social order.. However, and most interestingly, Hayek does not think matters end there. It is after all not the case that this order emerges *entirely* spontaneously – on the contrary, it requires what Hayek calls tradition.

In *Law, Legislation and Liberty* Hayek argued that 'Man has undoubtedly learned more often to do the right things without understanding why, and still today is better served by his habits than by his ability to understand.'[26] It is precisely because the spontaneous order is still *an order* that it cannot be the mere anarchy of today's liberal thinkers. Instead this order comes from tradition, and tradition is that tacit knowledge which allows the uncertain not to collapse into the wholly unknown. Hayek says not only can we not know the world, still less can we know ourselves – how much more then do we need and rely on past culture, habit and the processes that transmit these formations. Without that inherited and transmitted culture, individuality will collapse into self-absorbed solipsism and the impossibility of exchange, or else this drive may move outward, engendering social conflict and warfare.

Unfortunately, Hayek's overtly political or social thought contains none of the subtlety of his theory of knowledge or indeed his account of what he thinks the pre-conditions of a society really are. In Hayek's political economy there is a stark opposition between collectivism and individualism, and as such there is no tacit tradition or mediated knowledge to appeal to. In which case the arch anti-rationalist falls prey to his own critique, for Hayek must have the state or the collective in order to prevent individuals collapsing into themselves or into conflict with others.[27]

Indeed, if the whole emphasis of *The Road to Serfdom*, Hayek's most famous book and Mrs Thatcher's favourite of all his works, is the claim that we can construct rules to stimulate competition but not to achieve fairness, the question is begged as to where the habitual knowledge to construct these rules comes from. If the habit is absent, then it is either rationally already available to the human mind – in which case the planner is present in the market liberal and the perspective of perfect competition is *just as rationalistic and utopian* as that of the perfect society of the socialist. If it is not available, then competition and markets never occur. Even to conceive of society as spontaneous order is to construct it and shape it through non-spontaneous action, since this requires a non-spontaneous knowing of what is, and that in turn requires the very knowledge that Hayek denies is possible.

The market is not the guarantor of political liberty, as it is founded upon an individualistic premise that itself requires the presence of the state. And of course this is what was revealed with Mrs Thatcher. Simon Jenkins has tirelessly listed the massive state centralisation that took place under her aegis. He seems deeply and rightly bemused by this result, as if somehow it was in conflict with the premises of the original and founding vision. But it is not. If we configure society on purely individualist lines as Mrs Thatcher did, then we create a society where all social knowing and learning is ultimately aborted, as individuals cannot properly learn about history, culture or tradition, and instead become the plaything of their desires and their most primitive and uneducated drives. In a world without tradition, people as culturally empty carriers of rights require some sort of external authority to police them – and that can be and indeed has been only the state.

So paradoxically the great friends of state authoritarianism and the extension of centralised power are the liberal individualists, for it is they who most abhor tradition and it is they who most exhibit that 'homeless moral passion' which when coupled with 'rationalist fantasy' aborts all virtue.[28]

Mrs Thatcher, by endorsing an extreme individualism, undermined and destroyed the very associative traditions that are the only protection against the state. In this way the liberal in her destroyed and made impossible the conservation of what she most desired.

5 The Errors of the Left

The legacy of New Labour

While the election of New Labour in May 1997 was a
result of a moral and social exhaustion with the costs of
Thatcherism, on every crucial economic question New
Labour was the continuation, extension and intensification
of Thatcherism. This is not to say that there were no real
and genuine achievements in Blair's premiership – peace
in Northern Ireland, the intervention in Sierra Leone and
the establishment of a minimum wage. After that I struggle
to think of any, though the right to roam and the opening
of the natural legacy of our island to its inhabitants were
worthwhile reforms. But the other side of the balance sheet
weighs very heavily: the institutional, cultural and economic
damage to our country is very marked indeed.

It was Labour's first election victory since October 1974;
they got just over 43% of the vote and gained 147 seats and
a governing majority of 179. It was the largest majority and
the greatest number of seats that Labour had ever won. The
future story of Britain could have been radically rewritten.
But of course it wasn't, or at least it wasn't in the way that
was envisaged or indeed hoped for by the voters. Britain
didn't become more equal or more just or more noble, we
became more unequal, more unjust and under New Labour
more pious, self-righteous and self-congratulatory. We had

new hospitals but we couldn't keep them clean. We became multi-cultural and cosmopolitan but at the price of an open borders policy that at times looked designed to destroy the prospects and outcomes of the white working class. Focusing on the group it believed constituted the new middle ground of British politics, Labour eulogised a middle-class life defined by conspicuous consumption and the increase of debt-financed personal choice. This lifestyle had to be controlled by an array of policing, surveillance and audit powers. At least 25 Acts of Parliament and some 50 other measures have been introduced to achieve this since 1997, ranging from stop-and-search powers, sharing of government data, restrictions on peaceful protest and the extension of lawful detention.[1] You and I might only experience this change of tone when being roughly questioned by security guards about photographing our favourite buildings, or indeed arrested while train-spotting at a mainline station, or perhaps undergoing criminal records checks if we want to volunteer at the local youth club, but the erosion of democratic and civil freedom is real enough. Against this background of a genuine and growing authoritarianism, an insistent litany of New Labour boasts punctuated the decade: no more boom and bust, Britain is open for business, things are only getting better ... Meanwhile senior Labour figures were intensely relaxed about making the top 10% of the top 10% ever more wealthy, driven by New Labour's love of undirected markets.

This is not the place to write about Iraq and how that finally broke the Blairite hegemony and revealed New

Labour as shallow manipulators of truth and acolytes of whatever interest seemed the most powerful.[2] The Iraq War was a clear foreign policy disaster, but what is interesting from a domestic point of view is New Labour's inability to determine a separate British interest from that of the neo-con view of the world then prevalent in Washington. If we had had a more confident and engaged culture, one that was aware of its interests and the necessary autonomy of its institutions, then the insights of well-informed academics, the Foreign Office and the military – who would have to pay the price of war – might have been listened to.

The essence of New Labour is not upheaval or revolution, but continuing exclusion, social inertia and the stripping away of assets and opportunity from those at the bottom of society. Economically all that Blair and Brown did was intensify what Thatcher had initiated and what Major had confirmed: support the City. Increasingly focused on the economy inside the M25, Labour ignored all the lessons about diversity and a mono-economy that it had touted as a criticism of Mrs Thatcher. It foolishly ignored Will Hutton, who for a crucial time was arguing for a British variant of the German stakeholder model.[3] Unfortunately, through the twin axis of the unions and the markets, the established powers managed to derail an attempt to create a genuine alternative to the ongoing status quo. Yet, although Hutton was truly visionary in advocating worker share-owning and responsible participation, he partially under-estimated the need to create a new ethos as the precondition for a British variant of continental corporatism. In any case with total *lack* of vision, Blair and Brown believed in the idea that globalisation meant that the only option for Britain was to concentrate on what it did well and, since the only surviving prosperous industry was finance, every other economic possibility was sacrificed, including the very manufacturing base that Blair and Brown once denounced Mrs Thatcher for destroying.

In place of a genuine vision, we were promised by New Labour and Anthony Giddens – its intellectual architect – 'a third way'.[4] This was to be a progressive politics that charted a new middle between the old left of statist social democracy and the neo-liberalism of the new right. Yet what emerged theoretically, and later in practice, was not any new middle ground but a repetition and strengthening of the old left–right opposition unified as the worst legacy of both: the market state.

What Giddens argued for was the inevitability of globalisation and its inherently unchangeable character; curiously, given his supposed triangulation of both market fundamentalism and statism, Giddens seemed wholly to accept the neo-liberal variant of markets, as if the fact of their dominance precluded any other account of market exchange and how markets might operate. New Labour and its intellectual godfather believed that neo-liberalism was the only conceivable economic future, and that the progressive duty of government was merely to recalibrate the role of the state in the light of this determination.

It was New Labour's recognition of the manifest problems caused by the neo-liberal understanding of markets that led to its support of a strong centralising state. Giddens sought a renewed and recovered role for the state because he despaired of any other source or site of power – he wrote of social movements and associations of citizens as 'sub politics' and stated: 'The idea that such groups can take over where government is failing or can stand in the place of political parties is fantasy.'[5] This understanding of civic associations as merely special interest groups decries their real capacities and eulogises instead the role of the social investment state – having displaced society, the state will now provide the social capital to compensate for the damage that the market is doing. He looked 'instead for a synergy between public and private sectors, utilizing the dynamism of markets but with the public interest in mind'.[6] Just as the neo-liberal right accepted an unjust market and attempted to ameliorate its outcomes with injunctions to personal philanthropy, so the new left accepted an unjust market and attempted to mitigate its consequences through the state. It was supposed that only the state can deliver redistribution and the equalisation of opportunity. The end result of this theory is a massively powerful state squatting alongside a misappropriating and distorted market. And here we have New Labour's true legacy: not a third way between the two opposites of individualism and collectivism, but a union of the two, which excludes any sort of civil society.

And why exclude society? Society is the home of families, of culture and of established practices and tradition. It is where people are born, live, work and die. It is the world of the ordinary, of loyalty and of security. As individualists, New

Labour hated the world of tradition, ritual and established pattern. Instead it celebrated the world of glamour and the speed and innovation of the real movers and shakers: 'risk [Giddens tells us] is not just a negative phenomenon – something to be avoided or minimised. It is at the same time the energizing principle of a society that has broken away from tradition and nature.'[7]

Giddens in the late 1990s denounced modern conservatism for being committed to two mutually exclusive political positions: tradition and market fundamentalism. As he wrote: 'the continuity of tradition is central to the idea of conservatism ... Nothing is more dissolving of tradition than the permanent revolution of market forces.'[8] Yet New Labour embraced those very market forces and used the state as the new replacement for the society.

Essentially Blair and Giddens tried to create a third way without a third sector, but all they did was replicate and reinforce the state/market combination by unifying what they had hoped to transcend and using it to destroy all that most of us hold most dear.

Thatcher and Blair: the legacy and the continuity

From 1979 to the financial crisis of 2007/8, the story is less one of rupture between Thatcher and Blair than one of continuity. The fundamental economic settlement negotiated by Thatcher was not only accepted by Blair, it was intensified, augmented and celebrated. Indeed the Thatcher renaissance was only retrospectively constructed as a hallowed period during the warm glow of New Labour's growth years, when the left congratulated the right for creating the economic conditions for prosperity and the left celebrated itself for garnering that tax revenue to fund the new social-investment state. In this regard Blair and Brown were only following Anthony Crosland's injunction in the 1970s to go for growth, no matter what, and redistribute the proceeds later. In this way an increasingly monopolised financial sector which gamed the state was allowed to take root and grow. And of course grow it did; in fact the majority of GDP growth over the ten years since 1997 was in financial services, housing and the public sector. The only difference that Labour really made to the new right's legacy was to turn the now massively powerful state created by Thatcherism's hatred of left-wing democracy and institutional autonomy outwards, so that the centralised state could seek to manage everything via productivity targets and central dictates.

And of course the economy was not transformed either – yet Labour had imagined or at least pretended to something very different. In Gordon Brown's first budget speech as Chancellor in July 1997 he was very clear about what type of economy he wanted to create: 'It is essential that consumer spending is underpinned by investment and industrial growth. Britain cannot afford a recurrence of the all too familiar pattern of previous recoveries: accelerating consumer spending and borrowing side by side with skills shortages, capacity constraints, increased imports and rising inflation.'[9]

But in fact, Labour witnessed the manufacturing sector slip to a rump of 12.4% of overall output by 2007.

According to research from the *Financial Times*: 'The rate of decline in the manufacturing share of the economy under Labour has been 2.7 times faster than under Mrs Thatcher's government.'[10] Britain's overall economy has performed under Labour in almost exactly the same way as it did during the Thatcher and Major administrations. There has been no real renaissance in our rate of growth since 1997: it has averaged just over 2%, a little bit lower than under the previous regimes.

And in examining the rest of the Chancellor's first speech, it is hard to deny that skills shortages are still with us and may well have increased, and with consumer spending financed by credit accelerating rather than reducing, blowing asset bubbles throughout the economy, it is hard to see quite where Labour has met its own declared aims.

But perhaps most telling of all is the rising inequality under Labour stewardship – though some might claim the rate of increase has slowed, this is still an economy that has failed to balance enterprise with fairness.

The equality report commissioned by Harriet Harman found that inequality was higher now than in the 1950s, with the distribution of wealth far more unequal than that of income, wages and earnings.[11] The top tenth of households had wealth above £853,000 and the bottom tenth had less than £8,000, making the top tenth 100 times better off.[12]

Housing is another clear indication of current contemporary inequality. Those who were renting, whether privately, from a local authority or from a housing association, had the least total net wealth. Social tenant households, the report found, have median financial and non-property wealth of £15,000, which rises to £18,000 when including non-state pension rights.[13] Some 90% of social tenant households had total wealth of around £105,000.[14]

Those households that own their homes outright were found to have median total net wealth of £411,000. When housing and private pension rights were excluded, the median was £75,000.[15] In the ninetieth percentile for this category of households total wealth reached £1.23 million.[16]

All of which shows in stark relief who has benefited from the economic model of the last thirty years: the wealthiest 10% of society. Across a broad spectrum of indicators, it is the wealthiest 10% and those with the highest academic qualifications who still come out on top, despite government efforts to improve the chances of the very poor. With an increasing specialisation of the economy in certain sectors such as the service industries, and technological developments profoundly affecting the types of labour that are in demand, many low-skilled workers have been left far behind. It is also these workers who have the lowest percentage of asset wealth and it is their children who start life on a lower social standing than their peers, and who increasingly struggle with inter-generational inequality (as David Willetts has admirably pointed out) to escape the position into which they are born.[17]

Differences in equality have also become concentrated in particular areas of the country, as households in southern England, and London in particular, have benefited from rises in house prices, whilst growth in other areas has been less pronounced. Those already well-off individuals have become increasingly wealthy, passing this wealth and social standing on to their children, whilst those at the bottom end continue to be disadvantaged from birth.

Since the mid-1970s, inequality has widened significantly in the United Kingdom. Inequality has traditionally been measured through changes in incomes and changes in real annual wage growth. Looking at the Gini coefficient, a popular measure for income inequality, for the period 1979–2008, one can see a consistent rise in inequality in the UK. The Gini coefficient can range from 0 to 1, where 0 corresponds to complete equality and a value of 1 is the ultimate form of inequality where one person is receiving all income.

According to the Institute for Fiscal Studies, throughout the Thatcher years inequality rose dramatically from a value of 0.25 in 1979 to 0.34 at the beginning of the 1990s under Major's government. Following this initial peak, income inequality fell slightly throughout the early to mid-1990s, rising again under Blair's first term to peak at 0.35 in 2000–1. The level of income inequality went on to fall again in Blair's second term, which saw inequality levels return to those of 1997–8, only to rise again to reach 0.36 in 2007–8.

When compared to other OECD countries, the United Kingdom has also remained above average in terms of income inequality throughout the 2000s. Whilst the UK saw a Gini coefficient of around 0.34 in the mid-2000s, fellow OECD countries such as Germany had a coefficient value of around 0.29, the Netherlands one of 0.26, while Sweden saw a level of income inequality of approximately 0.24. These figures indicate a clear continuity in Britain over the last thirty years, where income inequality has risen dramatically, concentrating income gains at the top of the scale.

According to the Office of National Statistics' survey on Wealth and Assets, the total wealth in Great Britain, which includes private pension wealth, for the period of 2006–8 is estimated at £9.0 trillion. In this period, the wealthiest 10% of households were 4.8 times wealthier than the bottom 50%. The wealthier half of households for this period had 91% of the total wealth, while the poor half had the remaining 9%. This unequal distribution is reflected in the Gini coefficient for the distribution of total wealth, calculated for the first time in 2009, which was 0.61 for the period 2006–8.

A study conducted by the IPPR in 2002, which focused on personal rather than household wealth, found that while wealth creation grew at an unprecedented scale in the period 1979–99, from £500 billion to £2,752 billion, the distribution of wealth was increasingly concentrated among the rich. According to its figures, the wealthiest 2% of the population held 24% of the wealth in 1985. By 1996 this had increased to 26% and by 1999 it had reached 30%.

From 1978 to 1996, the IPPR study found that the percentage of people with no financial assets, no property or savings or capital of any kind, had doubled from 5% to 10%. The number of people in this position had increased the most in the 20–34 year-old age group. And this exclusion of millions of people from any access to financial assets remained at similar levels throughout the subsequent

Labour government, with the percentage of people with no savings reaching 34% in 2000–1 and 46% of individuals in the lowest income groups having no savings whatsoever, indicating that the economy over the last thirty years has done little to improve the ability of the very poor to acquire assets and accrue wealth.

One last and very striking statistic. For the years 2006–8, the ownership of net financial wealth was much more unequal than that of property and other physical wealth. Fully half the households in Britain owned a mere 1% of net financial wealth, while the top 20% owned 84%.

And indeed this fact is the most telling and the most troubling – for inequality is troubling less because of the disparity itself than because the lives of those at the bottom increasingly resemble those of a lower and abandoned caste. Indeed what we have produced over the last thirty years is capitalism for the privileged few, and indebted servitude for the many.

The original visionaries of the right wanted a society, an economy and a culture of widely distributed property, innovation and distinction. For them, the totalitarian logic of the statist left could be resisted by an enfranchised and liberated citizenry that could extend its independence and foster a truly free society because it participated in a vital economy.

Instead the last thirty years, under the aegis of both right and left, have introduced a new economic form via debt and low wages: serfdom. The radical politics of the future must address the needs of the new serfs.

6 The Illiberal Legacy of Liberalism

How then are we to make sense of these linked crises – the economic collapse, the erosion of society and the legitimacy crisis of all our governing institutions. What is it that binds all these things that are so often treated in isolation? Is there any single set of ideas that can account for our contemporary fate? For me the linking narrative is deceptively simple and almost terrifyingly complete. It is the triumph of a perverted and endlessly corrupting liberalism.

Now by this I do not mean to support a politics that is extreme or reactionary or kitsch. I am in part appalled by the legacy of modern liberalism precisely because I take myself to be a true liberal. I believe in a free society, where human beings, under the protection of law and guidance of virtue, pursue their own account of the good in debate with those who differ from them and in concord with those who agree. Since in this life we cannot know all that can be known and all human knowledge is conditioned by our own lives and the culture in which we are immersed, we can never transcend this condition and know directly and completely the ultimate principle of everything that exists. What knowledge we have is always limited, conditioned and mediated. It follows that fundamentalism of all kinds — religious, scientific or indeed nihilistic – is always predicated on knowing more than we can possibly know: whether this be the mind of God, or the once-confident claims of Soviet state planning, or even the widespread belief that there is no such thing as an objective truth at all. In this sense I am a liberal – I believe that any fundamentalism is both ethically wrong and epistemologically impossible. Because our mind is quite simply never in a position to know all that there is to be known, the last thing one can be is an absolutist who refuses all debate, discrimination and dispute.

But it does not follow that there is nothing to be known. Unfortunately, all too many British students, who have suffered the misfortune of ten weeks of bad French philosophy, or empiricistic analytic philosophy of a more homegrown kind, emerge from university with the deep and abiding conviction that there is no such thing as objective truth and that everything cultural is arbitrary. They carry into their twenties and beyond the view that any claim about truth is hierarchical and therefore synonymous with fascism and all manner of evil and conservative consequences. Happily convinced by the radical import of this message, too many of our talented young people give up on the possibility of transformative politics and assiduously work their way into the managerial and governing class of our country. Once there, with self-interest duly satisfied, they repeat and institutionalise the same compliant liberal nostrums, which ironically translate into increasingly centralised and bureaucratic procedures that exclude the poor and those who have not been so well-positioned or so well-advantaged to work the system.

While the idea of a universal relativism doesn't survive the first brush with serious rational reflection, such juvenile dictums have permeated our governing elite and undermined the foundations of all our great institutions. Recently, at a policy breakfast, the chairman of the trust set up to guard the reputation and mission of the BBC looked at me with wide-eyed accusation when I suggested that the BBC should not simply reflect the population back on itself (which after all it does not, since it rightly refuses to reflect back the values and beliefs of the BNP or the lynch-mob impulses that can follow horrible crimes), but recover instead the Reithian belief in the sort of people we British ought to be and what sort of culture we should have as a result. This appeal to the example of his great predecessor did not go down well. 'The BBC is not in the business of suggesting what people ought to watch or be,' was his response. But I replied that the BBC is already doing that in negative mode, since it is already saying that we ought as a culture to represent nothing very particular or distinct at all. Needless to say, the conversation moved blandly on to well-meaning but ultimately vapid questions about choice and value for money. The vital issue about the educative role of a crucially formative national institution had been shunted to one side.

This is an indication of the way in which a nihilistic liberalism has over a long period of time almost completely eclipsed classical and Christian traditions of political life and argument, which always rested on a dispute about what was objectively good, and about the practice of virtue required to realise them. It was never the case that these traditions thought that they had grasped the nature of the good life once and for all. However, they believed that a partial grasp was possible, and therefore thought that a sound polity must include at its centre a large space for the further discovery of the nature of the good life through discussion, innovation and practical experiment.

Ever since the seventeenth century, this tradition has been slowly rejected and eroded – at least in theory. Its critics, from Hobbes through Locke and Rousseau to Kant and Mill, have all argued that it is impossible for human beings to agree about the nature of objective goods and the true path of human well-being and of what makes societies flourish. This argument against the classical and medieval view of the true and the good acquired great plausibility in the wake of the religious conflicts that had torn Europe apart during the seventeenth century, especially the disastrous Thirty Years War, conflicts that often caused people to exaggerate their differences and to ignore the degree to which they still overwhelmingly shared the same Christian legacy and the same inheritance of Jewish monotheism and the Greek linking of the life of the city with the pursuit of a universally valid human virtue. The emerging liberal argument was simply this: if we cannot agree upon the good, then we must found society not upon the good but upon an idea of rights – upon people's permission to act and think as they like, to the degree that this does not interfere with the merely negative freedom of others to choose what they want also. In the case of Kant, by the end of the eighteenth century, respect for freedom has taken on a new sacred aura of respect for human dignity as such, but the same basic framework remains. All that can be held valid beyond individual freedom are the contracts into which individuals freely enter, whatever the content of these agreements. Justice now becomes a matter of sticking by the letter of contractual arrangements, while the spirit informing their substance is regarded as publicly irrelevant.

Later, to this contractual view of human relationships was added the idea that we can also agree about the minimum requirements for material happiness and that we can sympathise with each other in this respect. On this basis, according to Jeremy Bentham, society should aim for 'the greatest happiness of the greatest number' and any concern for individual rights must be subordinate to this quest.[1] In this way a tension between the 'deontological' foundation of politics in rights and the 'utilitarian' foundation of society in material happiness entered into the heart of liberalism itself. (Deontology is the theory of duty and moral obligation.) Most liberalisms since the time of Bentham in the early nineteenth century have been a more or less coherent or incoherent amalgam of the two. In the case of John Stuart Mill, a great scope is given to individual freedom, but only for the sake of ultimate utility.[2] Mill believed that the more people were free, the more an elite would come to utilitarian conclusions and manage society on a utilitarian basis. This included the view that one should promote supposedly 'higher' elite pleasures like opera over supposedly lower and more popular pleasures like going to the pub and making love. Mill had a kind of nostalgia for the idea of the good, but having refused all metaphysics and traditional religion, he could find no real basis for this nostalgia other than in a snobbery disguised by disingenuous empirical claims for the greater intensity of 'higher' modes of pleasure.[3]

In more recent times the key liberal thinker John Rawls, probably the most influential political philosopher in the Western world over the last four decades, appeared to make 'the right' much more decisive than mere 'happiness'.[4] He thought that the negative liberty to choose one's own good for oneself should be the central principle of political organisation, while trying to blend this with a Kantian respect for the sacred dignity of the right of others also to enjoy this freedom. To this end he allowed that the state had an obligation to engineer equality of opportunity and even to promote a certain equality of condition by compensating for natural inequalities. Any permissible inequality in society, such as the need to offer incentives for wealth creation, ought to be rigorously justified by reference to this equality in freedom. However, Rawls's understanding of the basic goods people require in addition to liberty was a fundamentally materialist one, very much in the Benthamite tradition. And his sense of the reasons why people choose different goods came down to the idea that we are the passive victims of our emotions and inclinations, ultimately rooted in our physicality. So while Rawls rigorously subordinated the good to the right, the exercise of right is only in the end for the sake of promoting material comfort and arbitrary personal preferences, which are but quirks of our bodily nature.[5]

So for liberalism, the praise of freedom as mere freedom of choice is always intimately linked to an account of human beings that is just as narrowly materialist as the Marxist one and just as dogmatically unwarranted. Rawls had no convincing vision of the good society or the good life. People would be satisfied by meeting their minimal needs for housing, food and transport, and preferred modes of pleasure. We were not supposed to reflect on any tradition-informed questions about true human flourishing.

It is for this reason that liberalism has promoted a radical individualism which, in trashing the supposed despotism of custom and tradition concerning the nature of true human flourishing, has produced a vacated, empty self that believes in no common values or inherited creeds. But in creating this purely subjective being, liberalism has also created a new and wholly terrifying tyranny. For, in order to strip people of their cultural legacy and eliminate the idea that people should enjoy degrees of prestige according to their nature and capacity for virtue, and by making everyone instead the same sort of individual with basic physical needs and rights, an excess of centralised authority is required. The rule of virtuous persons is displaced by the explicit control of a central state, which has a monopoly on the use of violence and must endlessly police, through more or less subtle modes of coercion, both the sanctity of contract and the ways in which one free individual may impinge on the liberties of others.

In this way the supremacy of the one lone, isolated individual quickly converts into the supremacy of the one, unquestionable state authority, which tends to manage and manipulate our negative liberties in the interests of the greatest happiness of the greatest number. But in reality this formula is an unexamined code for the strength of the state, for there is no possible calculus of human happiness. We can only make judgements between different kinds of happiness and we can only discriminate between different human claims to freedom if we have some basis for ordering lesser and more important forms of happiness and lesser and more important liberties. But this requires some teleological sense of the human good – that is a sense of what the ultimate end of human action might be. The truth of the matter is that even today many human individual and collective decisions still require a sense of the good. It is only in theory that liberalism has totally triumphed – even though this has had such widespread corrosive influence. The spending of council money on parks and libraries and cycle-tracks all assumes, in reality, some notion of local collective aspiration to an objectively good pattern of living. Decisions for or against abortion suppose some account of whether or not the foetus is a person, which presupposes that we have some notion of what constitutes a human person, which in turn involves an account of what constitutes the human good – even if this is taken to be a compound of mere negative freedom and happiness. And courts sometimes rule contracts to be illegitimate if they are substantively unfair, however freely they have been entered into. In this way liberalism has not only promoted bad things and weak ideas, it has also lied about all the good things that inevitably continue to take place and which alone uphold the possibility of human association.

Of course it seems bizarre to claim that liberalism ends in state authoritarianism. After all, is it not the case that the foundation of liberalism, the very ideal from which it springs, is the pursuit of liberty and freedom? The paradox is not singular, however, for one might equally note that one political ideology ultimately derived from liberalism, namely Marxist socialism, is also destructive of the very society that it should cherish.

For at the heart of contemporary liberal and socialist political models lies a revolutionary liberalism descended from Rousseau that at bottom cares a lot less for society than it does for the individual. Indeed, society, for the liberal, is the first and most basic trap or prison for the individual, the forum in which she is exposed to the potential violence and frustration of opposition. For Rousseau, the individual is radically free, an unencumbered atom for whom sideways association represents an immediate limitation on this original purity, a restrictive impediment to the full and free expression of individual will. Those organic social relationships with which an individual is confronted cannot provide identity or empowerment, but only imprisonment. Self-interest here trumps social engagement, and so a differentiated society offers only the possible limitation of the individual's freedom of action. Thus, for the individual, the first instinct is inwards, and concerns only the self: 'to watch over his own preservation; his first care he owes to himself'.[6]

For this vision of freedom, man most authentically reflects his nature when in isolation, and association represents his bondage. Yet this freedom is not just the philosophical expression of a mild form of xenophobia, of hatred of other people. Rather, any external claim on the individual is seen fundamentally as a limitation, even in the most primary of relational institutions, that of the family. Rousseau chillingly wrote: 'children remain tied to their father by nature only so long as they need him for their preservation. As soon as this need ends, the natural bond is dissolved. Once the children are freed from the obedience they owe their father, and the father is freed from his responsibilities towards them, both parties equally regain their independence.'[7] He thought that the family exercises a claim over the freedom of the individual in so much as it lashes individuals into relationships that demand corresponding duties and emotional commitments; for Rousseau, the solution is to deny the objective reality of such roles, such that 'fatherhood' ceases to be an objective state, but rather turns into an irksome temporary contract that expires once the child reaches the independence of maturity. Once the child has attained his majority, the father–son relationship becomes no more than a mutual agreement, to which both may (or may not) give assent; the wider family is no more than the assenting association of fundamentally disparate units. It would not require the greatest leap of faith to suggest that socialism's historic ambivalence towards the family springs from, amongst other things, this coldly individualistic account of familial and human relationships.

The dilemma arises, however, of how to uphold the precedence of the individual over and above the society with which he or she must necessarily engage. The answer is a two-stage path to modern tyranny – first collectivism and then the authoritarian state. The extreme individualism that underpins the liberal account of human nature in the end demands collectivism as a means of preserving the sanctity of the singular when confronted with the reality of others. If enduring human relationships – the family, corporations, communities – offer only subjugation, society must be stripped of its oppositional forces and of genuine difference in order to preserve this radical idea of liberty intact. Individuality cut away from human relationships and inherited traditions demands that, in order to preserve this extreme sense of identity, all individuals must be exactly like each other: this is exactly why John Rawls imagined that one could only construct a model for a liberal society by imagining a 'veil of ignorance' in which no one knows what identity or what social role they would occupy in any actual social arrangement. But genuine decision-making is always a reflection upon what we have received and what we owe each other: a fictional abstract subject, identical to all other subjects and free of all relationships, can only choose a society that preserves this formal identity and equality as far as possible. Such a society will be bound to become tyrannical: to purchase identical freedom for all at the price of a terrifying control of all by all, which will be exercised in the name of what Rousseau called the 'general will' by a tiny elite.[8]

Precisely because he conceived liberty in such individ-ualistic terms, Rousseau was forced to say that the price of sustaining a mutual recognition of liberty is to hand over all our rights to the power of the state. We then receive our rights to freedom back from the state in an enhanced form, supposedly, and together we participate in the mystical collective liberty of the power of the state itself. But in reality this conception of liberty leads to conformism and terror, as first the French Revolution and many subsequent revolutions have shown. Yet, in rightly attacking the revolutionary tradition, conservatives too often lose sight of the fact that the entire liberal tradition has fomented a dangerous creeping revolution – and alongside this a creeping terror and a creeping conformism, as we have so clearly seen with New Labour and its restrictions on civil liberties and association.

The alternative to this modern form of tyranny is a virtue society and a polity that constantly seeks to discern a just order of priorities between differential claims and between various associative groups in society for the attainment of various purposes.

Liberalism, then, paradoxically tends to promote a totalising unity within an overriding collectivist framework that nullifies opposition in the very name of negative freedom. For an authoritarian state claims only to intrude upon the will of the individual when it moves against those associations that are restrictive of individual freedom. By attacking potential constraints, rather than promoting specific goals, it seeks to insulate itself against opposition by perpetually eradicating anything that might prove a barrier to self-gratification. But almost any positively creative assertion of free action impinges in some way upon another person (even the plants I grow in my garden may threaten the neighbouring garden with too specific a kind of pollination or odour) and in this way can be taken to reduce the other's freedom of choice and scope for unhampered activity. Thus, the state is driven to homogenise individuality in the very name of individual diversity. Individual liberty becomes inexorably the 'general will' of the social whole and the only truly freedom belongs to that individual writ large – which is the state. Competing claims to loyalty, from customary tradition, localities and the family, are anathema to this modern state, because they are supposedly anathema to the unfettered freedom of individual agency.

In this way both state and individual conspire in modern times against civil society and all its institutions which are linked in some way to objective goals and the finding of the right roles for the right natures, and the right habitually required virtues in order to achieve these goals – whether we are talking about the local football club, the women's institute, the neighbourhood association, or the local school, church and hospital. Real freedom is based upon the inheritance of shaped possibilities that such groupings sustain. But liberalism tends to abolish the practice of free association that has been the nursery of British liberty and is the only possible nursery of any human liberty whatsoever.[9]

By contrast, once the state as the central power becomes the only association that unites the citizenry, then it is perversely through the state that one receives civic liberty and empowerment – and through the state that one loses it. The social relationships that historically have defined the social realm, in and through which individuals joined together in association to create commonly shared projects and confirm commonly held ideals, are now displaced by a state that controls the civic arena. By offering itself as the prime defender (because the ultimate representation of) the individual, the state can both enforce and claim the ultimate loyalty of its citizens, and legislate the civic arena accordingly.

Hence the current slow leaching of civil liberty is presented as the legitimate actions of a state seeking to protect its citizens. For the liberal, the state has become the ultimate expression of the individual and the exercise of freedom has become curiously fused with the will of the state – the individual is more 'free' by being more devoted to the centre. The utterances of any New Labour minister on matters of law and civil liberties are textbook examples of this process in action.

Because the individual and the collective have become alchemically blended in one, the single individual is continuously threatened with expulsion from that very society of which individuality is supposedly the very basis: everyone is every day a potential traitor and there is always a justification at hand for the latest extension of surveillance or control. That exercise of creative choice which the liberal system exists to legitimate, it must simultaneously be able easily to ban – merely because any actualised freedom of choice by one person inevitably threatens the potential freedom of choice of another.

Liberalism can therefore only accommodate society by making it replicate individual liberty. The complex web of relationships, the intimate ties of kith and kin that situate the individual within transcending frameworks of value and meaning, culture and tradition, are refused, and replaced instead by the nothingness of endless self-determination.

If conservatives are to have anything left to conserve, then they must grant that, in reality, this whole characterisation of the individual as radically unencumbered is plain wrong: the individual is always already part of a diverse interconnected web of relationships, and these define and empower the person, not ensnare and imprison her. The interlocking and interconnected order of horizontal and vertical relationships are thus not external impositions, but are rather constitutive of individuality itself. Those identities, from the most intimate to the most distant, all in some sense add to the uniqueness of the individual rather than detract from it.

The revival of the associative society, then, would bring with it a revival of those flourishing relationships that make up a society, and which both empower and protect the individual from the arbitrary sway of external power. For a free society demands an account of the common good that is cultivated organically from within rather than imposed arbitrarily from without, and it is this that trumps both the extreme individualism and the statist authoritarianism of liberalism. Once the common good is restored as the associative expression of commonly shared moral and social belief, then the very first question to be asked is not 'how do I protect myself from everybody else?', nor 'how do I ensure my own sensory happiness and cosy comfort?', but rather 'how do we look out for the needs of one another?'

In recognising society as forming the individual rather than being oppressive of individuality, the need for an arbitrary power policing the people according to the dictates of radical individualism simply dissolves. Shared accounts of virtue are allowed to flourish which look not immediately to the freedom of self-gratification – that toxic mix of inflexible formal duty and debased enjoyment – but rather to the well-being of society as a whole. Such a state of affairs more accurately reflects the central truth that individuals are at root relational beings, and only fully express themselves when conceived as such. Society in complex and various ways can protect the rights of both individuals and groups far more effectively than by the centrist control of the state. The latter, as we have seen, must always cancel out the very freedoms which it supposedly exists to protect. But a civil society built around the practice of virtue and exploration of the good can find ways to allow the real exercise of creative liberties by some in harmony with the same exercise of freedom by others. This is only possible if we have a collective ranking of social and moral priorities, continuously revised.

Such a claim appears deeply shocking and oppressive to the products of our contemporary education system and the liberal consensus. Is this not tyranny, they will ask? But I have already shown that liberalism produces a worse tyranny and does so without debate. There is, in fact, no real liberty without authority. But true authority, unlike tyranny, allows debate – a true debate about what we should collectively value, not the sham debate of emoting without meaning or understanding, which is what our media largely promote today.

And if this whole argument sounds abstract, do we not see the evidence of this paradoxical conundrum of liberalism everywhere we look in Britain today?

Across our towns and cities, the widespread breakdown of civility – binge drinking of cheap alcohol in late-opening pubs, late-night violence and disorder and the consumption of drugs by very young people – has been accompanied by a vast increase in uncontrolled surveillance by police and other security agencies. The London borough of Hackney alone has more than ten times the number of surveillance cameras as the city of San Francisco; New York has around 5,000 cameras, even after the terrorist attacks of 11 September 2001, while London has more than 400,000. In the UK as a whole more than four million cameras record us as we go about our lives. Even a generation ago, electronic surveillance of our movements, our computers and our mobile phones would have seemed fantastic, the concern of paranoid thrillers and the stuff of Orwellian nightmares – a Big Brother state. Yet this drastic augmentation of the state's power is the logical consequence not of some inherent failure of the British legal system and constitution, but of the massive over-valuation of individual rights by economic and political liberalism. Anything goes in the personal sphere – experimentation with sex outside of any meaningful relationships, with alcohol and drugs as a means to achieving oblivion, with forms of self-expression in the mass media, especially the tabloid press, that are to any objective viewer obscene and degrading – and into the chaos steps the strong state to control the results. It is this nightmare that the libertarian dream has created.

When, therefore, a serious though relatively minor terrorist threat raises its head, it is easy for the state to panic, because it no longer knows what is truly real or important. Heavy on regulation and light on ethos, a state that has become indifferent to the norms of civilised behaviour can only respond with excessive policing of the supposedly 'free' society that it exists to protect. Successive New Labour Home Secretaries have accordingly vied with each other to show how robust and muscular they are in response to terrorism and crime, with appalling consequences for our liberties, for the prospects of reform of criminals, and in some cases the treatment of innocent suspects.

This culture of individual rights has also grown up at the expense of very important group rights of religious and other corporate bodies that preserve and encourage values that may be at odds with the nihilistic culture of economic liberalism. Far from liberating individuals, this reduces their real scope for free activity, which can often only be pursued through collaboration in specific groups with their own customs and rules and modes of enforcement. By contrast a supposed monopoly of power exercised by the sovereign individual is really, as we have seen, a mask for the monopolising authority of the sovereign state.

PART II

Alternatives

7 The Restoration of Ethos

I concluded my diagnosis of what has gone wrong with Britain by suggesting that the corrosion of virtue through the dominance of liberalism was the deepest malaise of recent British culture, politics and economics. I now want to consider the possibility of the revival of a modern variant of virtue in Britain. The recreation of a genuine ethos requires a transformation in the role of the state and a refigured and renewed civic policy and civil economy, but these changes can themselves only happen if we can nurture individual honour and reciprocal trust through changed patterns of behaviour, a different approach to education and an altered conception of social equity and meritorious conduct.

One of the most difficult things in trying to write about a general cultural loss is that if the loss has been gathering pace for generations then few realise or believe that anything has been lost. If there is little or no cultural memory of what is now forgotten then the most that you are left with is a vague but still powerful sense of nostalgia. Most importantly, the loss of belief and practice associated with earlier models of virtue then becomes, to borrow the words of Donald Rumsfeld, one of the 'unknown unknowns': things so unrecognised that they are beyond our cognitive reach. Human history can be like this – there are civilisations in the past which we can learn quite a lot about because they had writing; there are others which had no writing but left some traces of their presence and others still whose very existence has left so little mark on the earth that we scarcely know of their existence at all.

Thus the call for a return to a culture of virtue in politics and economics hovers between a vaguely recalled history on the one hand and a belief that there never was such a history on the other. Hence any politics based around such a call can appear either as regressive, or as totally occult. I want to show why this is not the case.

Virtue is the means by which people fulfil the socially recognised goals that they are attempting to reach. Virtue is value and practice combined – if, for example, you believe in love as the basis of human relationships, then you can't treat men or women as dispensable items on the road to your own satisfaction. Virtue also implies a political context for ethics, as it imagines an objectively desirable future which can only be defined in inter-relational terms as a social order which distributes different roles to different people according to their different characters. At the same time, it also implies a very important educative dimension – a process of creating and inculcating in individuals the beliefs and practices that are required to realise virtue. The ancient Greeks called this process *paideia*; the modern Germans *Bildung*. In English the best equivalent would be 'formation'. Virtue as both political and formative is not subjective, since it believes that there is a common good under which all would flourish and prosper. But by the same token virtue does not imply a static collectivism either, because it realises that the good is not attained once and for all by assertion and prejudice – a group of individuals cannot for themselves permanently determine what is virtuous and impose it on society. This can produce only dogmatic ideology, whereas the genuine good can only be partially discerned, as was stressed in the last chapter, by the advancement of debate and the acceptance of disagreement.

So a politics based upon virtue and intimately linked to education is teleological, which means that it has goals, and is concerned with a future orientation. By contrast, modern liberal politics, for all its often meaningless talk of 'progress', is curiously static in character. This is because it thinks of humans as it supposes they irredeemably are, and does not in consequence seek to reshape them. Either it treats the human seeking of pleasure as a fundamental given, which must, it argues, govern all political consideration, or else it treats freedom of choice in exactly the same way.

We pretend that we do not need to be educated into true freedom and yet we all know that if we learn a difficult skill we develop a much greater creative capacity. It is the trained dancer who can be innovative, the classically trained artist who can achieve the authentically avant-garde. Still more profoundly, we know that if we make a bad choice in terms of pleasure or company that our future lives can become more and more constrained. The choice to take drugs, for example, can quickly turn into a habit that inhibits your freedom altogether. Liberty is manifestly positive and not negative: certain choices allow to you to become more free; others clearly prevent freedom. St Paul was right when he said that we are 'set free' only when we 'know the truth'. And so we have to know the truth about ourselves and each other if we are to choose wisely – though modern liberalism denies that such cognition is possible. For the liberal, to choose is the ethical act par excellence – but the idea that there should be some account of what you should choose is for that self-same liberal an illegitimate transgression on individual liberty. Yet unless there is such an account, liberty is enslavement and choice delivers no value – it is never the case that in deciding between good and evil there is a moral equivalence such that what is chosen, be it good or ill, makes no difference. What you choose matters.

The loss of a British culture of virtue has inspired this book. It is hard of course to pinpoint the rupture – the exact tipping point when the most crucial values were finally lost sight of. Perhaps, like rents in an old fabric, the material tore at points of particular pressure – be it war, social change or loss of empire. I can identify a series of critical moments, but what seems interesting is that often the initial tear was an intellectual one – made or initiated by a middle-class elite who tried to convince the mass of the population of the redundancy of their values and the poverty of their convictions.

In the 1920s the Bloomsbury group denied the objective existence of values and under the influence of G. E. Moore decided that the good was a quasi-aesthetic 'non-natural' and non-teleological property, glimpsed fleetingly in the ineffable instances of intimate friendship and pleasurable impression.[1] They implied that if only others shared this same effete value-set then liberation through self-affirming repudiation of accepted codes could then be possible. Lytton Strachey set the tone in 1918 with his *Eminent Victorians*, which decried, by disparaging its heroes and heroines, the whole Victorian age and its ethos as hypocritical and oppressive.[2]

The Bloomsbury painters (apart from Dora Carrington, who was informed by other influences) were no better. None of them was able to continue and radicalise a more authentic British tradition of painting, which was always about an objective and visionary natural world. They instead repeated and subjectivised decades later the main trends of European art, producing a post-impressionism that amounted to little more than pretty pictures of a private domestic sphere separated from the real world in which alone such values could be seriously incarnated and developed. They upheld only a subjective definition of goodness as an indefinable quality that has no reality outside the self: redefining the good as what is pleasing to the individual. By draining the good from current social codes and manners, the Bloomsbury group decried all existing norms as oppressive and regarded with ill-concealed contempt the practices and values of the working-class autodidacts whom they claimed to support. In this respect Leonard Bast, the Edwardian clerk of E. M. Forster's *Howards End*, embodies the class prejudices of the liberated bohemian class and the novel implicitly calls for the re-inscription of class hierarchy on a new basis of supposed secular sophistication, involving the protection of the world of the elite from a rising working class which aspired to a culture equal to its traditional practices and beliefs.

Between the wars, disillusioned members of the elite played a peculiar and decisive role in the destruction of British notions of virtue and of shared values. The First World War demonstrated that, if the British working class believed in a code and practised an ethos, then nothing could break their allegiance to each other and to those values. But by the late twenties and early thirties, the signs of a dissolution of a shared vision of the common British good were clearly visible in a revisionist valuation of the sacrifices made in that war, which in the mind of the common man had been seen as a noble victory over German militarism. The memoirs of the officers that became so canonical in our liberal culture – those of Robert Graves and Siegfried Sassoon – were profoundly disenchanted and despairing. Lloyd George's war memoirs, out to settle his scores with Field Marshal Haig, schooled British readers into thinking that they had suffered a terrible defeat rather than gained a bloody but necessary victory. Wilfred Owen's poetry, fine as it is, was that of an officer haunted by despair, and was elevated above the far superior and more heroically orientated work of the rank and file infantrymen poets – David Jones, Isaac Rosenberg and Ivor Gurney.[3] A significant faction of the liberal elite wished in their revolutionary bourgeois radicalism to reshape past triumph as current defeat.

This corrupting repudiation of tradition and belief returns time after time in twentieth-century British culture. In the 1950s and 1960s, it succeeds in converting the populace into nearly complete unbelief and that contemporary diligent solipsism which has exchanged the culture and ideals of popular excellence for shopping and a competition in personal gratification. The *Gormenghast* trilogy, published by Mervyn Peake from 1946 onwards, was a prophetic account of the Britain to come.[4] In its pages Steerpike, a ruthlessly ambitious kitchen hand, enters the world of the castle, where a noble family lives, obsessed with a bewildering litany of rules and behaviour, the meaning of which has long since been lost. Steerpike, as an attractive young nihilist, gradually exposes these codes and practices to ridicule and advances himself seamlessly into power, as all about him are unable to defend themselves since they have forgotten the logic and meaning of what they do. Steerpike consummates his destructive achievement when he burns down the library, thereby destroying the shared cultural record and the very possibility of the recovery of meaning. Finally he drives the old lord mad and insinuates himself as the dominant figure. He is the evil that must be confronted.

Likewise British culture of the 1950s, like the Bloomsbury group before it, willed itself to forget that the logic of its rituals depended on the reciprocal responsibility of the aristocracy and the mutual associations of the agrarian and industrial working class. Between these two great nineteenth-century political traditions, which formed their own accounts of virtue, the middle class used to articulate a culture of public service and acknowledgement of the greater good. However, this settlement was derided in the late 1950s by a self-hating cultural elite personified by Philip Larkin in his poetry and by John Osborne's 1956 play, *Look Back In Anger*. Both authors represented a minor grammar school/public school culture that deeply despised its own legacy, hated religion and gleefully repudiated the institutions of the past, just as the eponymous hero of Kingsley Amis's *Lucky Jim* is allowed to pour scorn upon earnest provincial seekers of culture and defenders of local custom. These angry young despisers of mythology also taught the British middle class a contempt for the notions of virtue and tradition. Such disdain found mass expression in the late 1960s when a newly decadent middle class became addicted to its own pleasures and engendered the professional advocacy of value relativism, individual rights assertion and state multi-culturalism.

This fragmentation of a shared national culture in turn helped to license a self-aggrandising right-wing piety among the newly pre-eminent and virtue-free middle class, justifying their own economic advancement and self-importance. After virtue and tradition had been repudiated by both left and right in the late 1960s and 1970s, public values became a form of unrestrained liberal individualism that believed only in its own assertion of personal will and subjective desire. The circulation and propagation of this emptiness was accompanied by the rise of a bankrupted low culture of utilitarianism aimed at the working class, and by assertive, rights-based advocacy for the newly individuated middle class. The working class were first provided with a semi-pornographic tabloid press in the early seventies – the first page 3 girl made her appearance in 1970 – and the public presence of pornography and the delighted destruction of taboo by progressives has intensified ever since. In 1974, the BBC series *The Family* gave birth to reality television with a portrayal of a week in the life of a family that endorsed a view of working-class life as hopeless and debased, ignoring the grace and honour of much proletarian existence. This kind of low realism has by now colonised much of our nightly television viewing, reaching its nadir with the staged banalities and catfights of Channel 4's populist hit *Big Brother*, up to and including the broadcasting of casual sex between the 'housemates'.

Far too many in our governing elites – be they in the BBC, in Parliament, in the banks, in social services or indeed education – have been promoting exactly this cultural mix for decades. It is they who have produced the culture that has destroyed our financial system, caused the ethos and professionalism of our public services to haemorrhage, produced expensive politicians of low calibre and laid waste the traditions that are, or were, the cultural bedrock of our country.

What the behaviour of both bankers and MPs exemplifies is that, like the denizens of Gormenghast, they have forgotten the meaning of the station they occupy, and of course so have we. All of us now patently lack any common account of the sort of people we should be. This is our contemporary 'gothic' crisis: the crumbling citadel full of empty pageantry sceptically and sentimentally embraced is already prey to the forces of a cynical self-advancing nihilism. It is clear that mere procedural reforms cannot be the answer to such a situation. There is no point in changing the institutions or their rules if the values we enthrone within them are the same values that have corroded us in the first place. Projects for constitutional reform, no matter how worthy they might be, do not get to the heart of the matter.

The real task is to recreate and refashion the original culture that a vapid and unhinged middle-class liberalism has destroyed. We need to recover what we owe one another in respect of our history, our people and our shared civic home. So more democracy is not enough of an answer, even if it is part of the answer. This is particularly so if by democratising we merely extend the absence of virtue that characterises so many of our governing elite and so much of our culture to more and more citizens. *Big Brother* may have a democratic flavour, but that does not make it either morally good or culturally desirable. And just because it is neither it is, of course, not truly democratic or empowering. Many can achieve excellence in real athletic, dramatic or musical skills; only a tiny minority will ever compete for the dubious privilege of never being thrown out of a fictional televisual homestead. Nor will simplistic assertions of the rights of the people prevent the dominance of the executive. We need to deliver the ethical content necessary for a change in behaviour; only then can our institutions flourish.

To achieve this we must recognise both dimensions of a good politics. A virtue-based politics is one in which both hierarchy and democracy coexist and each is the precondition of the other. Without free democratic debate there can never arise a seriously examined and tried-out recognition of abiding values. But without a hierarchy of objective values, and of people embodying degrees of such value, democracy will become identified with self-interest and eventually corrode, as we see in Britain today.

How can this be so? How can such a seemingly bizarre paradox really hold good? In two specific ways. First, democracy is not an infinite abyss. We don't vote about everything and we don't vote concerning what we should vote about. Thus, before the people decide, they are presented with various points of view and some points of view occupy more public space and gain greater support than others. This appears to be unfair, but the answer to this conundrum cannot, as a matter of social possibility, be a democratic one. Otherwise we would have to wait for a collective vote before we were allowed to say anything at all. It is at this point that all democratic and republican (in the broadest sense) polities have recognised that they rely crucially upon the role of public education. The voices that have most right to be heard before we vote are educated and virtuous ones – the voices that will put different points of view before us with integrity and after careful consideration of alternative positions. These are the voices which should be listened to. In the not so distant past they included honourable statesmen like Disraeli and Gladstone, the leaders of voluntary associations, energetic priests ministering to their flocks, local trade union leaders, mothers helping each other with childcare, and local charities and many others. But today, this claim that we should respect and honour virtue tends to meet with charges of unwarranted elitism. And what is the upshot? A new culture in which even 'the first speakers' who await the response of the people are also permitted to speak only by democratic decision? Very far from it. Instead the upshot is that the old educators are replaced by the new persuaders – the advertising executives, the spin-doctors, the pollsters, all the contemporary sophists. We need a new Socrates to denounce these manipulators. Such people do not offer us honest alternatives in elections: instead they seek to trick us into supporting them, or try to second-guess public opinion in order to adapt to it. This further enshrines a politics of resignation before the lowest common denominator of human opinion and behaviour. Democracy therefore requires a hierarchy of persons of genuine education – of true formation in whom knowledge is combined with virtue.

This is not an unjust elitism, for equality itself requires hierarchy if its end is to be met. Equal distribution of goods requires an agreement as to a hierarchy of true goods. Do we, for instance, want an equality of hair colour or height, or do we want an equality of assets or income? Even to decide on which goods such an equality might distribute is already to exercise a hierarchical preference for the better over the worse and the more over the less important. For where there is no such agreement, we can only mediate disagreement through the formal game of an unfettered market competition. Again, this claim will usually meet with the liberal protest that such agreement is impossible and that what I am advocating is a system in which some people impose their arbitrary preferences upon others. But, once more, let us consider the actual upshot of accepting pluralist disagreement about values and we will see that it has generated a far worse arbitrariness and a far greater indulgence of power and vested interest. For a market competition between competing goods has led inexorably to the imposition of certain values by the monopoly winners in the marketplace. Merely formal fairness as to the rules of the game leads in the end to a massive substantial unfairness. By contrast, all human equity requires some human consensus as to the ordering of values – why else would we consider that all children should be educated and not be given a daily choice between school and the amusement arcade?

But it is one thing to establish the case for virtue and a hierarchy of virtuous persons and values, it is another to create its content and initiate and shape its practice.

What are the preconditions for the revival of an honourable culture? Well, David Cameron outlined one of them in a speech in early 2009, when he said: 'I believe that the central object of the new politics should be a massive, sweeping radical redistribution of power: from the state to citizens; from the Government to Parliament; from Whitehall to communities; from the EU to Britain; from judges to the people; from bureaucracy to democracy.' What Cameron is here gesturing towards is an older Tory tradition of intermediate structures and the politics of community and reciprocity. Instead of the vertical sanction of the state, which citizens can only experience as an act of external coercion, a good politics requires the horizontal sanction of our peers, friends and colleagues. Crucial to a revival of virtue is the restoration of genuine liberty, which must be organically embedded in particular social formations with particular privileges and duties.

Under liberalism, freedom is formal and procedural. A revival of groups and genuine intermediary associations, by contrast, renders liberty both real and specific. The ordinary isolated person can never really enforce their freedom against the state, since their litigation on any matter can easily be, and often is, overruled, ignored or derogated. The language of rights all too frequently appeals to an assertive and aggressive middle class whose penchant for lawyers only reveals their failure to understand the common basis of law. For genuine rights can only ever be appeals to mutual understanding and the sharing of duties and obligations. Rights based merely on self-possession will endlessly proliferate and then the real questions become: how do we balance one right against another? How do we enforce the active duty of one without which the claim-right of another is a mere dead letter? How, for example, do we balance out the rights of men, women and children? Or how can we fulfil the right of children to be educated by inculcating in all adults a true sense of the duty to provide this education? One does not need to deny altogether the validity of the language of rights. The point is that it quickly evolves into issues about the just distribution of goods and of the need for virtuous education into a sense of duty.

So the first and overriding precondition for the restoration of a good ethos is the restoration of civil society, of intermediary associations and alongside them a culture of reciprocally interlocked rights and duties. This requires a renewal both of local government and of companies in ways that will be outlined in the following two chapters. It requires in addition the encouragement of the role of all sorts of voluntary associations.

But it also and fundamentally requires a renewal of education. So far I have explored the political aspect of virtue; now I must turn to its other aspect, which is 'formation'.

In the ancient and medieval worlds, and still to some extent during the eighteenth-century enlightenment, politics and education spun round in a virtuous circle. Education was intended to fit people to play a part in the life of the city; politics was intended to form virtuous citizens. Hence the polity itself promoted schooling and the political forum was itself the highest school of humanity. Here there is an interesting balance between the social and the personal: neither the collective good comes first, nor the individual good. Rather both matter, the good of the city in time and the good of the individual, including the eternal well-being of his or her soul and the reputation of the individual and the familial line.

However, with the advent of modern liberalism this beneficial circle has been broken. Education still prepares people for the political arena, but politics ceases to be a form of education for the good. We have already seen the logic whereby individualistic liberalism develops into worship of the state. One corollary of this is that the state gradually becomes the sole educator and the sole purpose of education becomes the state's well-being. This is most of all exemplified in the thinking of J. S. Mill, for whom the point of education is to produce an elite that will realise the correctness of the principle of the greatest happiness of the greatest number. Here the only true goal of politics is the banal one of being either materially satisfied or aesthetically pleased. As we saw in the previous chapter, even liberty is to be promoted insofar as it promotes this realisation. But becoming educated is an end in itself because it conjoins knowledge to virtuous practice. If the true political goal is one of virtuous flourishing and a continuous debate as to the nature of the good life, politics itself is part of the educative process and in consequence should not wish to subordinate the process of education to itself.

This can sound very abstract – but it has a direct practical consequence. It slowly becomes normal to grant the state a monopoly over teaching as well as over violence. Taking those two things together, one could say that the state alone wields the cane! And appropriately enough, a set of desiccated schoolmasters lay at the heart of Gormenghast, that great fable of modern Britain. It is nothing short of incredible that we think it normal for the state to be able to require by law that all children be educated, and only according to standards which the state lays down and most commonly in schools where the state imposes a narrow syllabus. This syllabus is increasingly conceived in utilitarian, functionalist terms, such that children are only to learn what will benefit the state, including the state by way of the market. Moreover, children are subject to a bizarre discipline whereby they are not allowed to focus on any topic of interest for too long.

This discipline surely mainly serves the purpose of churning out children as modern political citizens, because it is clearly detrimental from an educational point of view.[5]

So Mr Gradgrind still stalks school corridors, even if he speaks the New Labour language of targets, skills, outcomes and pluralist equality. For this dominant outlook, education is about inscribing the blank slates of childish minds with the procedures of an information economy and a late modern technocracy. It is a matter of inserting them within a pre-given space and certainly not of developing their latent talents nor of attending to their particular characters – despite the fact that this is once more disastrous from a pedagogic perspective.

Yet the really bizarre thing is that as soon as Mr Gradgrind, the school organiser who probably doesn't actually teach much in our time, has vanished down the corridor, Miss Jean Brodie enters the classroom, even if she'll tend to admire Obama more than Mussolini these days. For alongside a strictly objective technocratic approach to the sciences and to 'skills', there survives in our schools the romanticism of the 1960s which dominates the teaching of literature in particular and which still ensures that there is little concern for grammar and punctuation. To this can be added a total disdain for every historical canon, unless it be one relating the history of some beleaguered minority or other. In this quarter of the curriculum self-expression still rules. Just as the reductive right informs our economy and the destructive left our culture, so this division is reflected in our schools and universities: the right rules in terms of science and discipline; the left rules in terms of the humanities and the persistent culture of moral relativism. As a son of one of my friends pointed out to me, the trouble about the latter is that children get the message that no progress is possible in either arts or ethics, because they are encouraged to believe that what they already think is as good as it gets. They are educated into uncertainty – for the modern humanities have already wholly bought into the teenage myth that truth is relative.

As I have already argued, state technocratic education derives from the Benthamite turn given to the enlightenment. But where does 1960s' child-centred education come from? Surely from the romantic reaction to the enlightenment which began with Rousseau. A modernity that rejects religious transcendence is bifurcated in a contradictory way: sometimes it stresses the dominance of human artifice and so one gets education as a set of technical procedures; but it equally stresses the priority of nature, which gets treated like a substitute divinity. The latter is what happens with Rousseau: he sees all education and culture as tending to weaken and corrupt, just as he regards all society as contaminating individual purity. So, for Rousseau, the real goal of education is to unleash the genius that is already there in the child.[6]

Here then is the clue to the strange combination that we find in our schools: Gradgrind pure facts to be trotted out on the one hand and sheer Miss Brodieish self-expression on the other. Once again these are two halves of left and right liberalism in covert collusion, whereas the real alternative is education into the good. For if there is no transcendent value in any sense, then all one is left with is the given variety of nature on the one hand and the imposition of artificial norms on the other.

By contrast, an education into the good locates the third term between nature and artifice, between time and space, between the child and the teacher, as residing in the idea of tradition. Children should be inducted into a living tradition and not merely taught facts. And only thereby will their unique individual creativity be truly unleashed. Both facts and originality matter and they are not alien to each other. By the same token, the uniquely English (and to a lesser extent Scottish) segregation of the arts and the humanities should be brought to an end, as it is bad for both and bad for students. Nor should young scholars in universities be allowed to know everything about Hitler and nothing about Plato. We need to restore humane education in a new sense if we are truly to educate people both as citizens and as human beings.

The role of tradition is inseparable from the idea of the good because it makes neither the given child nor the teacher's expertise absolute, and so keeps them both in play. This implies that what is absolute lies beyond either, and here we are close to Plato's idea of learning as recollection and Augustine's idea of learning as illumination. In a sense children do 'recall' something when they learn something, if they are to 'see it for themselves'. But this is not to recall something simply innate. Instead it is to have a dim inkling of the entire truth with which human beings are – despite it all – still kin, even though they can never altogether understand it. It is for this reason that religious ideas of a transcendent God seem to be uniquely able to achieve both a sense of objective truth and to sustain an educational balance between the child and the teacher. Here lies the deep reason for the otherwise perplexing persistence of the role of faith schools in education today. This is not to say that there can be no secular approximations to this sense of transcendent truth and goodness. But some such proxy is required in order to achieve the balance I am talking about.

Without any belief in the objective good, further bad educational consequences follow. Truth gets separated from virtue and we run the risk of merely training clever criminals or tax-evaders rather than honourable citizens. Also we risk causing psychological damage to children by presenting them with an incoherent melange of fact and opinion, science and arts, and fragmentary insights, never correlated. It is far better for children if a teacher presents them with some holistic and inspiring version of reality which they can negotiate, even if they ultimately modify it or reject it in favour of another version.[7]

But what are the practical consequences of these reflections? I have already indicated one – the need to move much further away from over-specialisation too young and judging people too early, such that natural differences in rate of educational development are not taken into account. A second would be the need for the re-professionalisation of schools. Teachers should be left to teach and not be endlessly checked up on. They should be allowed to devise their own diverse syllabi. A third would be the need for all-age education in order to allow education to keep pace with politics. We should revisit the 1930's 'village college' idea which survives in Cambridgeshire and make all schools also providers of adult courses. A fourth consequence is the need to shift education away from the sphere of the state and towards that of civil society, with teachers and parents far more in control, and to allow for far more diversity of types of school. A choice between types of schools should be allowed to all parents, however poor, and they should no longer be the prisoners of their geographical areas. How to achieve such equity is admittedly problematic, and current Tory proposals to offer both a pupil premium in terms of funding per pupil to those in disadvantaged areas, and an ability to institute and create schools from the bottom up, offer real measures to meet some of these needs. One additional idea might be to involve universities, which could coordinate local resources and continuously make up for the deficiencies of some schools in some areas. This measure could further promote a professional ethos by making general use of graduate students as teachers – and overall we need to move to the idea of primary and high school teaching as being something that many people will perhaps do only during their youth. Teacher fatigue and high turnover is a problem that needs to be admitted and acted upon.

If all or even some of these things were implemented, then we might start to produce a generally valuable mass education. For up to now mass education has in many respects made people more stupid. It results in an equal disparagement of the subtleties of folk culture and of complex metaphsyics –

leading in general to a triumph of the middle-brow and the bourgeois where plausibility always wins out over truth and depth. Indeed, when many of the working classes educated themselves, they often had a knowledge of Shakespeare, Milton, Bunyan and the Bible which meant that they were far more genuinely 'formed' than their descendants today. This is not to be nostalgic – for we need in future a mass public education that will be able to surpass those old standards which now put us to shame.

If we redefine education as formation in the good, then this will open us out to genuine ideas rather than to dubious 'ideals', which are the stock in trade of falsifying ideologies. For ideals are purely abstract – so either they are irrelevant to practice or else they license the terroristic condemnation of every existing practice in the name of a phantom purity, as happened with the French Revolution and under Maoism. Genuine ideas, by contrast, can be practically participated in and are only known – to the degree that they can be known – through an experience of such practice. It is the interplay between ideas and practices that constitutes a tradition. Because ideas can be somewhat realised they are not simply vacuous. But because they cannot be totally realised they can still exert a critical pressure. In this way a belief in the transcendent idea of the good alone allows both objectivity about values and a liberal openness to free discussion of value. Otherwise one has either a tyranny of fixed value, as with fascism and communism, or else the contemporary tyranny of liberal subjectivism.

The best human products of good formation, which is also formation in the good, are those people who can combine knowledge with virtue. It is in those people above all that we can repose trust – and, as we have seen, the democratic process requires such trust in such people. The political left often says that we cannot leave everything to trust – and they are right. We need democratic checks upon our leaders. To deny this would be naive. Yet the left is also naive when it implies that we can dispense with trust altogether. The truth is that democratic checks must always be supplemented by an encouragement of trustworthiness in human leaders. Social groups and human associations need to have the capacity to judge potential leaders shrewdly – to discern their capacity for truth-telling and honesty. For the alternative to good leaders is always bad leaders – even within democracy. And our culture under-estimates heroic leadership because it has given away so much to the state that there are too few citizens left who have the experience of autonomous organisation and leadership. Because the state or the monopolised market deprives all of us of group activity we can no longer recognise the importance or possibility of leadership. Good leadership is crucial to successful human organisation, and while our rulers trumpet their own capacities as leaders, their courage and decisiveness, the fact is that in modern government and bureaucracy the leading roles have been monopolised by technocrats and placemen too scared to take risks or trust their own judgement.

This must lead us finally to a brief reflection on the role of inequality, which is one of the implications of a politics of virtue. Certainly the virtue of all should be encouraged and certainly the most crucial virtue – charity or love –

can be exercised by all. Yet those who exercise talent with virtue in any mode or degree, or who exemplify charity in a supreme way in their capacity for justice and prudential judgement, deserve appropriate privileges and sometimes a certain hierarchical elevation. Again, as with leaders, the alternative to this virtuous hierarchy is not no hierarchy at all, but rather the dominance of evil men or women, time-servers and exploiters of public benefit to private ends.

For almost no-one believes in literal equality of outcomes for all. In which case, the key to achieving greater equality and equity is paradoxically the acceptance of justified inequality. This was already firmly grasped by the very egalitarian liberal thinker John Rawls. But Rawls could only admit inequality for instrumentalist reasons such as increasing economic wealth through the spur of incentive. The problem here is that the beneficiaries of such a policy need not be virtuous men or women, and so will have no interest in keeping their wealth at the level of this social benefit. Furthermore, I would argue that the virtuous are entitled to the means that will give an appropriate and wide scope to the exercise of their virtue, both for their own sake and for the sake of their direct and personal (rather than indirect, as for Rawls) influence upon the rest of the population. Finally one cannot restrict this benefit, as Rawls does, merely to the unfortunate – it must in justice be to the benefit of society as a whole.[8]

Rawls tended rather curiously to think that natural inequalities were a kind of injustice that society should rectify. But any natural talent is surely a potential benefit to all which should be developed and not suppressed through forcible equalisation. In this respect one can also defend certain kinds of inherited privilege to the degree that what is passed on from parents to child is a tradition of honourable duty as well as material comfort and social status – and is this not exactly what we see and value in our armed services? Again the alternative to this mode of inherited privilege is not no privilege – for short of tyranny no measures of death tax (however desirable they might be) can ever abolish the imbalance of inheritance altogether. The alternative will be the inheritance only of material wealth and moral brutality. So, rather than attempts to achieve equality of opportunity by constantly cancelling out the benefits of achievement from one generation to the next (and so wasting much individual talent and social energy) we need also an attempt to produce greater economic equality among the living. And part of the way to achieve this is to justify inequalities in the name of virtue. For the justifiable wealth acquired by virtue will prove far less productive of ostentatious houses, expensive yachts and private bank-accounts than the unjustifiable wealth of the irresponsible rich, who have prospered only according to the rules of the game of equality of opportunity and who see no need for reciprocity in return

With the demand that we accord both trust and power to the trustworthy, formation – genuine education – has circled back to politics and the virtuous circle of virtue is once more complete. Let us work to make it once again complete in contemporary British practice.

8 The Moral Market

How would a new politics of virtue relate to the economy? In this chapter, I argue that we cannot have a moral society without a moral economy, and that a moral economy, rather than inhibiting the free market, is actually its precondition.

This argument directly opposes the two dominant ways of thinking about markets and morality. On the neo-conservative right, capitalist free markets are seen as ethical exemplars, because nothing is more moral than pure freedom. On the liberal left, by contrast, markets are seen as amoral but necessary – as utilitarian mechanisms for providing certain basic material goods. On this account, truly ethical considerations can only moderate the scope of market influence with non-profitmaking civil associations and state welfare provision.

The problem with the first view is the problem with liberal ethics in general, as already described. Any supposed exaltation of the sacredness of human freedom involved here is exposed in practice as a mask for the justification of the restriction in the freedom of others by the advancement of self. The problem with the second view is that amorality is contagious. If much of life is dominated by naked individualism this then decisively shapes our behaviour. Moreover, modern capitalist markets were only established by seizing control of areas of life that had previously involved only production for the sake of self-sufficiency or else for reciprocal exchange, for example agriculture. These markets sought more profits by appropriating the non-profitmaking sphere.[1] Hence there is nothing stable about the 'market sphere' and recent history suggests that its natural desire to extend itself tends to eclipse any well-meaning attempts to limit its functions. These attempts are made yet more difficult by globalisation, since local society and national governments cannot hope to contain the global market.

Today it appears more *realistic* to try and achieve a moral market than to limit an amoral market by a more bureaucratic and interventionist state. It is also a far higher ethical aspiration. The liberal left would say that a capitalist market in some things is tolerable but not in others – not, for example, in health, education, human body-parts, goods that affect life and death. Yet nearly all commodities affect human well-being – whether material or spiritual. Why do we so easily accept a raw competitive trade in food and shelter (without which we could not survive), and yet we baulk at a naked trade in medical care? An economic exchange is always involved in any economic interaction – even within the welfare state we all pay for doctors and we all pay in some fashion or other for midwives and for funerals. But in these latter cases exchange is moralised because we think that this good is a good for all and so we fund it through universal taxation. However, could we not moralise all economic exchanges, without welfare, in various different and appropriate ways? Can we not ensure a basic just distribution at the level of the economy, thereby minimising the need for political *re*-distribution in order to correct economic injustices? This is all the more desirable because redistribution is necessarily always limited and unstable, and involves the additional coercion of the state. Besides, because the market logic seeks always to expand its scope, redistribution is a bit like trying to push back the tide with a broom. Welfare merely licenses an original immorality by limiting the market's more unacceptable social consequences and welfarism reinforces a utilitarian, impersonal and individualist understanding of human goods.[2] It is also subject to cyclical cutbacks when the need to re-generate a return on capital once more takes precedence over an equally cyclical need to replenish consumer demand.

For these reasons then, establishing a moral market is desirable. But what exactly would virtue within the marketplace mean? In the broadest possible terms it would mean that, while prices and wages would continue to be the outcome of supply and demand, supply and demand would be subject to ethical considerations. This is true to a certain extent today: when we decide what to produce and what we want we are not only concerned with economic factors. To some degree people already produce what they think is desirable or have an interest in – people rarely open their own restaurant just to make money, it is also because they delight in the preferential exercise of their culinary and hosting talents. And people discipline their desires not only in relation to their income but also in relation to what they believe to be good for them and for others, as many consumers now limit what they buy to fairtrade or organic products precisely because they do not wish to profit from certain outcomes. I would argue that these other, personal considerations of extra-economic value or sympathy be given social as well as private recognition and become economically valuable as a result.

First, this would involve a deliberate effort at ethical education of both producers and consumers about the wider social costs of certain activity, be it the purchasing of hardwoods from the Amazon or the denial of healthcare to the indigent and the poor. Second, it would involve the gradual creation of a new economic culture in which more was at stake in the making of contracts than simply the satisfaction of two isolated self-interests. Adam Smith supposed that sympathy is marginal to the operation of the market, because when I buy meat from the butcher neither of us is at that moment concerned about the other's well-being. Yet this is only true of a certain kind of contract within a certain kind of market.

By contrast, all the evidence shows that, for most of human history, contract has often had an aspect of mutuality about it, an echo of primitive gift-exchange, where the economic bond established also a personal bond, and self-interest did not entirely exclude a concern for the other. Even today this has not vanished entirely: I may decide to shop at my local butcher rather than at the hypermarket because I want to keep that shop's livelihood going and because I think that small concerns like it are good for the elderly who can't drive and good for the fair treatment of local farmers. Likewise I may seek out products which are (at least in theory) 'fair-traded'. And quite often, in fact, a good deal for the producer and his workers is also a good deal for myself. The firm that cares for its employees' welfare is more likely to care for the quality of its produce.

It is therefore not a naive fantasy to suppose that elements of sympathy and trust can enter into economic transactions and that the search for an economic good deal can go hand in hand with a search for social solidarity. Indeed Italian traditions of political economy have recognised this ever since the eighteenth century.[3] And this combination can be institutionalised in realistic ways. Already, the non-profit sector of the economy is significant and because it is a genuine part of the market, its practices and assumptions cannot be neatly corralled but tend to leak into the practices and assumptions of the profitmaking sector also. Thus one increasingly sees the rise of hybrid enterprises, such as social enterprises where a large segment of the profits is systematically donated to charity and where an acceptance of this direction is part of the very pre-condition for share-holding or stake-holding.

The idea of contract as enacting a shared horizon, rather than fulfilling individual, isolated desires can be secured through the idea of the 'civil enterprise'.[4] In a civil enterprise, there is a cooperative partnership not only between share-holders, managers and workers as stakeholders, but also between these and the regular consumers, who can also enter into partnership in various ways. In this way the one-sided favouring of the worker – often in a very utilitarian way – by the traditional cooperative is overcome. Instead, the importance of society and of establishing personal relationships can be seen *as goods in themselves*. People come to enjoy their 'loyalties' to a certain style of production and product as much as they do the products.

Through civil enterprises, a new type of market regulation becomes possible via shared ethos rather than state imposition. This can come into effect by example and influence – when the ethical firms turn out to be more economically successful than non-ethical firms. Second, we need to stop seeing all contract as amoral and grounded in mutual egoism; once this notion is overthrown, there will be less inclination to form monopolies. This is already true at a local level in many parts of Europe, because small and medium-sized local firms are often content with sufficient profits and a relationship of reciprocity with their suppliers and consumers. The small-scale clothes maker in one northern Italian city is not very concerned about buying out his fellow-maker in another town because this would actually compromise his market identity which is closely bound up with the high quality and distinctiveness of his products. It is not that market forces are not operating here, it is rather that qualitative considerations really do enter into market exchanges. By contrast, where the element of sympathy is elided and the typical economic actor is supposed to be indifferent to its employees, its customers and the nature of its products, the logic of the enterprise must be the drive towards total victory and so to monopoly. But at this point of course, market logic has contradicted itself and a competitive market has been abolished. The argument then is that an ethical attitude towards salaries, prices and product quality is actually allied with sustaining market competition, whereas a total refusal of this logic tends to abolish the market in favour of oligarchic corporate control, which tends to become quickly allied to, or synonymous with, the bureaucratic operations of the state.

The neo-liberal model of the capitalist market is far too open to the pursuit of bad practice – buy as cheaply as possible, sell as dearly as possible, produce goods with the least possible expense and labour and the shoddiest possible quality. If this gives a market advantage — in part because of uneducated consumers – then gradually bad practice will crowd out good practice and so enthrone bad practice at the expense of the free market itself. But through the proper operation of the market the opposite effect can be achieved. Good treatment of workers, consumers and products can actually give a competitive advantage, because people will select for social value as well as value for money. In this way you can achieve a 'crowding in of the good and a crowding out of the bad'. Good practice and good habits can gradually drive away bad ones. This will not tend to generate a monopoly, even of the good firm, because there is not the same kind of drive to relentless expansion as with the non-sympathetic operator. And before the point where monopolisation has been reached it is likely that good practice will have been copied by other businesses. This then effectively gives rise to a market competition in virtue as well as in profits – and both would be in harmony. The better the product the higher the social gain and the greater the monetary and societal profit.

We all know that quite quickly CAMRA defeated the big brewers and, for a time at least, saved many independent pubs. This is because it successfully combined market logic with a desirable aesthetic and moral logic. And John Lewis has been more successful than many of its rivals, without seeking totally to destroy them, by its relatively ethical approach to staff, consumers and the nature of the products it trades in.

Here, then, one can argue something interesting and slightly paradoxical. The logic of monopoly is grounded in individualism, even though it leads to collectivist economic oligarchy. But the logic of anti-monopoly is just the reverse. It sustains some diversity of firm just because, from the outset, it admits more relationality and cooperation. Thus the civil partnership is a kind of small-scale benign 'monopoly' because it involves people banding together who subscribe to certain standards, and by including consumers within partnership it tends to circumscribe a certain reliable and constant body of consumers who remain mostly loyal. It is only through this relative 'monopoly' that perverse monopolisation is prevented, because the ethical business has set up a counter-logic to the crowding-out of good practice by bad. The key to this counter-logic is that good treatment of workers, consumers and products can actually give one a competitive advantage because people will select for quality and reliability as well as value for money.

I would also suggest that the moral market could be actively encouraged by the formation of 'free guilds' or voluntary professional associations. The trouble with guilds in the past, when membership of such bodies was often compulsory, was that they frequently encouraged monopoly, corruption and the exploitation of consumers. If an innovation was achieved and a competitive advantage developed, the guild defended that innovation against all other future advances. Thus guilds, whilst sustaining standards, also inhibited progress and advancement. But if membership of a guild guaranteeing that certain standards of fair practice had been met was voluntary, then this would not inhibit rival competitors, while membership of the guild could secure a competitive advantage, in the way that exhibiting a fairtrade or social enterprise brand does today. Moreover, such guilds might be flexible about their vocational scope, which is crucial in a world where new vocations appear every decade.

Once, through all these means, a new economic ethos had been established, it would no longer appear socially or politically acceptable to engage in economic activity in order *only* to achieve a profit without also producing some sort of social benefit. In relation to ecological issues we are already starting to develop this sensibility. Unfortunately this awareness is obscured by the tendency to speak of environmental questions in overly scientific and economistic ways which conceal from view the fact that what we find really intolerable is the destruction of the physical world in ways that destroy also the quality and depth of our human existence, including our natural human concern for the flourishing of plants and animals. (For a world in which there was no real wildlife would impinge dramatically on my sense of well-being and fulfilment.) Thus, in terms of the environment, it is not really an issue of survival at all: in reality and in spite of global warning we and the planet will not die. It is rather that the way we will have to live will be intolerable if ecological collapse is allowed to continue. We will find life unbearable if the beauty of nature and closeness to the earth has been altogether removed. Ecology is above all a *human* issue, and if we can see this then we should be able to see that there are issues also about social ecology which impinge upon economics. For if the destruction of nature only for profit is intolerable, then so also is the destruction of human hope, human comfort, talent and creativity. Given the emergence of such a new ethos, it might well be that at the limit, issues of fair pricing, proper remuneration for work and quality of workmanship could become issues for local rather than central jurisdiction. An economy based on trust can be an economy that requires less state intervention, but it will remain the case that formal contract is something underwritten and only sustained by law. Yet once we have decided that sympathy is both ethically and economically a valid aspect of contract, there is no reason why the law should not also recognise this aspect also. Common economic goods should be known primarily through the operations of a 'civil economy', but the law would still have a role in securing contracting parties against the worst violations of those goods.

But is all this still not too utopian and in conflict with the proven working of the free market? Not at all. The moral market would alone establish a genuinely free market, since a successful free market, not a market mis-identified as a purely individualist endeavour, is in fact already founded upon, and productive of, sympathy, reciprocity and the extension of ownership.

The main reason for this is simple. The free market does not only embrace supply and demand, it also embraces the role of the firm.[5] For a long time economists have been aware of this, making the fashion for 'neo-liberalism' among politicians rather outdated. For neo-liberalism recognises only the individual actor. In consequence it must view the firm as but an instrumental contractual collaboration between individuals. Viewed this way, nobody within a firm can trust anyone else – and this has increasingly come to be the case within the economic sphere as within the bureaucratic sphere. But if no one can trust anyone else, then much energy must be constantly wasted on everyone within a firm keeping an eye on everyone else and making sure that individuals do not bleed the firm dry as, on this anthropology, they could naturally be expected to do. Of course this has the consequence of reducing the energy that can be spent on enterprise, while in an atmosphere of distrust no-one's entrepreneurial and creative drive is likely to be fired up and no-one's desire to forward the firm's activities is likely to be promoted.

It follows that the promotion of trust is actually in the interests of the free market, just as good moral practice can be ultimately more successful in the marketplace than bad, amoral practice. This suggests, as many economists have long known, that the firm is not best conceived as merely a contract between isolated individuals. Instead, the firm is crucial, as it corrects the inadequacies of the model of classical economics. First, while it is true that the market delivers exact information in a way that cannot be mapped from the centre (as Hayek rightly said), it is also the case that this information often arrives too late to be of use to the individual. I can discover that no one wants my toy wooden horses, but my consequent switch to toy wooden elephants remains a market gamble. This is one reason why individual producers are often at risk from innovation – they simply lack the ability to map the future accurately; instead they tend, if they are successful, to maximise what they do have, which is often a small, reciprocal market. If, however, you have more ambition then it is better to join a firm (or even start one), not only in order to share the risks, but also because a firm tends relatively to 'control the future' by establishing a certain habit of consumption amongst many people and a better permanent pattern of innovation. The firm is then always already in some form a cooperative enterprise, though mis-identified as an individual actor by a neo-liberalism that has always misunderstood the economic value of relationship, group activity and sympathy. In this way the very existence of the firm interferes with the classical individualist 'purity' of the market. For, in one sense, the firm reduces competition since it reduces competitors, but in return produces a higher standard of goods than would have been possible on the basis of a purely individual production. This is why it is firms rather than individuals that tend to be trans-national and successful because the activity of the group around the common end of excellence and product innovation will always have more ability and capacity than a single individual.

And this is why for the most part I favour mutualist or cooperative structures of ownership and reward. Because the firm is never just the managers – though the managers may be the most important members and so should be rewarded more – it is always a strangely communal endeavour. Indeed, where capitalism does not work is where – in the case of mega-mergers for example – managers often game both owners and workers in order to maximise their own short-term advantage against the long-term interests of everybody else. Recognising this fact allows us to remove the false lenses through which we have been observing economic activity in order to recognise that, insofar as the free market has been *both* successful and good, it is because it already includes the very ideas and notions that I am arguing for.

The second reason why the moral market can succeed is that the market is not stable over the long term and does not achieve a perfect equilibrium between demand and supply. Instead, over the long term, any specific mode of supply or demand will tend to atrophy through exhaustion, boredom, change in fashion or failed gambit due to the way in which the market always informs us 'too late'. A collapse in supply can in consequence lead to unfulfilled demands, while equally a collapse in demand can lead to a crisis of over-production or sterile capital.[6] Against these entropic tendencies, the firm based upon trust again provides a relative surety.

Even classical economics recognised one mode of entropy: the law of diminishing returns based upon 'declining marginal utility'. This law states that the more we get of something the less we need it or are excited by it. The fiftieth diamond brooch from the fifth husband will likely bore even the most feverish gold-digger. This is yet another example of the way in which the pure market, as conceived by fully 'classical' utilitarian liberal economics, tends to undermine itself in the long run. For sooner or later we all get bored, and for this very reason one exponent of this economics, John Stuart Mill (and John Maynard Keynes in his wake) suggested that eventually we will reach a point of satiety when all have enough and a no-growth economy will end the era of economic domination over society. Of course this idea of a final dialectical work performed by capitalism is just as foolish as that of that other great liberal, Karl Marx. For capitalism will engender endless new needs.

But should one then say that a moral economy would be able to discriminate between better and worse need and so would be able to pronounce 'enough'? Should a moral economy be anti-growth? Not exactly. Rather a moral economy can suggest both a way to counteract the law of diminishing returns *and* a more valid mode of unlimited growth.

How is this so? It is quite simple. We only get bored by lollipops. We get less bored by proper food and still less bored by good paintings and less bored yet by the activity of painting. The same applies to going to the theatre or to acting in a play. Creative and relational goods are not subject to the same entropic processes as ones of mere sensory satisfaction.[7] And yet these are still commodities in one of their aspects. Hence the more an economy is turned towards the production of creative and relational goods the more it counteracts diminishing returns. In this way too a more moral economy is a more stable market economy. Yet at the same time we can see how the infinite growth of such goods is only to be welcomed, since they enhance rather than destroy our natural and social environment.

In essence, liberal market economics is based upon individualism but generates monopoly. It theorises stability but generates entropy. By contrast, an economy of virtue guards against both monopoly and entropy in the multiple ways that we have seen. Likewise a liberal economy tends to promote centralisation, whereas an economy of virtue protects both the locality and the centre. This is because the 'circle of trust' tends to extend only so far, or if it reaches round the world, in the case of a big corporation, does so in a way that is not trying to destroy all local enterprise and all local integrity. Indeed the model for future corporate activity is exactly this: a sympathy between the things that only a trans-national can produce and the locality and economy in which they are manufactured. Thus corporates will make and market products for the regions they are in and try to produce a diversity of suppliers, not least because that builds economic resilience into the supply chain and extends the benefits of ownership and trade to more actors.

An economy of virtue promotes a 'principle of economic subsidiarity' which favours production and delivery at the geographical level and in the mode (profit or non-profit) that is most appropriate for businesses and society. In both cases a new kind of market advantage can accrue because the economic gain from sympathy extends not just horizontally between players at the same level but also vertically between enterprises of different size and scope. This makes markets that include sympathy more not less productive. Certainly we must always guard against a local protectionism that could deny access for local consumers to more desirable or more excellent products from elsewhere. But the demand for such protection often stems from illegitimate and state-sanctioned subsidies that impede a competitive and open market. By contrast a truly competitive market would allow and license competition between localities, rather than the current situation where all too often it is just trans-nationals which can compete while local enterprises cannot. Indeed it is the development of the infrastructure of mass trade in the market economy and the collapse in the price of transaction and transport that allows, perhaps for the first time, a genuine global competition between localities.

The role of economies of scale is not here denied, but it is balanced by specifically economic as well as ethical considerations which favour greater diversity in the majority of circumstances. And the more one prices in the true externalities of economic trade – be it pollution, healthcare or the social costs of wage serfdom – the more one will guard against monopoly and vested interest.

Hence the final paradox is that the dominance of the individualistic profit motive ultimately destroys the market, whereas commerce as a mutually sympathetic endeavour sustains it in perpetuity. The free market is the upholder of genuine liberty on the basis of reciprocal exchange.

9 Creating Popular Prosperity

We have seen that the primary task of renewal is to restore ethos and then to imbue the economy with an appropriate version of that ethos. This is far more vital than state redistribution. However, the state still has a crucial role to play in encouraging and enabling a fairer market. Two aspects of that role for Britain in the future will now be detailed.

Re-localising the economy

Many now agree that we need to democratise credit. Yet, despite efforts by the government to boost lending to small and medium-sized enterprises following the credit crunch, there is significant evidence to suggest that lending has in fact declined.

The government's quantitative easing programme poured £200 billion into the economy, with the intention of providing banks with more capital to lend. As Chancellor Alistair Darling put it in 2008, 'Banks need adequate capital, so that they can keep on lending to people. That is why today the Government have established a bank recapitalisation fund.'[1]

However, contrary to claims by the British Bankers Association (BBA), lending rates have not recovered enough to keep pace with local demand.[2] Despite recapitalisation measures, the Bank of England has found that credit flow to British businesses fell for most of 2009.[3]

Following the failure of major banks to extend credit in the aftermath of bank bailouts, the government's temporary Enterprise Finance Scheme was launched in January 2009 to provide a guarantee that credit would continue to flow to the economy, by subsidising the risk to lenders. The scheme guarantees lenders 75% of loans between £1,000 and £1 million, in exchange for which the borrower pays a 2% premium on the outstanding balance of the loan to the Department for Business, Innovation and Skills (BIS). The programme is available to qualifying UK businesses with an annual turnover of up to £25 million, in most sectors until 31 March 2011.

This 'Real Help For Business Now' stimulus failed to deliver during the recession. Despite pledging up to £13 billion in support, loans drawn down amounted to only £405 million.[4] Crucially, no loans were issued under this scheme during the worst quarter of the recession, Q1 2009, when 5,110 businesses were declared insolvent.[5] A survey by the Institute of Directors (IOD) found that, of a sample of 300 businesses that had applied for bank credit, 57% were refused and 20% resorted to using credit cards to finance their business. It also found that, of those businesses refused credit, 83% were not offered information on the Enterprise Finance Scheme.[6]

The Bank of England has noted that the lack of available credit will have a disproportionately negative effect on small businesses.[7] Approval rates for new borrowing fell for smaller businesses, between Q1 2008 and Q1 2009. This, combined with reduced demand for finance, has meant that lending has been 'markedly lower' than in Q1 2007, before the recession.[8]

Many of the issues inhibiting growth in lending to real businesses, and therefore growth in the resilience of the British economy, are related to the banking structures. Banking in the UK is highly centralised, as the market is dominated by four monolithic providers: RBS Group, Barclays, Lloyds TSB and HSBC, which together account for approximately 80% of lending to the SME market. The largest of these is the main provider to one quarter of all SMEs.[9] Meanwhile nearly 60% of SMEs have used only one main source of financing, while fewer than 10% have used three or more providers and fewer than 2% used four or more. The annual rate of bank switching is just over 2% across all types of business.[10]

Compare this to a region where banking is less concentrated. In 2005 the Lombardy region of Italy was home to 183 different banks – these having increased in number, against the tide of wider Italian and European trends, in the five years between 1999 and 2004.[11] Compared with the UK banking sector, banks in Italy generally, and the Lombardy region particularly, are significantly more heterogeneous in terms of size, ownership and services on offer.[12]

This variegated banking system has sustained an equally variegated distribution of business ownership as well as a globally competitive, resilient economy. With a GDP over €33,000 per capita and unemployment of only 4.3% at the height of the crisis in 2008, Lombardy is considered one of the 'four engines of Europe'.[13] As important as their high levels of income and employment, the 9.7 million people of Lombardy own over 825,000 businesses.[14] These businesses are primarily small and medium-sized, with 55% of businesses having fewer than fifty employees.[15]

Many businessmen and academics in the region attribute the success of the economy to the localised financial structures, frequently citing in interviews their strong local ties to banks as an important factor in their success. For their part, local banking officials take great pride in having sustained high levels of lending during the crisis ('unlike the unscrupulous UK bankers'), despite the increased risk of extending credit during a recession.

This civic pride and sense of responsibility is not simply a cultural difference, but a structural one. Not only do more, smaller banks increase competition, but their proximity to the community provides information which mitigates lending risks and, as importantly, strengthens the bonds and sense of mutual responsibility between lenders, borrowing businesses and the communities that they both serve.

The introduction of legislation modelled on the US Community Reinvestment Act (CRA)[16] would certainly contribute to keeping money in areas most in need of it, by facilitating the partnership of high street banks and intermediaries to deliver affordable credit. This kind of banking, at grassroots level with a focus on close relations between lender and borrower, combined with innovative financial instruments and a supportive tax framework, can begin responsibly to lend increasing sums into communities desperate for investment: '[The] impact of the CRA has been instrumental in the expansion of the community development field in the US ... The US Low-Income Housing Tax Credit and other tax credits have brought new investment into areas where "the market" was not operating effectively.'[17]

Unless we are going to go along with the perverse logic that says the poor will never own and should be prevented from doing so, which is what the FSA seems to be recommending in arguing for a tightening mortgage lending rules for those lower down the economic scale, then we need a new era of available but responsible lending.[18] Moreover, according to a study entitled 'The Community Reinvestment Act: A Welcome Anomaly in the Foreclosure Crisis', in keeping with its mission, the CRA actually deterred irresponsible lending, with banks subject to CRA requirements 66% less likely than other lenders to originate a subprime mortgage loan, even though they were 16% less likely than other lenders to deny a loan application.[19]

Recapitalising the poor

G. K. Chesterton once remarked that the problem with capitalism was not too much capital but too few capitalists. Chesterton's point is clearly resonant today. We live in a country in which, as David Cameron put it in 2009, 'the winners have taken all'. If Disraeli's great achievement was the extension of the political franchise, then his greatest failing was the lack of an attempt to develop a political economy for the poor. If Conservatism had abandoned the defence or vested and landed interests and offered the emergent industrial worker something more than low wages, then state socialism need never have happened. By the early 1890s, the Primrose League – the monarchist and pro-Empire Conservative association founded in memory of Disraeli – had well over a million members and enjoyed wider support amongst the working classes than the trade union movement. The inability to generate an appropriate form of economic management for the waged worker has united Conservatism every since.

The clear task facing the Conservatives of today has to be the radical extension of the economic franchise. Why? Because we face serious economic injustice. The poorest in our society own and earn disproportionately little, are hit hardest by recession and inflation, and are excluded from actively participating in the financial market. Our benefits system breeds dependency. If the sum of Britain's household assets were distributed equally among us, each person would own in excess of £137,330.[20] The reality is very different. The poorest quarter of Britain's population own less than 1% of total assets, while, at the other extreme, 3% of households possess one-sixth.[21]

While we have witnessed strong credit-financed economic growth since New Labour came to power in 1997, the fact remains that this growth has benefited some far more than others. Between 1997 and 2007, the poorest tenth of the population have actually seen their income fall. Some 40% of the total increase in incomes over the past decade has gone to the wealthiest 10% of the population.[22]

Just as the poor benefit least during the good times, they get hit the hardest during the downturn: the least well-off are paying a disproportionately high price during the recession, when the evidence suggests that the boom in consumer credit did not benefit them as much as wealthier borrowers: only £16 billion of £232 billion debt was subprime.[23]

More widely, Centre for Cities says that many of the cities that have been hit hardest are places still suffering from the legacy of industrial restructuring and previous recessions. This is widening the gap between cities.[24] 'The difference between the highest and lowest ten cities in terms of their [benefit] claimant count has widened by 70% since the start of the recession.'[25] In Hull the unemployment roll swelled by 16,000 names during the recession compared with just over 700 in Cambridge.[26]

Paradoxically, but perhaps not surprisingly, life at the bottom often costs more. Some 3 million adults lack a bank account or the ability to access credit from reputable sources.[27] This results in an inability to borrow at reasonable rates, while zero access to direct debit facilities often means that poor households end up paying a 'poverty premium' of around £1,000 per year. This includes paying 150% more for basic goods, such as an oven bought on credit; spending 10% more on gas bills and 8% more on electricity bills paid through pre-payment meters rather than by direct debit; and being forced to pay greater home and car insurance for residing in deprived areas.[28]

Economic attenuation is further compounded by parallel social phenomena. According to a 2001 Home Office Citizenship Survey, people living in the most deprived areas were twice as likely as those living in the most affluent areas to say that they 'never' had friends or neighbours round to their houses, and 'never' went out socially with friends of neighbours. Similarly, people living in households with an annual income above £75,000 are twice as likely to volunteer as those living in households with an income under £10,000.[29] The ramifications of these high levels of inequality are not confined to deprived neighbourhoods. The bad consequences permeate wider society, with all manner of negative indices being worse in more unequal societies than in more egalitarian cultures.[30]

All of which serves only to remind us that we need a new economic model to target those left behind, one that works through local communities and civil society. We need innovative ideas to craft a wholly different capitalism that will redistribute wealth, create multiple centres of wealth and innovation and substantially reduce welfare dependency. We require a new political economy that ensures that everyone in society begins to accumulate the capital they need to lead fulfilling, independent lives.

At first sight this sounds both very attractive and highly unlikely – how could it be achieved? How could an associative society be formed, considering how fragmented we are, and how could we construct a viable economy that sought to realise this vision? Well it is far more realistic than one might suppose. By enhancing the role of charities, social enterprises, housing authorities and community trusts, people from all backgrounds can begin to accumulate the capital and assets they need. There are, in fact, a burgeoning number of schemes already working to facilitate such an economic model. What follows is an outline of the ideas and schemes that, if promoted and encouraged by central government, could begin to foster the society we desire.

Re-directing pension tax relief

One of the problems facing policy-makers is how to encourage individuals to generate assets (such as pension savings) in a way that is compatible with a progressive distribution of tax receipts across society. Typically, asset policy has relied on the employment of financial incentives to encourage saving, investing, home and business ownership, and other asset-generating activity.

The problem with these asset-building incentives is that, despite encouraging individual well-being and pro-social behaviour, these policies typically suffer from limited take-up and deliver socially regressive outcomes, concentrating benefits on high earners and those who already hold assets. This has meant that, with the exception of programmes such as the right-to-buy scheme or the child trust fund, policies designed to generate widespread asset ownership have often further excluded those they were designed to include.

This can largely be attributed to certain features of incentive uptake. First, those most likely, and in the best position, to take up a given incentive, are typically already financially included and asset-holders. Secondly, tax-based incentives are inherently regressive, benefitting high earners who already pay more tax.

In the worst-case scenarios, low and medium earners end up subsidising asset-creation for the top few per cent. This has been the case for pension tax relief, on which 25% of government spending has been concentrated on the top 1% of earners. This amounts to almost £10 billion in tax relief per annum for the percentile of the population earning more than £150,000. The TUC argues that this has meant that taxpayers spend two-and-a-half times more on pensions for the top percentile of earners than on retired public servants. According to this report, 'The cost of providing tax relief on pensions in 2007/8 was £37.6 billion according to HMRC figures – ten times the net cost of unfunded public sector pension schemes that are not backed by an investment fund. This is estimated by the Treasury to be £4 billion this year.'[31]

Of course, pensions are an important type of asset for everyone in society to hold. For individuals, a pension provides income and protects against poverty in retirement, while also reducing dependence on state provision in old age. This explains why states are so willing to subsidise pension spending, as the cost of supporting state-dependent pensioners is large and growing quickly.

In 2007/8, 60% of all benefit expenditure in the UK (£74.9 billion) was directed at people above state pension age.[32] This problem is only set to grow as 34% of the total population have not generated any savings at all for retirement, and a further 13% of the population are considered to be saving too little. Some 44% of the public intend to rely on state pensions as their primary source of retirement income.[33] According to a study by the Association of British Insurers conducted in 2002, the total shortfall in current pension saving is £27 billion per annum.

However, attempts to subsidise pension savings through tax relief have accrued benefits to those on the highest income level. Up until changes introduced in the 2009 budget, every pound that an individual invests in a pension is excluded from their nominal income used by HMRC to assess their tax deductions.

It is easy to see how the benefits of such a policy are concentrated on high earners. For those who pay the basic rate of tax, 20%, every pound contributed to their pension saves 20p in tax; in this sense, a pound of pension savings 'costs' the saver only 80p. However, for top earners, those earning over £150,000 and paying up to 40% tax on income, each pound saved into a pension saves 40p in tax. For every pound so saved, 40p accrues to a high earner rather than contributing to tax revenue.[34]

The current overall sum spent on pensions tax relief is some £27 billion and it subsidises the already rich such that for basic-rate taxpayers to get the return that a millionaire gets for £600 they would at present have to pay in £800. This is a hugely regressive system that could with a little ingenuity be transformed into the foundation for a truly just savings culture.

We should recover this amount and direct it instead into a genuinely progressive matched savings programme that favours asset-creation for the poor rather than asset-augmentation for the rich. If we credit the pension pot of the already wealthy, then why not credit the savings products for the poor – this credit could go into a specified ISA product that gradually topped up with matching funds so as to provide those on the lowest incomes with an almost immediate resource that could help limit the use of loan sharks or the usury of doorstep credit. These matched savings could – like the Tory pupil premium for schools – favour those at the very bottom of society: on the basis of available data we have the resources to give the least well-off a double-matching, thereby massively increasing the savings ratio. Suddenly, as with child trust funds, a new mass savings culture could be created. And, with some short-term savings achieved for those who are most vulnerable, we could also allow the roll-over of matched savings (once a certain level had been reached) back into pensions, and give the basic rate of relief for the sum transferred. And all of this would be a massive reversal of the asset-stripping that has taken place at the bottom of society – it would be a genuine re-capitalisation and if made available from the current pensions tax relief it would cost nothing.

Massaging the bail-out

Currently the public sector is underwriting the UK bank bail-out to the tune of perhaps £1.4 trillion. When these now public assets are returned to the private sector, the public should be recompensed. For no longer should we accept the socialisation of risk and the privatisation of profit. Therefore we need to return the true price of risk to the private sector and stop collectively underwriting the private sector through the gaming of the tax base. So has this principle of a public return yet been conceded by politicians? Happily yes – George Osborne has recently announced that, under a Tory government, the public will be allowed to share in the return of assets by accessing shares at less than their true market value. Clearly this move is intended to endow and kick-start a new savings culture. However, I worry that the fate of such an intention will be similar to the perverse legacy of the great privatisations of the 1980s. Many of the shares were quickly squandered on holidays or just cashed in to make ends meet and no popular capitalism or new savings culture was established

Perhaps a better use of the money would be a seriously radical recapitalisation of the poor. Why not convert the return into investment vouchers for those at the bottom of society? They could, for example, be given such vouchers for the sake of starting or contributing to social enterprises (so that they can benefit twice over) in order that they can invest in something that will make a difference to them and their community. Of course, many people are not naturally skilled in this sort of entrepreneurial endeavour. However, this circumstance can be obviated by making such investments associative in character. In order for them to be activated people would have to group together to build social as well as investment capital; in this way they would gradually constitute bottom-up investment groups. Moreover, we could then seek to develop a 'dragons' den' environment – where a variety of social enterprises could compete for these investments in a specific area, so that popular market competition of a benign and socially beneficial kind can finally take root at the bottom of society.

Asset transfer

Local councils own property worth some £250 billion[35] and in 2009, the Audit Commission found that only one in fourteen councils was an exemplary manager of its assets.[36] 'Asset transfer' is a means of transferring council-owned property into the hands of local communities. Communities should be able to acquire property – at market or discount rates – and then use it as a base to deliver local services that have been opened up to the third sector, such as health provision for asthma sufferers or those recovering from a heart attack. Alternatively such buildings could shelter social enterprises such as those dedicated to getting the long-term unemployed to work or even a local shop on a retail-bereft estate that could function as a new community and retail hub. This has tremendous benefits for communities. First, it eases some of the financial pressure on social enterprises – with their new assets, they are able plan for the long-term and are no longer dependent on short-term grants and the increasingly onerous manner of applying for them. Redevelopment of one building can provide a catalyst for other inward investment and create jobs. By so doing, those who bought at the bottom can increase the asset value of what they purchased and begin to create an asset base of their own.

The Wolseley Community Economic Development Trust is a case in point. Following extensive public consultation in early 1994, it was recommended that redevelopment of a derelict site in inner-city Plymouth should include retail, office/light-industrial units and a community resource centre. The site was purchased from Devon City Council, for management by Wolseley Community Economic Development. The costs were met by local public bodies and the EU. The site development created the desired office and retail space, and community resource centre, as well as major employment and enterprise opportunities for those living locally.

A fundamental element of the project has been the involvement of the local community. Regular design meetings gave way to a community forum and a local skills' register was established to provide employment for local people throughout the development of the site. Anyone living in the Wolseley Trust catchment area can be a trust member for free and then elect the management board.

Asset transfer is a tangible way in which councils can support smaller social enterprises, and thereby improve local services, by returning publicly owned and often ill-managed land or assets to the communities they serve. However, present legal dictates often frustrate this outcome. Local authorities will argue that they are under considerable pressure to reduce council-tax levels and therefore need to sell to the highest bidder, regardless of the social benefit. For example, Stroud Common Wealth Ltd was a partner in a mutual bid for the 72-acre Standish Hospital site, but the Department of Health accepted a substantial bid from a healthcare firm instead.[37] Unless or until we challenge or broaden the 'best-value' legislation which tends to force councils into this position, many enterprises that could generate far higher social returns and so save on the costs of dysfunction will not be able to prosper. In short, we need a new mode of measurement that recognises the social gain in disposing of assets to social enterprises and factors that into tender or right-to-buy considerations

There are a number of ways to encourage asset transfer. The Audit Commission recommends that councils review their property holdings and get rid of surplus or under-utilised property.[38] All councils should be required to publish 'property maps', which would detail all council-owned property. In the same way that the Conservatives envisage the public scrutinising council spending, the public should be able to challenge council use of buildings, placing the onus on councils to justify their use of them. Social organisations and charities should be encouraged to submit proposals detailing how they would use the property, which could even be on a time-shared basis, with night or weekend use when the building was empty. And councils would have to respond publicly to these requests, giving reasons for the rejection of an application. We need councils to be willing to transfer property to the community, to see the process as a form of community empowerment, rather than power and resources ebbing away from local authority and central control. To realise this, central government should impose a legally binding duty on local authorities reasonably to consider asset transfer to social enterprises by emphasising the social rather than the monetary return. Currently, there is such a duty, but councils are free to interpret it in their own way and often cite the need to gain maximum financial returns as a reason for rejecting applications. Qualifying this by measuring social return should aid matters considerably. Successful applications for asset transfer should be published, and available for other groups to access. This will encourage consistency, which should improve council–community communication. Applications should be able to be tracked through the decision-making process so that applicants know what stage their proposal is at. Democratically elected figures in the council, or elected members of the community, should be consulted more during the process. The powers of the Asset Transfer Unit[39] (an organisation set up in 2009 to provide advice and materials to interested parties) should be strengthened, turning it into a court of appeal for transfer claims which have been rejected, by granting it the power to enforce its rulings. The government could also encourage organisations that promote asset transfer, such as community land trusts, cooperatives and development trusts.

Community land trusts, cooperatives and development trusts

Community land trusts (CLT) are non-profit organisations that exist to acquire land and property for the community and use them to deliver public services, such as affordable housing. An example is the already mentioned Stroud Common Wealth Ltd, in Gloucestershire, founded in 1999. It acquires land to provide affordable housing, workspace, amenity, food growing and conservation. Stroud Community Agriculture Ltd, one of Britain's most innovative community-supported agriculture ventures, leases 23 acres, employing three part-time farmers and growing food for 95 members. It builds on cooperation and mutual support, so that the risks and rewards of farming are shared between the farmers and consumers. The consumers commit to supporting the farm and providing a fair income for the farmers, allowing the farm to be developed.[40]

A cooperative enterprise allows communities to invest in local businesses. Individual shares can be issued for as little as £5 and marketed to as many people in the community as possible, giving them all a personal stake in the project and enabling them to engage with each other. Such enterprises can also act as a hook to attract wealthier supporters living outside the area.'[41]

Cafédirect plc, the UK's largest Fairtrade hot drinks company, raised over £4 million in 2004, with more than 16,000 people applying for a share prospectus and each investment averaging about £1,000. A community in Slaithwaite, West Yorkshire, pooled resources to buy a greengrocer's which was on the verge of closing. A cooperative was formed and sold £10 shares to members of the community – over 100 people invested in the business. These members now own and control the business and can stand for the board.[42]

Slaithwaite is on a relatively small scale, but with more assets and resources, communities can be encouraged to form development trusts. Headingley Development Trust (HDT) was founded in 2005 by residents of the Leeds suburb and by early 2009 had a membership of around 800. Membership is open to all; members have one vote and are eligible to stand for the committee. HDT has established a new farmers' market for Headingley and a scheme to bring local houses into community ownership (60% are owned by private landlords for student lettings). In 2006, the trust began negotiations with Leeds City Council to bring a former primary school into community ownership and develop it into an enterprise, arts and community centre. In all 291 members invested in HDT, raising £105,000, in addition to which money was raised through a combination of loans, grants and council funds. Community involvement was critical to realising funds from the council. The property was transferred in 2009.

Community allowances and time-banking

It is clear that the welfare system is outdated and needs to be flexible in order to reflect the contemporary labour market. A Community Allowance is an alternative model to help the long-term unemployed on Jobseeker's Allowance. It would work like this: community organisations in deprived areas often have money to create part-time jobs, frequently of short duration, but are unable to recruit local unemployed people because those people fear the economic insecurity that often results from taking on part-time work. If they do, they risk losing benefit as the system cannot cope with small amounts of part-time work – benefits can be frozen and families left without any support at all. The unemployed, meanwhile, are trapped in a welfare system that penalises them for taking tentative steps back into employment. Happily, from April 2010 anyone on Employment Support Allowance or Incapacity Benefit will be allowed to earn up to £92 a week without risking their core income or housing benefit. But that still leaves the 900,000 on Income Support for incapacity not included, as well as those on Jobseeker's Allowance and lone parents and carers.

The Create Consortium has proposed that the unemployed be granted the ability to work for community organisations in their local area, which could pay them, on top of their benefits, a maximum of £4,305 (or the equivalent of up to 15 hours a week on the minimum wage) over the course of one year. They estimate the cost of a pilot of this Community Allowance at £69,000, but predict that the initiative will generate £92,000 of investment in jobs in the local economy.[43]

This means that socially worthwhile work will get done in places where it is most needed and the unemployed will gain invaluable experience and skills in a supportive, rewarding environment, and not be forced to enter the unregulated job market, with the lack of pensions, references and other disadvantages that accompany that lack.

Time-banking is a system whereby members of a community can exchange skills, using time as currency; for example, an hour of gardening could be exchanged for an hour of teaching, with no money changing hands. Time-banking provides an innovative way to enhance association, and by building a network of support, it creates new communities, as well as consolidating existing ones. While it seems that time-banks must necessarily be kept small, since they are reliant on long-term communities staying settled so users can build up and then spend credits, they could potentially be integrated with public services for the genuine empowerment of users, for the improvement of service delivery and effectiveness.

Adjustable business rates

If areas that are officially designated as deprived had the power to adjust their uniform business rates and freehold rates, it would go some of the way to tackling financial exclusion. It would reduce the number of empty buildings and shops, which would in turn lead to a reduction of crime and anti-social behaviour.[44] A recent article by the Associated Press noted that the current tax system on property (the former reduction in rates available when a property was empty has been scrapped, but vacant land is only subject to minimal rates) had increasingly led owners to knock down unused buildings rather than pay the tax.[45]

Local communities in 'deprived wards' should be able – given enough signatures – to call a vote to adjust the uniform business rate and council tax so that more of the tax burden falls on landowners (freeholders), rather than occupiers (leaseholders). The increase in freehold rates (and complementary reduction in leasehold rates) would be decided by the community – residents and business-owners – in consultation with the local authority. Tax gained from this would be earmarked for regenerating the area and fewer businesses would be lost due to hikes in rates (rather than lack of sales/viability). If landowners chose to sell rather than pay the tax, prices would fall, which would attract investors from outside the area or give residents an opportunity to purchase land (through cooperative groups or community land trusts). In short they could become hubs for the coordination and increase of flourishing local activities.

Community development finance institutions

Currently, banks and building societies offer very competitive rates of interest for personal credit, but their 'credit scoring' criteria make access to credit difficult for people who are in receipt of benefits, particularly tenants. Companies who will lend to tenants on benefit, usually by 'doorstep cash loans', charge rates of interest of up to ten times the amount that a bank or building society would charge. A customer borrowing £1,000 from a mainstream lender over 12 months would have to repay the loan plus, for example, £106.88 (Lloyds TSB[46]) or £139.24 (Halifax[47]). Mainstream lenders do not lend less than £1,000 to customers, meaning that people wanting to borrow less than £1,000 are forced to borrow via home-collected loans and other cash-based loans, where on a loan of £1,000 over 12 months, interest accruing can reach between £750 and £875.[48] The Financial Inclusion Taskforce estimates that there is an unmet demand for small-scale affordable credit of around £1.2 billion per year.[49]

Community development finance institutions (CDFI) channel responsible funds into those neighbourhoods most in need. In deprived communities, where major banks have withdrawn their services, CDFIs are able to provide life-changing support to people and entrepreneurs desperate for credit. Since 2003, CDFIs have lent roughly £250 million into poor communities in the UK, creating and sustaining more than 86,000 jobs.[50] Often CDFIs and financial trusts employ traditional banking principles of pursuing close relationships with clients and lending responsibly. An organisation such as East Lancs Moneyline, an industrial and provident society set up in 2001, provides loans, savings, advice and information to individuals who struggle to get credit from high street banks and building societies. It is already helping over 10,000 people by providing access to more affordable loans.

If CDFIs had sufficient capital, they could begin to develop a hybrid, profit/non-profit programme model to deliver capital, advice and support for small and medium-sized enterprises (SMEs) in low-income communities. SMEs provide more general skills training and their employees' wages tend to grow faster over their first two years of employment when compared to larger firms. Moreover, because they have fewer employees, SMEs provide workers with more opportunities to upgrade their skills since, out of necessity, employees tend to have a wider scope of responsibilities.[51] In these cases, CDFIs could also stipulate certain conditions that promoted social returns, for example that if the company were to be sold in the future, a certain percentage of the sale price be divided among the company's non-management employees.

It is crucial to channel responsible funding into deprived areas – which, given the dexterity with which the benefits system can be played, are clearly populated by people with entrepreneurial flair – and to provide, alongside financial resources, advice and expertise to maximise their talent.

Savings

The Conservatives have pledged to maintain child trust funds (CTF) for children in low-income families, whilst seeking to abolish the matching payments for those on higher incomes given the present climate. The CTF is a personal fund for a child, started by a contribution by the government, which cannot be touched until the child is over eighteen. They are designed to promote saving among young people and to allow children to start adult life with some capital behind them, when they might otherwise not have done.

CTFs are one of the most vital ways that we currently have of building an asset base for the poor. More than 4.5 million children already have open, active accounts. Approximately 70,000 are opened each month and 2 million parents are saving for their children each month. Monthly amounts being saved for children seem to have increased from £15 to £24, a huge 60% rise. Families from all walks of life are embracing the CTF by engaging and saving, including low-income families, 30% of whom add monthly to their child's CTF. Some 97% of the CTF government investment goes to families with household income below £50,000. The abolition of the CTF mooted by all the main parties is a classic own goal – it is the most successful savings product available and the savings from its abolition are so small as to be questionable.

Prior to the introduction of the CTF it is estimated that only 18% of children were having long-term savings made for them.[52] Since the CTF has been introduced we can compare the number of people now saving into them each month which determines the effect on the 'savings rate'. Across the market, as defined by trade association statistics the number of people topping-up their child's CTF account is 27.4% – an increase of 52%.[53]

The Children's Mutual calculates that £250 from government at birth and age seven, plus the average top-up of £24 a month and 7% p.a. growth (minus charges) over the eighteen years, will give a 'financial springboard' at eighteen of £9,750.

One myth is that better-off families are embracing the CTF and others are not. However, profiling tells us that, for example, of the families whose income levels would put them 'just above welfare dependency', 30% of their children's CTF accounts are having money saved into them every month.[54] What is more, LSE focus group research confirmed that low-income parents would not swap their child's CTF for an increase in weekly Child Benefit.

The funds are a key foundation for building assets among the poorest in our society. We must consider increasing the ratio of government to parental contributions, or means-tested top-ups – possibly linking to performance/attendance at school, or for civic participation and volunteering. The lack of take-up by many of the very poorest families must be examined in order to make CTFs more efficient.

Banks could also promote savings – some current account providers operate initiatives such as rounding up any purchase made by debit card to the nearest pound and putting the rest in a savings account. JobCentre Plus outlets and Post Offices could automatically suggest savings programmes to users when their benefits increase. Likewise income tax refunds could be automatically transferred into savings accounts unless otherwise specified.

Financial literacy

The benefits of increasing financial literacy should not be underestimated, for both individuals and the country as a whole. MyBank, a charity working to promote financial literacy, recently conducted qualitative research in Brighton & Hove and found that many older participants in the study stated explicitly that if they had possessed the skills necessary to manage their personal finances earlier in life, it would have encouraged them to aspire to greater educational goals. Some went as far as to say that they would have gone to university if they had recognised the benefits of saving at an earlier age.[55]

Scrapping the Education Maintenance Allowance (EMA) would fund financial literacy classes in every comprehensive school in the country. The EMA is a controversial programme that provides financial support to students from low-income backgrounds who stay in education. While its aims are laudable, evidence suggests that these financial rewards are ineffectual: the number of young people who are NEET (not in education, employment and training) rose in the last quarter of 2008.[56] Margaret Eaton, chair of the Local Government Association, has claimed that the EMA has failed to tackle drop-out rates, and that the billions spent on benefits for young people was 'money down the drain'.[57] Additionally, from 2013 all young people in England will be required to continue in education or training to seventeen. In 2015, they will have to continue in education or training to eighteen. Bonuses paid on top of the weekly EMA for good behaviour or excellent attendance cost about £100 million a year. To provide one teacher (on a salary of £25,000 per year as an example) for a financial literacy class in every primary and secondary school in the country would cost roughly £573 million yearly, the same figure currently misspent on the EMA.[58]

One of the best methods of combining saving and financial education for adults is in the workplace. Financial literacy workshops, as well as savings schemes in which a small percentage of employees' wages go into savings accounts, where contributions are matched by the employer, could all be used to increase savings. The Central Provident Fund (CPF) in Singapore is used by citizens for a range of purposes such as home ownership, insurance, hospitalisation, retirement and investment in real property and financial assets. Working Singaporeans and their employers make monthly contributions to the CPF and these contributions go into accounts which earn a minimum risk-free interest guaranteed by the government.

Social investment wholesale bank

The Cabinet Office is currently considering a Social Investment Wholesale Bank, which would concentrate on supplying funding to the non-profit sector. The bank would be an independent social investment vehicle, created using the capital from dormant accounts with founding capital of at least £250 million, and an annual income stream of £20 million for a minimum of four years. Note, however, that the bank would only use an extremely small percentage of the total unclaimed assets from dormant accounts, most of which will go towards developing youth facilities. In fact, there are some concerns that the bank could be underfunded, as the government had said in 2008 that the bank could be established with as little as £40 million.[59]

There are existing organisations in the microfinance field which are operating extremely well, but simply lack the credit to expand. Rather than establishing another institution would could distort the market, what is needed is a way of increasing the resources of CDFIs and other microfinance institutions (when they need additional resources), as well as providing the necessary incentives for research and innovation in the field, developing new financial products to attract further mainstream capital.

Divestment strategy

By June 2009, financial sector interventions had cost the public sector £141.3 billion in debt.[60] Taxpayers now have a huge stake in the financial sector and the Conservative Party claims to be 'committed to divesting the Government's bank-holding to strategic effect and in the wider public interest'.[61] Mark Hoban, Conservative shadow minister for the Treasury, says that, 'If [the Conservatives] gain power, one thought would be: are there ways ... of increasing competition by breaking up the banks we own?'[62]

Between them, three banking groups (Royal Bank of Scotland, Lloyds Banking Group and Barclays) hold 77% of UK deposits and 40% of UK mortgages.[63] Both Lloyds Banking Group and Royal Bank of Scotland, which are majority-owned by the taxpayer, have been formed by a series of rapid mergers, and the acquisitions have not yet been fully integrated. Divisions could be spun-off independently, creating new localised building societies and banks, sold to smaller rivals, or merged with or taken over by CDFIs. A fundamental principle of these new financial institutions, would be to consider social value.

Newly created institutions could prove to be exceptionally powerful vehicles. They would provide affordable loans to viable businesses and access to responsible credit for those in deprived communities, as well as enhancing financial inclusion and promoting a savings culture. They would be given the freedom to generate and trial innovative new techniques. The use of mobile banking could be exploited as a means to target those without bank accounts. Telephone network providers could build on their market image and either provide banking services themselves or enter into partnerships with financial institutions.

Inflation

The Conservatives will consider including house prices in the range of data when calculating inflation, ostensibly in order to avoid another house-price bubble, but as George Osborne has acknowledged, 'there is considerable debate about whether the current Consumer Price Index inflation target reflects the true cost of living faced by consumers'.[64] With news that energy bills in the UK could increase by up to 60% in the next seven years,[65] and the number of households living in fuel poverty (spending more than 10% of income on fuel) in England likely to reach 4.6 million by the end of the year,[66] house prices are not the only set of statistics that should be looked at when calculating inflationary pressures.

A Necessities Price Index (NPI), which would measure average wage per annum and minimum wage per annum against the costs of energy bills, food staples such as rice and wheat, fuel and transport costs, would be a significant advance for those at the bottom. An inflation figure which took these into account would be far more accurate in detailing a picture of the pressures faced by those on low income. The food basket would be comprised of items generated by yearly surveys of those most financially vulnerable, and would add a particular weighting to fresh fruit and vegetables, to ensure those on low income are able to obtain healthy foodstuffs.

Post Office

The Post Office offers an incredible infrastructure which could be used both to revitalise local economies and to re-capitalise the less well-off. Post offices are small businesses, offering essential services to the local community and generating footfall for surrounding shops and businesses – 97% of small businesses think post offices have a crucial role to play in the local community, and 82% of members of the Federation of Small Businesses say the closure of their local post office would have a significant impact on their business, in most cases leading to business closure.[67]

There is widespread agreement that the Post Office must be modernised to meet future challenges. The Post Office should not be saved from privatisation for nostalgia's sake, or just to protect a 'valuable part of Britain's heritage', it

231

should be revamped and modernised for the twenty-first century, placed under the control of its employees and the communities it serves. Under no circumstances should a profitable Post Office branch face closure.

We should consider mutualising the Post Office through the creation of community-owned companies, led by front-line workers and customers, that would deliver services, led by front-line workers and customers, tailored to the specific community they were located in, stripping away layers of needless bureaucracy created by middle management, and harnessing two powerful forces: the insight and dedication of postmen and women and the great affection for the Post Office still felt by citizens and communities. The new civil company would have all the back-office responsibility, but also full budgetary delegation. It would have a structure similar to community interest companies, with an asset lock that prevents external expropriation. Essentially the Post Office would be re-configured as numerous cooperative branches operating via franchise under an umbrella organisation. We could even operate it as a cooperative franchise with the universal system being underpinned by local ownership.

The users of services would own a stake in the civil company, providing accountability as well as efficiency. They would play an increasingly active role as designers, implementers and evaluators of services, including co-ownership, and a seat at the board table. For example, local food producers could join the civil company alongside local food retailers, and initiate a food distribution service using the postal delivery vans.[68] Wholesalers for independent producers believe that large retailers will obtain a natural price advantage over them on a scale of 1–2%.[69] By coming together in a cooperative partnership, independent producers can use the extensive delivery network of the Post Office, using an enlarged version of the 'box schemes', where a producer or distributor delivers a box or bag of produce direct to customers, or to community distribution points. The over-centralisation of food systems has meant the loss of local distinctiveness, traditional varieties, craft production, and a sense of belonging to the community. As a result, access to fresh and seasonal food is difficult in many communities, leading to poor diets with serious implications for long-term health. In addition, money leaks out from local economies as it is siphoned off by distant food businesses.[70] Additionally, UK car manufacturers could be contracted to develop energy-efficient, hybrid postal vans which are capable of transporting both mail and food suppliers to retailers.

By granting ownership to employees and service users, post offices could tailor their services to meet the demands of the local community, offering new services where there is clear demand. For example, with more than 600 filling stations closing per year, motorists in some rural areas are being left up to 30 miles away from their nearest forecourt.[71] Hybrid post van-buses (as already used in the Highlands and Islands) could be procured from UK manufacturers for post offices in rural areas, where transporting mail could be combined with fixed route bus services, demand-responsive transport or a food distribution network. A revitalised Post Office would thereby help support local communities, combating the rise of food deserts, where a lack of food distribution results in a lack of availability of fresh fruit and vegetables in areas where no supermarkets are situated.

Socially useful backstop leverage ratio

In addition to creating new banking institutions and reconfiguring the role of the Post Office, a Conservative government could explore how to incorporate blended value investment (BVI) into the banking sector.[72] The arguments for a limit on banks' ability to lend is an economic one, but by blending it with a social objective, David Cameron can make take a powerful step to achieving his idea of a form of 'capitalism with a conscience'. According to the Bank of England, the capital composition of the major UK banks incorporated just under £200 billion of Core Tier 1 capital.[73] A small percentage of that mandatory capital base could be invested in secure 'blended value investment bonds'. Investments could take the form of the case studies already mentioned, or they could be bonds ranging from one to ten years, guaranteed by the government on the model of the loan guarantee, where, on issue, a percentage of the bond (up to 20%) would be granted to charities, and the remainder lent to housing associations, social enterprises, cooperatives and mutuals at a reasonable rate of interest. For example, from a 5-year bond of £1 million, £200,000 could be granted to charity, and the remainder loaned at a rate of 6.25% per annum, so that on maturity the bond would deliver the original sum (with the possibility of returning a profit). This could be pioneered in the socially orientated banks formed from the divestment of the public stake in Lloyds and RBS. If this requirement was to be expanded to encompass all major UK banks, requiring them to hold 0.1% of their Core Tier 1 capital in BVI bonds, a sum of £20 billion would be unleashed, resulting in up to £4 billion worth of grants to charities. As well as providing much needed capital to credit-starved communities and entrepreneurs, it may provide a 'nudge' to mainstream banks to enter this field, so that if they were to establish branches and lend into these communities, the sum of Core Tier 1 capital they would be required to hold in BVI bonds for example, would decrease in proportion.

The principle of putting reserve capital to social use through blended value investments should also be extended to the public sector, with the explicit understanding that it is there to incentivise and thus attract private capital. For example, total local council reserves are estimated to be £15–20 billion.[74] The investment and loan portfolios of Community Development Finance Institutions totalled £331 million in 2008. If just 1% of council reserves were channelled into CDFIs, it would nearly double the pool of funds available to these institutions, which in many ways perform a public service by providing responsible and much-needed credit to poorer communities.

Government guidelines urge councils to 'balance risk and potential returns'.[75] This advice seems to have led to 127 local authorities investing a total of £953 million in Icelandic banks.[76] Now is the time to rewrite these guidelines, incorporating a duty of local authorities to put part of their resources into social projects in their area. According to a report by the New Local Government Network, over 80% of local authority directors of finance support the case for creating a council mutual fund, potentially resulting in a fund of between £389 million and £2.8 billion.[77] Alternatively, a small percentage of council reserves could be used to purchase BVI bonds, or used to guarantee all or part of the loans made by CDFIs, which would reduce the cost of borrowing for the latter. Through this process, banking can be re-orientated towards an interaction built on trust rather than financial modelling based on extrapolated data, which ends up excluding those who need the service.

Microfinance has the potential to bring millions of people out of deep poverty, but 'the industry needs a new group of financiers capable of increasing the amount and various forms of capital available in this market by an order of magnitude – and to do so without stemming the flow of donated capital to Microfinance Institutions where such capital is the most appropriate fuel for their development.'[78] Microfinance business needs many billions of dollars to fund loan portfolios so that hundreds of millions of people can begin to create income and wealth and ultimately raise themselves from poverty. Similar demand for capital exists in the Blended Value Investment segments that would fund affordable housing and community development, environmental protection, health, education and related services for the poor.[79]

The debate about micro-finance seems stalled with evidence that there seems no real gain in terms of securing business success. In other words, the provision of credit via micro-finance give no greater guarantee of the success of the business. However, others look for stability of returns and pension funds, predominantly seeking secure returns on investments, have begun to move more resources into micro-finance. PGGM, manager of the €70bn Dutch healthcare industry pension fund is committing €200m to microfinance, while ABP, one of Europe's biggest pension funds with about €180bn in assets, has invested €180m with a view to increasing this amount again in the next few years. The draw for investors: micro-finance has paid out returns as high as 20%, while fulfilling an aim to lift households out of poverty.[80]

Restoring the local economy and re-capitalizing the poor are just two examples of the way in which we can re-infuse virtue into the market. Just distribution in the first place can minimise the need for the artifices of redistribution. And to reiterate: this just distribution establishes and does not inhibit genuine market freedom.

10 The Civil State

In order to put a virtuous society at the centre, we require not only a mutualist civil economy, but also a civil state in which professional responsibility has been restored to individuals and collegiate groups.

It is hard to underestimate the challenge faced by our public services today. Not only must they contend with ever-increasing public expectations and an ever-evolving society, they must do this in the face of the biggest shock to public finances in living memory. With our annual budget deficit due to hit £178 billion in 2010, and quite probably exceed that in subsequent years, the crisis is real.

Our current model of public-sector reform is not up to this challenge. Over the last ten years, our public services have experienced a real terms funding increase of 55%, financed by an increase of 5% of GDP in public expenditure since 2000. Yet public sector productivity has continued to fall, as has been seen.

Funding is not enough; the only way to see real improvement is if the system is re-structured. To this end we need to harness two powerful forces: the insight and dedication of front-line workers, and the engagement of citizens and communities. Too often these forces have been under-exploited or set in opposition. We need a new model that instead utilises them. I will argue that ownership is that model, and that ownership, realised differently for different groups, can be a part of what constitutes the necessary innovation for renewal of our public sector and our public services.

Unless we allow nurses to ensure that hospital wards are clean, unless someone takes responsibility for abused children, unless the single mother can obtain her benefits quickly when she loses her part-time job, then British citizens will carry on dying unnecessarily from MRSA, scandals like Baby P will continue to occur, and vulnerable members of society won't seek the part-time paths out of welfare they so desperately need for fear of losing all income and security. Similarly, services cannot hope to respond effectively to the needs of the people who use them, unless these people can make clear what they want from the public sector and take an active role in its delivery. Engaging providers and recipients enables ordinary people to make a difference and minimises the costs and burdens of ineffective management. It is the future of public services.

Engaged workers and citizens also make public services cheaper. Empowered staff are better at cutting costs and correcting failure than those managed by command-and-control methods – as has been proved in the private sector, in businesses such as John Lewis. Wasteful middle management and damaging accountability and audit structures can be reduced. Examples of this approach applied in the public sector suggest that empowering front-line staff to drive service improvement can result in very significant savings: in certain areas it can be in the order of 20–40%.[1] At the same time, citizens who take an active interest in their health and welfare initiate behaviour change and cost the state less, far less, than passive and de-motivated recipients.

Engagement is a hard thing to achieve. The very structure of our public services militates against it. Trying to achieve true engagement in existing structures can feel like a partial fix in a hopelessly compromised system. Front-line leadership is a scarce commodity in large multi-disciplinary organisations with centralised cost-control and management by target. If conducted under these auspices, user involvement is not co-creation but the choreographed rubber-stamping of top-down decision-making.

But there is a way forward. We can energise front-line staff and citizens – and multiply the impact of their vocation and excellence in public-sector services – through the power of shared ownership. In a new model of public-sector delivery, services could be provided by social enterprises. These would be led by front-line workers, owned by them and the communities they serve. These new social businesses would exchange (often illusory) economies of scale for the real economies that derive from empowered workers and an engaged public.

To deliver this, a new power of civil association should be granted to all front-line service providers in the public sector. This power would allow the formation, under specific conditions, of new employee- and community-owned 'civil companies' that would deliver the services previously monopolised by the state. Central to this power would be the obligation to ensure that full budgetary delegation of all the supporting services goes along with this new responsibility. The new civil company would be organised as a social enterprise, with the scope and flexibility to allow different structures according to local conditions. Such structures could be community-interest companies with an asset lock that prevents external transfer of the resources of the new organisation, or a partnership trust along the lines of the John Lewis model. This latter structure allows employees to benefit from their employee position at the company – by getting a dividend as their share of the profits – but the actual shares stay within the trust and cannot be transferred out. The additional advantage of a partnership trust model is that it allows not only partnership with its own members but external organisations or companies – so the idea of a joint venture between an employee trust and a private-sector contractor can be envisaged.

Governed neither by the public state nor the private market, this new civil association, whatever form it takes, would localise responsibility, capture agency and promote ethos. It would do this by spreading the ownership of publicly funded provision, revolutionising public-service delivery for the benefit of all.

The imperative for change in the management of public services is now recognised by both right and left, but a full engagement with, and an analysis of, the failed consensus has yet to take place. J. K. Galbraith wrote that it behoves the left to be much smarter about business and management than the right. If (in an earlier age) it was nationalising economic basket-cases or (as now) using state agencies to bring services to the citizens, it ought to have some pretty sophisticated ideas about how to run public services. Unfortunately, this has not always been the case. Old Labour was too quick to dismiss management and all its work, while New Labour's public-sector critics have argued that it has been too smitten by private-sector management and the theory that free markets necessarily promote rational choice. But this latest swing is not specific to the left or the right. With few exceptions, the debate over different methods of improving our public services has been abandoned to a purely market-driven approach, whose domination of the speaking parts is so complete that, in the middle of the greatest management meltdown in history, management responsibility for the financial crisis is entirely shielded from question. It is as if there is no market in markets – we are told that the market mechanism has only one instantiation and only one means of operation. Yet, under this model, in resource-allocation, risk, product-design, accounting, reward and governance, the visible hand of the financial and banking sector got every single aspect of management wrong. Yet not only is there no investigation, no critique and no market alternatives on offer to the model that has got us here; the same model that caused the crash is now expected to get us out of it again. This is especially poignant in the public sector, where accelerated 'reform' is certain to mean more market-based discipline (in an ersatz copy of the failed model) in the form of competition, choice and contracting-out.

Market versus statist thinking is a crude false dichotomy, based on an ideologically grim vision of human nature which has led both sectors into today's cul-de-sac – in which every problem can only be addressed by prescribing larger doses of the treatment that got us into the mess in the first place.

The management model that has come to dominate – from the A-grade journals that shape the academic research agenda to the management consultants and eminent advisers who influence government policy – is the neo-liberalism of the Chicago School economists whose line of descent goes back to the radical individualism of Smith (of the *Wealth of Nations* rather than *Moral Sentiments*), Locke and Bentham. Before he died, Milton Friedman consoled himself for (he judged) Chicago's relatively small influence on economic practice with the knowledge that 'judged by ideas, we have been on the winning side'. He was right. Almost all the social sciences – sociology, law and social psychology as well as economics – have been colonised by Chicago economics. This is especially true of management, which in its efforts to be recognised as a real science has been as consumed by 'economics envy' as economics has by that of physics, to its enormous detriment.

For the radical individualist (the figure the Chicago School extols as the foundation and zenith of political economy), the ideal organisation is the 'marvel of the market', where individuals contract with other individuals coordinated by the price mechanism. In this view, companies are a second-best option, the product of a kind of market failure that still produces a collectivist residue. In this market, morals and ethics don't count. Famously, what puts dinner on the table is not 'the benevolence of the butcher, the brewer, or the baker ... but ... regard to their own interest'. The dismissal of the ethical dimension and assumptions of strong self-interest are carried over into neo-liberal views of the company where, given human imperfection, the problem of organisation is as much about preventing people doing bad things as encouraging them to do good.

In the private sector, these beliefs found their justification in what critics saw as the cosy corporatism of the 1970s. After twenty-five years of easy living after the Second World War when they could sell everything they made, managers and companies had gone soft. They seemed more interested in building corporate empires to shore up their own status and prestige than in making money for shareholders. The prescription was straightforward. Companies would be run as strong hierarchies, with managers disciplining their underlings with sharp incentives and sanctions. Manager-agents in their turn would be aligned with owner-principals through the use of incentive pay, typically stock options. Self-evidently, following Milton Friedman, the sole responsibility of the corporation was to maximise returns to shareholders. A vigorous market for corporate control would ensure that managers who succeeded in this enterprise attracted extra resources, while those who failed would be ejected and their companies taken over. If there was an activity that another company could do more efficiently, outsource it; if its entire business was less efficient, then the company should put itself up for sale.

This was the age of the raider, the break-up and the deal. A token of the change: in 1980 the total value of US mergers and acquisitions was less than 2% of GDP, by 2000 it had reached 21%. Equity-based remuneration for suitably self-interested company executives exploded in proportion. According to Standard & Poor's, stock options granted to US executives – non-existent in the late 1980s – were equivalent to 20% of all corporate profits in 2002.

In the state sector, the same principles applied. As James Buchanan, a leading light of public choice theory, put it, '[state employees and politicians] act no differently from other persons the economist studies'; that is, they can be assumed to be as self-seeking and narrowly self-interested as anyone else. In this view, it is perfectly legitimate and predictable for people to pursue their own interests; therefore the problem is not motivation but organisation. If public services are self-serving (one reason why state spending always goes up), it is because they are monopolies delivering producer-designed services to weak consumers who lack purchasing power or the ability to choose.

As in the market sector, the solutions seemingly followed directly. Privatisation was one answer, but if that was impossible because of dependence on tax finance, the next best thing was for the state to simulate a competitive market. If services are producer-dominated, create strong purchasers (the purchaser–provider split). If there is lack of choice, establish competition. In other words, bureaucratic hierarchy is replaced with competing market institutions within the state as well as across its boundaries.

It is hard to over-estimate the force of these prescriptions, particularly in the UK, which has been one of the most radical proponents of the neo-liberal state. By pushing back the boundaries of state ownership and absorbing into it the disciplines and relationships of the market, they have ushered in the most profound changes to public administration since the nineteenth century. Notably through the various governance codes, all heavily based on agency theory, it has also overseen the absorption of neo-liberal principles into the bloodstream of the corporation. Unfortunately, the remedies brought by market individualism have turned out to be more destructive than the problems they were supposed to cure.

The elusive 'magic of management' is synergy: to get more out of the resources at its disposal than went in. The distinctive mark of the present management model is to do the reverse. In the market sector, Wall Street and the City of London are full of firms staffed by people with the highest academic and business qualifications who are collectively so witless that they have not only burned their own houses to the ground but almost brought down the whole edifice of capitalism. As Alan Greenspan admitted sadly to the House Oversight Committee in October 2008, 'I made a mistake in presuming that the self-interests of organisations, specifically banks and others, were such that they were best capable of protecting their own shareholders and their equity in the firms.'

In the state sector, any gains from increased spending have similarly been nullified by induced organisational stupidity of a different but equally debilitating kind. With the aim of cutting costs, consultants have introduced Fordist, computer-driven programmes centred on the mass delivery of standard packages from whose awful results they are shielded by, in Robin Murray's words, a complex 'diseconomy' of knowledge. In cases such as the NHS, the purchaser of the product is not the same as its consumer. This creates a challenge for the system: how do you ensure high quality outputs? Under the current structure, the purchaser is more likely to pay attention to senior managers and political masters, on whom jobs and prospects depend, than weak consumers. One well-rehearsed response is to institute specifications and targets, and penalties for failure to meet the standards. But, as has become abundantly clear, targets not only deflect attention from equally important but non-quantifiable aims, they also induce gaming, mis-reporting and an emphasis on process rather than hard-to-measure outcomes.

The resulting regulatory arms race has some remarkably paradoxical consequences. The first is that the market solution generates a huge and costly bureaucracy of accountants, examiners, inspectors, assessors and auditors, all concerned with assuring quality and asserting control, who hinder innovation and experiment and lock in high cost. Thus, the neo-liberal model that pretends to eschew the state repeats the statist outcomes of audit and control in the very markets that claim to be free of them. The second is that this model of control harks directly back to the tight supervision, separation of execution from decision-making and emphasis on compliance of Taylor's 'scientific management'. The third is that, in a self-fulfilling cycle, such management runs the danger of generating the very opportunistic behaviour that justifies another turn of the supervisory screw (the 'supervisor's dilemma'). The fourth is that public service institutions can only work if they are sustained by the kind of professional ethics and commitment to standards that public-choice theory denies.

There is a more productive way of looking at organisations than pursuing the sterile market-versus-state debate. Traditionally managed organisations in both the public and private sectors grew up as fundamentally closed systems – that is, they are machines that operate with limited interchange with their environment. They are instrumental, designed to carry out certain tasks, and planned and managed from the top. Consumers function as essentially passive receivers of products and services. To reduce their vulnerability to changing conditions, as Galbraith noted in *The New Industrial State*, such firms attempt to adapt the environment – for instance through heavy advertising and lobbying – rather than the reverse.[2] This is the typical pattern of mass production.

Open systems, on the other hand, recognise that uncertainty and change render traditional command-and-control ineffective. Instead, the aim must be to adapt continuously to the environment. Instead of top-down, such organisations aim to function 'outside-in', as John Seddon puts it. The consumer is a source of intelligence, as are suppliers and competitors. In production terms the goal is to make to order, at the rhythm of market demands, rather than to make to a company-defined schedule or plan.

Open systems are organic rather than mechanistic, and require a completely different management mindset to run them. Strategy and feedback from action are more significant than detailed planning ('Fire – ready – aim!' as Tom Peters wrote); hierarchies give way to networks; the periphery is as important as the centre; self-interest and competition are balanced by trust and cooperation; initiative and inventiveness are required rather than compliance; smartening-up rather than dumbing-down. I intend that the structure I propose meets these baseline requirements.

In the mid-1990s, with the emergence of ideas like public-value theory, and thinkers like Peter Senge and his notion of the learning organisation, there was a brief moment when new thinking in the shape of joined-up management and the learning organisation seemed to have a chance. But, all too quickly, these experiments were shut down by the deterministic certainties of an invigorated pure-market approach and the growing tyranny of the capital markets. In the grip of those false certainties each new excess – the dotcoms, Enron, the banking crisis – seemed to reinforce the pessimistic assumptions at the heart of the model, leading to all-enveloping webs of external regulation, that by emphasising formal controls perversely make organisations less adaptable, more stupid in systems terms. It is time to stop trying to make a broken model work – what Russ Ackoff calls the misguided attempt to 'do the wrong thing righter', which just makes us wronger – and set out on a different, more hopeful but at the same time more realistic management path.

Overcoming inefficiency and disempowerment

This ideological journey is of more than just academic interest. Its most practical legacy is two severe and structural problems in our public services. On the one hand, we have a demoralised public-sector workforce, sick of command-and-control and suspicious of anything described as reform. On the other, we have a track record of declining public-sector productivity that bodes ill for future attempts to restore the public finances. These two problems, it seems, are intrinsically linked and need to be solved together.

According to figures released by the Office for National Statistics, public sector productivity declined by 3.4% in 1997–2007 – compared with a rise in efficiency of 27.9% in the private sector.[3] The Centre for Economics and Business Research values this relative loss at £58.4 billion per annum, equal to the national VAT take.

The major parties now agree that, in order to resolve the fiscal bind that the government finds itself in, the public sector needs to spend less. But experience tells us that cutting services without reforming them is counter-productive. It degrades quality even further, and pushes services into a meltdown phase that requires urgent remedial spending further down the line, leading to more waste and expense. The real imperative is then to innovate before one administers cuts, because only then can one protect public-service outcomes and genuinely save money.

Labour came to power with a mandate to invest in and reform the public services. Its sweeping electoral victory and subsequent re-election were seen as signs of public and political consensus in support of public spending. The argument that public investment could be a positive social force had been won. The major increases focused primarily on health, transport, education and criminal justice and drove public spending from 37.4% of GDP in 1999 to 41% in 2005 where it remained until the financial crash – which on account of the resulting recession means that public spending will on certain figures hit 80% of GDP in the next year and perhaps even 100% by 2015.

Having made the case for public spending, the incoming Labour government in 1997 now needed to deliver visible results. From its perspective, having identified the outcomes it wished to prioritise (reductions in heart disease and cancer mortality rates, increased literacy and numeracy, an increased proportion of offences brought to justice and so on), public services just needed to deliver. And deliver they did: there was a rise in public-sector output during this period.

Centrally set targets became the mechanism to increase delivery, providing quantifiable benchmarks to assess progress.[4] The intention of this system was that once public confidence and public-sector capability had been built, detailed targets would be replaced with fewer, high-level outcomes, and public-sector organisations would receive more discretion to act.

But the vision of a reformed public sector in which committed front-line workers enjoy autonomy can seem remote. Public-sector staff frequently find themselves trapped in what was intended to be a transitional stage, an interregnum which seems neither particularly efficient nor particularly modern.

The NHS Staff Survey in 2008 bore these concerns out. Only 27% of staff believed that managers involved them in making important decisions, while only 26% believed their employers valued the work that they did. Only 15% believed that communication between trust headquarters and front-line staff was effective. Most alarmingly, 18% believed that their trust did not regard patient care as a top priority, with 27% giving an ambivalent answer.[5]

This is a problem for two reasons. First, it builds resistance to change. Staff who resent the imposition of top-down controls are likely to see any attempts to increase productivity as further unwelcome disruption. Change fatigue is a serious issue in the NHS, local authorities and beyond. Second, it is self-perpetuating. Julian Le Grand, an influential adviser to Tony Blair on public-sector reform, famously asked what motivated public sector employees: were they knights – honourably committed to the public good – or knaves – primarily interested in personal gain? One of the observations springing from this question is that a system that over-emphasises knavish motives – through crass incentives or rigid targeting – will accentuate them. Or to put it another way, you get the behaviour you plan for.

The combination of a public-sector productivity shortfall and a disengaged workforce presents us with a serious challenge: how do we improve our public services and reduce their cost in a climate where inefficiency seems built in to our delivery models and where, after much meaningless and costly innovation and relentless calls to modernise, the staff are justifiability suspicious of change?

Change

There are two powerful forces that can address this dual problem of low productivity and disempowerment. The first is front-line leadership, where staff both personify and own the service they deliver and the second is the involvement of users and communities such that the passive account of mere recipients is challenged and contested by proactive users and shapers of service.

Front-line leadership

The first powerful force that we must harness to transform our public services is the energy and motivation of front-line staff. Their disengagement is not just a human resource issue: it is a fundamental bar to real improvement. When important decisions are made based on front-line expertise, public services can draw on an often neglected source of knowledge. Front-line staff frequently confront problems or become aware of opportunities long before strategic managers. Many of the most important issues affecting productivity and efficiency are not vague questions arising from a detached, bird's-eye view, but detailed questions of implementation and execution. Worker involvement improves morale and builds trust, reducing the need for intensive supervision and monitoring. Increased employee involvement would help to cut organisational waste. And, as John Seddon argues in *Systems Thinking in the Public Sector*, bringing decision-making and service design to the point of delivery can generate vast savings for any service.

A critical flaw of the current system of public management is its disproportionate focus on controlling worker productivity and budgets – a fixation that actually undermines efficiency. The problem is that this strategy fails to distinguish between 'value demand' and 'failure demand' – between productive work and waste.

'Failure demand' is the valueless, cost-creating work generated by the failure of an organisation to deliver services that from the customer's point of view actually work. Examples of failure demand include: 'I don't understand this form' or 'Why haven't my benefits been paid?' This can be contrasted with 'value demand', which is productive. Examples of value demand include: 'I would like to apply for benefits' and 'Can you fix my window?'

Thus failure demand is demand on a service that stems from the failure to solve the problem in the first place. If you have to call back your telephone provider six times to solve one problem that should have been solved in one call, then that service is experiencing usage levels five times higher than need be the case. And in some organisations demand as a result can be six, eight or even ten times what it should be. According to Seddon, failure demand in banks typically runs from 40–60% of total demand and in local authorities it has been found to reach as high as 80%.[6]

By focusing on reducing cost – for example, by using offshore call centres – and time – for example, by setting targets for customer call lengths – the amount of unnecessary demand exponentially increases. A council where employees are under pressure to address problems in a limited amount of time means that someone needs to contact the council multiple times to solve one problem. Similarly, benefits, housing and immigration applications rejected to meet quotas, and arrests made to meet targets create unnecessary demand in the form of appeals, repeat applications, police, court and prison time, and so forth. This extra demand often falls on other agencies.

Empowering employees and their managers with the flexibility to design against local demand has resulted in efficiency gains of over 400% in council services that have followed the recommendations entailed in John Seddon's work. In one authority, capacity for housing repairs rose from 137 jobs per day to 220 in four months. Over the same period, the number of repairs requests rose from 141 per day to 279, and the number of jobs completed on first visit rose from 42% to 57%. Seddon's work implies that the savings from this kind of change can amount to a staggering 20–40% of costs.[7]

The benefits of employee ownership

Employee ownership is nothing new in the private and voluntary sectors. Indeed, there is a long literature recounting the benefits of employee ownership of profitmaking organisations.

The defining attribute of employee-owned companies is that employees have a controlling stake in the business. This may involve employees owning shares individually or 'common ownership', where assets are held indivisibly in trust rather than in the names of individual members – for example, the John Lewis Partnership.

John Lewis is the UK's largest employee-owned company. No employees own shares in it; the 69,000 members of the John Lewis Partnership's staff are all 'partners' in the business and, as such, are entitled to a share of the annual profits. The bonus has ranged from as low as 8% of employee's salary to as high as 24%, depending on the Partnership's financial performance.

The employee-ownership structure is reinforced by a strong democratic culture. Every store has an elected branch forum, which addresses local issues. Stores also send representatives to district councils and the Partnership Council, which holds the chairman to account, develops policy and agrees changes in governance. The Council can trigger the removal of the chairman through a two-thirds majority vote. The Partnership has in addition a written constitution, which begins, 'the Partnership's ultimate purpose is the happiness of all its members, through their worthwhile and satisfying employment in a successful business'. Employees report high levels of happiness and satisfaction.[8]

The employee-ownership model offers several distinct characteristics, which the public sector could benefit from:

- Less risk-aversion (compared to the public sector) and therefore greater potential to innovate;
- Greater entrepreneurialism (compared to the voluntary sector);
- A greater sense of mission (compared to the private sector);

- An open, egalitarian culture.[9]

Employee ownership inspires loyalty, commitment and creativity, benefiting the company and improving the level of business and financial literacy amongst employees. Evidence suggests that widely dispersed ownership has a powerful effect on productivity, as has already been noted This approach seems to pay evident dividends. In the five weeks up to 2 January 2010 sales at John Lewis rose 15.8% in total, or 12.7% on a like-for-like basis against the same period last year. Still more encouragingly, takings are 10.4% higher than in 2007, the year before the credit crisis.'[10] These increases seem to compare well with the competition. Against the 12.7% increase at John Lewis M&S – saw like-for-like sales up 0.8% in the three months to 26 December 2009; Next saw like-for-like sales up 3.2% in twenty-two weeks to 24 December; Shop Direct had sales up 6.3% in six weeks to 1 January; finally Sainsbury's reported like-for-like sales up 3.7%, excluding fuel, in the thirteen weeks to 2 January.

This opens a number of possibilities for the public sector. Where the governments of the 1980s and 1990s sought to outsource services to the private sector, this raises the question of 'insourcing', devolving ownership and responsibility to the employees of services themselves, without some of the potentially disempowering and dis-incentivising effects sometimes associated with outsourcing and privatisation.

As with other councils around the country, Newcastle City Council had a legacy of reform, following the introduction of compulsory competitive tendering under the Tories and best value surveys under Labour. While these reforms had delivered efficiencies, the pressure to save money had engendered a culture of short-term planning and savings. Outsourcing was a typical case: preventing future savings and leaving a democratic deficit. Structurally, decision-taking and responsibility in the council were deferred upwards from the front-line to managers. Backroom tasks were isolated from the rest of the service, and each service had separate IT systems, with little communication.

When faced with having to outsource services still further, the council organised a public tender to compete with a private bidder (BT). The public tender took a 'business approach' – requiring 'rigorous thinking about the best ways of allocating limited resources to meet social goals' – but differing from the private bid in that it offered 'a model based on the maximisation of public benefit not profit, subject to the cost savings constraint'.

Organising a public tender for services was no small task. Crucially, it entailed union engagement and leadership, managerial ownership and a general acknowledgement that 'the status quo is not an option'. Creating the plan for redesigning more efficient services required participation from all levels of public-sector workers. Front-line staff developed 'workers' plans', generating new ideas for products and methods of delivering service. This also entailed a radical shift in management style. Managers were expected to take on a facilitating role for largely autonomous teams – adopting the ethos of 'managers as servants'. Rather than driving the agenda, managers relied on worker initiative and creativity.

Ultimately the public tender was accepted and is set to deliver £28 million in savings over 11.5 years, which was greater than the private bid. The reformed customer service centres it produced have a 95% satisfaction rate and 98.4% of benefits claims are processed correctly. Financially, this has resulted in reduced costs of administering payroll and benefits processing and an improved council tax collection rate.

Employee ownership could also offer a way to mitigate some of the pay issues of particular types of public-sector work. In 2008, the mean gross annual pay of a public-sector employee in the UK was £23,943.[11] However, 1.5 million of these public sector employees were paid less than £7 per hour (23% of the total workforce in the UK earning less than that amount).[12] This figure accounts only for workers employed directly by the public sector, and therefore does not include staff employed by contractors working for the public sector. Of the 1.5 million people working directly for the public sector and earning less than £7 per hour, only 300,000 were under twenty-five years old. This low level of remuneration may go some way to explaining falling productivity levels, as well as dissatisfaction over a lack of recognition of good work amongst public-sector employees. Employee ownership has the potential to transform workers from wage labourers to common owners of the services that they deliver.

The public sector needs to capitalise on this potential for building productivity by giving providers a tangible stake in the services that they provide.

Collegial quality

Front-line workers also have an important role to play in ensuring that services are high quality. New Public Management has agonised over the question of how to stop incompetent or even criminal staff from abusing the system. The spectre of 'the next Shipman' hangs over most decisions on how to police workers in positions of trust, and has led to an increase in auditors and inspectorates. Front-line leadership here offers an alternative.

More engaged public-service professionals who take responsibility for their services and their wider teams are less likely to stand by in cases of misconduct than disempowered workers who assume that intervening is the job of a manager or a regulator. Research by MORI and the Improvement and Development Agency casts light on this phenomenon. Examining employee attitudes within different local councils, the study found that staff in the most successful councils share a common set of characteristics in that they have a say in management decisions, they are able to use their initiative and creativity, and to contribute to planning their own work and they are kept well informed of organisational developments and change.[13]

The report found that excellent and good authorities, in contrast to fair, weak and poor ones, 'value and recognise their employees, by allowing them greater input into the decision making processes of the authority, and perhaps, as a consequence, providing more room for individual creativity to flourish'.[14] Other factors, such as satisfaction with pay and workload, had a much more limited (if any) correlation to positive outcomes.

This clearly emphasises the importance of employees engaging more with managerial decision-making. When asked how to improve trust in the management of their organisation the top three responses given by employees are: 'frequent and honest communication', 'more meaningful consultation', and 'a greater voice in decision-making'.[15]

The contribution of engaged and trusting employees to performance cannot be underestimated. The Society of British Aerospace Companies' Human Capital Audit, found that high-performing firms benefited from 62% more value-added per employee than other businesses. The high-performance model places great emphasis on keeping workers informed and involving them in decision-making.[16]

They are also best-suited in the first instance to assess the success and failure of their peers. An organisation where workers are committed to collective goals can effectively self-regulate against free-riding knaves, when empowered with appropriate mechanisms. Horizontal structures of regulation, such as peer sanctioning, staff hiring and firing, democratic wage and bonus setting, build on existing relationships of trust and solidarity amongst co-workers.

A new structure for empowering public-sector workers must include mechanisms for joint decision-making and the mutual regulation of co-workers. As a recent study found, 'The vast majority of workers have a good idea of what fellow workers are doing (a pre-requisite for co-monitoring); that workers paid shared capitalist compensation are more likely than other workers to act against "shirking" by fellow workers; and that worker co-monitoring or anti-shirking behaviour is associated with higher worker effort and better workplace performance.'[17]

Social experiments have found that individuals in cooperative situations will sanction defaulters even when it is not in their individual self-interest to do so, due to strong social norms of reciprocity.[18] One of the reasons commonly attributed to the success of micro-lending projects around the world has been the efficacy of peer sanctions in group lending.[19] Together, employee involvement programs and shared compensation improve outcomes such as job satisfaction, attitude towards the workplace, and the likelihood of staying with an organisation. The best outcomes occur when organisations combine pay for company or group performance with an ownership stake in the organisation and employee-involvement committees. This supports the notion that these policies form a complementary package of employee–management relations.[20]

By empowering front-line workers to make more decisions and to hold each other to account, not only will services be more productive, but the need for managerial and audit-based supervision will be drastically reduced.

A mobilised public

Giving front-line workers a meaningful stake in the services that they deliver is a necessary but not sufficient step towards addressing the challenges facing the public sector. Overhauling our rigidly structured public services will also require us to change the way that the public interact with the services that they receive – not just as customers but also as stakeholders, designers, deciders, implementers and evaluators.

There are four main routes through which members of the public can influence their public services:

- Representative political democracy – affecting change through the ballot box and elected representatives;
- Consumerism – through market-like arrangements in the public services;
- Participative democracy – through self-organisation in unions, churches, third-sector organisations, and suchlike;
- Involvement as co-producers.[21]

In the cross-party neo-liberal consensus that has emerged over the past three decades, public sector reform has focused on the first two of these – seeking to empower citizens as constituents and as consumers. When these conflict, reform becomes seen as an intractable right–left dichotomy between a consumer approach that grants consumer sovereignty at the risk of inequality but with a focus on individual satisfaction, and a social-democratic approach which emphasises equal treatment and due process, at the expense of outcomes.

What unites these models is the assumption that services are provided by professionals and guaranteed by the state – while consumers and citizens nominally feedback by exercising choice and voice. Gone, or reduced to supplements, are the great intermediary institutions of British life and the non-professional contributor. In keeping with the scepticism of civil society that has become the founding myth of modern liberalism, these two approaches expect little active involvement by the public at large.

The public stake

A remarkable number of successful private-sector companies today – including Amazon, BMW, Google, Harley-Davidson, Honda, IKEA, JetBlue and Whole Foods – attribute their success at least in part to turning the traditional conception of shareholder interest on its head. Looking past their own shareholders, these organisations extended significant stakes to employees, customers, suppliers or society as a whole. These same 'firms of endearment' have uniformly outperformed the rest of the market, returning eightfold the S&P500 average on investments.[22]

This progressive private-sector practice has an analogue in public-management theory. Public-value theory, developed in the 1990s as a response to managerialist and consumerist approaches to public-sector reform, which, in attempting to emulate the private sector through the introduction of quasi-market mechanisms, put consummate emphasis on end-user satisfaction. In doing so, these approaches to reform ignored the wider contribution (the 'public value') that the public sector adds to communities.

Public-value theory (as opposed to public-choice theory) calls for the inclusion of the general public as stakeholder in public organisations, challenging the role that market-based reforms assign to the public-service manager. Rather than serving a primarily bureaucratic function (implementing political directives), managers are seen as entrepreneurs maximising public value – in the same way that private-sector managers attempt to maximise profit for shareholders.

The success and widespread popularity of safer neighbourhood teams is a concrete example of how a structural change that gives meaningful discretion to the front-line of a public service to solve problems can give community members a tangible stake in their local services. In 2004, the police were among the most heavily inspected and highly regulated of public services, subject to hundreds of Statutory Performance Indicators as well as a strict National Crime Recording Standard. As a result, police were spending (and continue to spend) nearly half their time in the office, between 20% and 30% of their time on paperwork and only 14% of their time on patrol – with just over 1% of their time spent on foot in the community.[23]

Safer neighbourhood teams – which vary locally in size, powers and jurisdiction (the Metropolitan Police have one team per ward, generally consisting of one sergeant, two fully sworn officers and three community support officers) – were introduced as a counterbalancing tier of policing, largely free from central control. As such they have increased time for community interaction, partnership work, street patrol (community support officers on average spend 75% of their time on patrol) and therefore visibility. They also report having increased discretion to solve locally identified problems with flexible responses. These teams are specifically mandated to communicate and work directly with their stakeholders: local people, community organisations, crime-

and-disorder local partnerships and local councils. These stakeholders set the agenda and priorities for local teams – often including addressing problems that do not directly affect crime or disorder, such as working with councils to establish facilities for children or adolescents.

Crucially, safer neighbourhood teams incorporate simple but essential mechanisms that give local people a seat at the table as stakeholders, directly involved in setting priorities for, and evaluation of, their local team.

The benefits of user participation

Opening public services to public stakeholders offers an often lauded but seldom tapped potential for direct participation in shaping the services that we use and delivering the social outcomes that we desire. While engaging service users in new ways has long been considered desirable, it has proven extremely difficult to realise in practice.

There have been a number of reasons for this. Genuinely treating the public as partners requires, by its very nature, flexibility in the way services are delivered. One prerequisite for developing partnerships between the front-line and the public is sufficient autonomy for the front-line to respond to demand. Structures which create excessive aversion to risk or overly pressurise performance at the expense of personal relationships render user-engagement meaningless.

The most immediate benefit of public participation is a reduction in the cost of inputs (such as labour). For this reason, many public services have made use of volunteers throughout their history – a practice common in, for example, nursing and fire-fighting.[24] The value of these contributions is enormous: according to Carers UK, volunteer carers alone save the state £87 billion per year – more than the entire NHS budget.[25]

However, public involvement improves services not just at a delivery level, but also at the level of design, decision and evaluation. There is a strong demand on the supply side for meaningful partnerships with the public towards the co-production of services. For example, as part of a recent initiative, Diabetes UK had 60 expressions of interest and 31 applications for three pilot programmes aimed at involving users in decision-making.[26]

What is needed is a system that will give the public, as individuals and as client groups, a literal stake in their service providers. The state must enable new associations of service-users, community members, voluntary contributors and existing social organisations to take ownership of their services, as partners with direct influence over providers.

When the Sure Start programme was first implemented in 1998, it was to feature 200 local programmes, concentrated in deprived areas, but with participation not confined to poor families. The initial aim of Sure Start was to blend core programmes of early education, play and health (child and maternal), with a view to reaching out to families who might initially be inclined to shun services offered. In recognition of the fundamental role each individual associated with the programme had in tailoring services to best suit their specific community, local projects were granted relative autonomy, with user involvement in decision-making a crucial ingredient, allowing the possibility of extra services such as debt counselling and benefits advice to be added if there was felt to be a demand on the ground.

The initial structure of Sure Start was a partnership between statutory agencies (local councils and primary care trusts) and the voluntary and private sectors, with funding ring-fenced and guaranteed for ten years. The principal focus was child development, building on extensive research that suggested outcomes for children from disadvantaged backgrounds were to a large extent influenced by early-childhood experiences. Because it was predominantly operating in deprived areas, with the associated difficulties in parent participation, Sure Start was initially run on community development principles, structured to allow local people to participate fully in determining content and management, realising that without local input, the scheme ran the risk of being perceived by parents as another quick-fix initiative from Whitehall. Because of the time needed to persuade sceptical parents to become involved, the programmes developed relatively slowly. As a result, centres began to lose their autonomy as their services became more uniform, with directives being set by the centre. The Department for Work and Pensions began to wield an increasing influence as Sure Start centres evolved into places simply offering childcare so mothers could return to work.

Public engagement is not only about participation in the supply of public services, but also about members of the public taking ownership of their personal and shared social environments. For example, a safe environment can be created by citizens enforcing behavioural norms, acting as witnesses, supplying information and minimising personal risks. Similarly, active parenting is essential to the effective education and health of children and personal ownership of health could lead to a sharp decline in key risk factors such as smoking and obesity

The idea of empowering front-line workers is not new, nor is the idea that user involvement is a good thing. But it is remarkable how little practical headway these two ideas have made in our public services. Why? A number of government policy documents have declared their support for harnessing user engagement and front-line leadership to improve public-service design and delivery. The 2008 Cabinet Office white paper 'Excellence and Fairness' extolled a variety of methods for achieving world-class public services, including: 'empowering citizens not only by further extending choice, but also by strengthening accountability mechanisms and radically increasing transparency ... unlocking the creativity and ambition of public sector workers to innovate and drive up standards in partnership with service users ... [and] less micro-managing and more strategic leadership from central government'.[27] Lord Darzi's NHS Next Stage Review[28] went further, promising healthcare professionals the freedom to establish their own social enterprises, a freedom which has already been taken up by clinicians in central Surrey.

Organisations ranging from Monitor, the NHS Foundation Trust regulator,[29] to the Design Council[30] have stressed the importance of users and front-line workers, and of course the public sector as a whole has a long history of public consultations and staff surveys. Reports suggest the NHS employs close to 34,000 people in patient advice and liaison services, dealing with complaints and public engagement, at a cost of approximately £600 million per year.[31]

But neither the endorsement of the Cabinet Office, nor the signal action of the Department of Health, nor for that matter the work of a raft of smaller organisations, has yet unleashed the transformation that I believe is necessary. This is because it is simply not credible to promise empowerment to staff and control to users when the structure of the system militates against ownership. Real incentive and real reward should be built in to the models considered and an advice and application unit should be there to facilitate and advocate for such solutions. The fact that most of our public services are still owned by government or their corporate contracting-out partners, rather than the people who use them or the people who work in them, sends an unspoken message of disempowerment more clearly than any putative endorsement by policy-makers.

Ownership is the crucial means by which true leadership by front-line employees and real engagement by users of public services can be achieved. When both users and front-line can have a stake – a genuine share of ownership – in the organisations that deliver public services, then the benefits of real engagement will result. This has radical implications for the way we structure our public services and the role that the state plays.

Ownership is a good, but too often in the public sector it is a limited good – ownership is concentrated at the centre, and the centre shows every sign of wanting this restricted situation to continue. Where ownership is given up, most notably when services are outsourced, the ultimate owners are generally not employees or service users but corporates (and typically, because of the nature of the procurement process, large ones). Since there is only one big state and few big companies, a public monopoly often passes to private oligopoly and in neither situation is the employee or end user offered a stake in the company or an alignment of their interests with those of the provider organisation.

My solution is different: the offer of a new power of 'civil association' to employees and users as already mentioned. Any self-organising front-line group of professionals who thought that they and their clients would do better by themselves in an alternative model of public provision would be granted this power. It would allow a group of staff in the public sector to self-organise and constitute a new civic organisation. Crucially the budget (including where appropriate budgets for support services and non-fixed overheads) for providing those front-line services would go with the self-organising association. Thus, if the application to be a new civic association was granted, the new organisation would benefit from the resources that had previously been spent internally to provide the service.

As these new civic associations would typically be established according to how services are delivered, they would offer a powerful boost to leadership by the front-line. The new organisations will put the real needs of service delivery first, and will allow for the stripping out of middle management and for clinicians or other front-line workers to play the leading role. The organisations will themselves be responsible for many of the functions associated with the worst aspects of command-and-control, such as internal performance management, staffing, and even pay. The most illustrative model for these new civil companies (though it is by no means definitive) would be the model of the community interest company (CIC) that was first legislated for in 2005.[32] Such companies are more radical forms of a company limited by guarantee – they have an asset lock that prevents the transfer out of the company of the public assets of that company. They exist in the company for the public good and for no other benefit. However, there would need to be a form of returning covenant for these civic companies, so that if the company failed the disaggregated assets would return to the centre. The hope is that the cost savings engendered by such organisations would in part be returnable to those companies to enable both service improvement and increased staff remuneration.

Ownership is and should be an incentive – the precise shape of such a reward can be determined later – but I see no reason why some dividend or profit share should not be distributed to company members. One reason why few employees in the NHS have currently applied to run their service as a social enterprise, even though that power was offered in 2008, is that the incentives are just not there and the risks are perhaps too high. Hence I would offer employees an asset lock on their present pensions so that their future was secured and I would offer them a profit-share in the savings and efficiency they were able to generate. If people are to work harder, they should be rewarded. Indeed one of the most notable things about employee share options is that if they are offered just to senior management then their effect at best is utterly negligible or at worst completely disastrous. Research strongly demonstrates that share options only really scale up productivity gains for a company when they are offered to all staff rather than just some.[33]

An additional advantage of structuring these new 'civic companies' along CIC lines is that it enables the sector to avoid the costs and downside of contracts, compliance and auditing. A CIC trust model would enable the whole public sector to structure itself along the lines of a limited liability partnership – where partners at the centre decide the appropriate budgetary allocation without the need for contracts or cost specifications. This structure would allow a matrix of common interest to pervade the whole sector and would prevent sectional interest from trumping shared interest.

However, we should not at this stage specify the precise structure of these new civic companies. We need to be open to the idea that ownership is a diverse good and that the same good can be realised differently by a number of different structures and instantiations. For example an alternative model for civic companies would be the partnership trust model, as evinced by the oft-referenced John Lewis. This also injects as an incentive the opportunity to earn bonuses, the opportunity to make creative trade-offs in terms and conditions of employment, and the incentive to do deals, such as mergers and acquisitions, which the asset-lock model of CIC would frustrate. The partnership trust model of employee share ownership has the advantage therefore of allowing expansion, which I would argue is likely to propagate best practice and create multi-function enterprises that enjoy economies of scale. Trust ownership, I would also argue, guarantees long-term, responsible ownership. With a trust, you therefore don't need an asset lock. In fact, an asset lock will frustrate mergers and combinations, which is what the public services need.

A realisation of our 'power to associate' along the lines of a partnership model would mean suitable public service businesses being transferred into companies majority-owned by 'partnership trusts', that operate for the benefit of present and future employees (and as we shall see, citizens). The emphasis on majority-owned leaves open the possibility of minority ownership by investors, user groups, management and employees individually, or indeed private-sector operators and others – whatever best suits the circumstances. A majority share could perhaps be given to clients so that the crucial notion of co-ownership and co-production could be maintained.

Happily, in February 2010, the Conservative Party announced that it was already adopting many of these ideas and so developing perhaps the most innovative approach to public-sector reform that we have so far witnessed. However, they have not yet taken on board the further suggestion that recipients of services from the companies should also sit on the boards to prevent them being dominated by vested interests.

For the other vital principle behind these civil companies is that they should be co-owned with citizens who use their services. This combined ownership model is essential to ensuring high-quality, responsive service, and unleashing the second force for improvement: public involvement. The right of the public to co-own their services is a powerful way to ensure their voices are heard, and in turn makes them more likely to engage with issues (such as healthy living or self-care) that affect the effectiveness of the organisation. Now it is likely and indeed desirable that the public users of the service will not own that service in the same way that the employees do. As I have said, ownership is a diverse good and can be realised differently. The vision I have is one where users have a veto or commissioning power, so that if the services they receive are not of the standard they require they can veto budget streams from the originating centre. Users can and should be represented on the boards of these civic companies – as commissioners of the services that they are receiving.

The balance of ownership between workers and the public is particularly important. Giving ownership of commissioning or decommissioning to service users prevents these organisations becoming captured by producer interests. The public in a given community are best placed to know what services they want, and empowered users are better equipped to hold public servants to account. The other side of this coin is that the role of front-line professionals in running the organisation mitigates the risk that delivery of services will be inadequate in areas where community ties are weak or where citizens lack the assertiveness to demand high quality.

The closest parallels to these organisations are NHS foundation trusts and the thousands of social enterprises that form from the interaction between communities and people who deliver services. There are, however, important differences. The unit in which the new model is expected to work would typically be much smaller than a foundation trust: an individual care team or benefit office could take advantage of the policy and localise its structure and implementation. And the organisations would be more central to core public services than many current social enterprises. But in spirit the initiatives have much in common.

This does raise important definitional questions: what parts of the front-line, and what sections of the public service can most effectively disaggregate and form a 'civil company'? Evolutionary and behavioural psychologists tell us that there is an optimal size for human group behaviour. Roughly speaking this appears to be around 150 people – any more than this and horizontal sanctioning and ethos building begin to suffer from the old managerialism and the rise once more of sectional interest and disengaged piece-work by workers and staff. If we are to avoid reinventing the bureaucracy and really gain the intensive enhancement that I believe is possible, then our emphasis must not be on scaling up but on scaling down, and bringing this innovation to bear on every locality and every part of the public sector.

That means producing something that can work on the small scale so that its universal applicability delivers gains to the widest possible constituency. Our aspiration should be 'mass micro' – innovation that when repeated across the public sector can yield a macro-gain. What we want to attain is the most effective public sector organisation possible. At the core of the decision process must be the question of whether the public good is best served by economies of scale or by a small, more attentive, engaged and dedicated service?

A public sector reformed on this basis would generate a radically flatter management structure, which removes the artificial distinction between management and professionals, and where workers and employees take up responsibility and engagement with their colleagues, the company's aims and their clients' needs. It would be a structure where peer-to-peer motivation builds ethos and expertise and replaces vertical sanction. The most important operational decisions, from resource allocation to staff scheduling, would be made by those with intimate knowledge of delivering the service in question, and the remit and responsibility to seek out efficiencies. Financial transparency, autonomy and effective cost management would be a company priority and a specific member responsibility. Employees would no longer be de-skilled and de-motivated by long years in the same job, staff could be re-invigorated and enthused, and intrinsic motivation could be fostered rather than taken for granted. The very nature of this new type of association will mean that staff learn new skills and develop a new civic agenda that allows them to innovate, manage and act far more effectively than before.

I have argued before for a massive redirection of budgets and responsibility to the front-line of public services. This itself would be no mean feat, as it requires a complete reversal of decades of employee distrust and the embedding of a centralised management as a result. But such an intention, while honourable and right, is insufficient to deliver what is needed. Delegated budgets remain a vague platitude and an unfulfilled promise unless some real power of association and formation is given to the front-line so that it can disaggregate its budget and assume power and cost responsibility for public-service delivery without asking the permission of the centre. This proposed reform offers the shift of power necessary to make this a reality.

In all of the above ways, the principle of association can be infused into the public sector, just as it can into the market. The economy and the state can start to meet in the middle-ground of civil society, such that economic, political and social purposes will no longer be artificially divided, as liberalism wrongly demands – so leading to tyrannies of the purely political and the purely economic over the social. To stress civil society in this way is not to abandon the state (it is after all the 'civil' component in the phrase) but to encourage a partnership of state and society in which government operates for the benefit of social relations, rather than social relationships being suppressed in the interest of oligarchic control.

Conclusion: Why Red Tory?

For many of us, much of what we value is broken. And while some indeed value above all else their wealth, their houses or indeed themselves, in the end what most people value and care about is each other. And it is our relationships, our families and our wider society that have been atomised, attenuated and almost lost over these last thirty or forty years. In a world where some people are so alone that they die in their homes and only the smell of their decomposition alerts their neighbours to their presence, our social recession hits those at the bottom the hardest. But the loss of society knows no boundaries of class, education or aspiration.

For the last thirty years, in order to save our country we have turned to both the market and the state as if each or either could solve the endemic crisis within. But this has come at a huge cost. Under the auspices of both the state and the market, a vast body of disenfranchised and disengaged citizens has been constituted. They have been stripped of their culture by the left and their capital by the right, and in such nakedness they enter the trading floor of life with only their labour to sell. Proletarianised and segregated, the individuals created by the market-state settlement can never really form a genuine 'society': they lack the social capital to create such an association and the economic basis to sustain it. As the state drains power from society and markets descend into monopoly, wealth is centralised and accrued to the corporatist elites who run the present dispensation. The effect in each instance is the same: the weakening and destruction of the social bonds that create the communities within which we can flourish and prosper.

The contemporary political settlement has embraced with equal rigour a social liberalism and a statist authoritarianism; thus what it advocates in the private sphere it represses in the public. How did this happen? The foundations of contemporary authoritarianism were first constructed both during and following the Second World War, when the state became entrenched in the everyday lives of its citizens. At first this was a benign intrusion, enabling the state to become directly involved with the mammoth and necessary effort of post-war reconstruction, but it codified a centralised management and provision of society and subjected society to state dispensation and control. In this way, the state, instead of augmenting the social world as it was, nationalised a previously mutual society and reformed it according to an individualised culture of universal entitlement. Dispensing resources and services became a managerial task founded on a centralised and utilitarian account of need, rather than a locally specified service that could establish mutual and reciprocal arrangements better suited to the needs of recipients and their communities. The citizenry was treated as a homogenous mass to be serviced, rather than a diverse web to be engaged.

By contrast, the generation that followed the 1968 social 'revolution' had imbibed this state-sanctioned and state-supported individualism and, having been emancipated by consumer capitalism from all the pre-existing forms of social and reciprocal bonds, they were happy to transfer the public logic of state-sanctioned individualism to the private sphere of their own maximisation and self-realisation. For this reason the left moved very quickly from an individualised state entitlement to its individualised expression in the market and, with the infinite logic of the 'politics of desire and self realisation' to accompany this project, the new mass bohemians invalidated all things and demanded a world made completely anew. Custom, tradition, family and community were shrugged off as an oppressive limit on the subjective demands of individual agency, as the left eschewed all its former wisdom and continued apace its abolition of society.

The irony was that, with 'society' refused, the state had to step into the ever-widening breach. If an isolated individualism now formed the basis of society, then the state had increasingly to pick up the costs of this liquefying vision. Broken families, failing marriages and rising levels of violence, poverty and dysfunction, all passed out of civic order and onto the balance sheet of the state. As society fragmented, the cost of policing this consequence passed over to government. During the 1980s and the 1990s the agencies of hard and soft social control were employed to recreate the order and community that had been dissolved. In the eighties this was the hard agencies of law and police, in the nineties the explosion in surveillance, from CCTV and DNA databases to the relentless demand for CRB checks and the proposed ID card scheme. At the same time management consultants and productivity targets proliferated in the public sector, and progressively began to dismantle ethos and professionalism in the name of audit and control.

The great tragedy is that, in the unleashing of the freedom of the 1960s, it is those at the bottom who have suffered most acutely. A neo-liberalism in part generated by the left has torn through the social fabric of those communities least able to cope with the unfortunate consequences. The dramatic rise in broken families, in single-parenthood, absent fathers and unwanted and unloved children – all these affect the life chances of the poorest the most.

There has been an undeniable boon in the creation of employment opportunities that comes in servicing this supplicant class. The welfare state in itself is a vast body of employment, ranging from the front-line staff administering benefits to the professionals at the top managing the whole scheme. In essence, the social underclasses have become a product, the careful supervision of which gives constant opportunities both for employment and career advancement for those claiming, no doubt sincerely, to assist. Once commodified, the need for careful stewardship becomes critical, and leads those in charge to prioritise according to the maintenance of their resource, rather than the elimination of it. Herein lies the great tragedy of the welfare state: it produces a managerial class whose interests, however unconscious or unintended, are intimately tied up with the eternal perpetuation of the problem they purport to address.

*

What, then, is the solution? We must restore society, and the individuals who comprise it, over both state and market as the sovereign site of our renewal. Society is more free when served by market and state, and less free when it is ruled by them. Entrance into the market must be widened, to release vast swathes of the population from the servitude of low-paid wage labour. The disenfranchised must be re-enfranchised, and to do so they must have something to trade – one cannot safely enter the market with nothing but labour to sell.

Wealth accumulated into the hands of a small elite is not wealth stolen from the masses, as the more enthusiastic revolutionaries would have us believe. It is the restriction of wealth, a closed shop on capital that confines access and ownership, distorting the market for the benefit of the few, rather than the good of the many. Rather than attack even modes of valid wealth as if we want to level down to poverty, we need instead to open up the arena and manner in which wealth is presently accrued. If we can restore power and control over their circumstances, and open up a path to new assets for the dispossessed, we have a chance of creating a true civil society.

Of course, to facilitate such change we must question the role of the state. A radical ideological and operational overhaul is required. Welfare assistance must no longer encourage passive dependence but move towards independence and economic empowerment through the extension of ownership, not least with the ability to capitalise the recipient's own welfare streams. In addition to which, associations of citizens should run and manage their own commonly-held and commonly-used services. Local people would have both a stake and a voice in the local services they engage with: the state of ownership, and the ownership of the state, would be extended to the masses.

The state–market relationship is symbiotic. As the role of the state grows, it becomes more reliant on the stability of the market – and the tax receipts that provides – and the market then has to be managed primarily for maximised profit. These interests are not wholly economic, however, but also encompass the social agenda of the state, and its maximal delivery. For big business is best able to absorb the cost of the bureaucratic burdens and social aspirations of the state – of health and safety regulation, of ever complex tax returns, of holiday pay, of sickness pay, of pension contributions and of national insurance contributions. Big business is the friend of the state, because it both funds it and is capable of delivering its agenda.

But if society were policed by itself, by shared commitment to social and moral norms, there would be less need for heavy central regulation. And the less the regulatory burden, the easier it becomes for smaller agents to enter the marketplace, and the more momentum gathers behind those social and moral constraints that regulate and make possible exchange. Injecting new blood into the system will initiate a genuine competition that tilts the system away from the rent-seeking interests of the few and towards the more holistic interests of the many.

If the state were to support the independent and the local alongside the national or the global, it would not need to be so dependent on London's finance industry. Equally, the British economy would not be wedded to a single market, susceptible to the unpredictable winds of global finance, but would spread wealth widely throughout the sectors, creating a truly resilient and plural economy, capable of self-sustaining in the face of the collapse of any one particular segment. People would no longer need to leave the North for the job markets of the South. Population could spread more evenly, as opportunities and genuine access to wealth and markets, to careers and the good life, could be found beyond the boundaries of the M25.

For, in opening up the economy beyond the capture of the state by finance, in investing in the citizenry and furnishing them with the assets and opportunities to become wealth creators and not economic dependents, a more diverse and therefore more resilient wealth-creating sector would flourish, bringing back into the fold the multiplicity of skills and talents lost in the meritocratic ordering of society towards the one goal and one aim of City finance. Local economies would bloom as their populations entered into wealth-creation and asset-ownership of their own, in so doing simultaneously adding to the economic vibrancy of their locale, as well as the cultural and associative relations to be found in such engagement – all would be genuinely involved in society, and would have a real stake in both its economic and social health.

We need a sustaining form of social conservatism, for only it can provide the bedrock upon which to stabilise the society it seeks to transform. It must avoid immersing the individual in a formless mass of relationships, whilst simultaneously recognising the claim of the common good over the free agency of the individual. By situating its thinking within the local constraints of culture and tradition, we can engage with society through those shared realities and common identities that unite even the most diverse of communities. This requires a radical rejection of categories now so ingrained within the left and the right, those universalised impositions of abstract notions which have such little commitment to, and thus such little traction within, the societies they address. Rather, socialism needs to embrace genuine difference, to plough the local identities of disparate communities and to celebrate precisely what it is that, for all the obvious multiplicity, genuinely unites commonly shared structures and ideals. This requires a denial of centrally imposed homogeneity, of externally conceived social and ethical norms, of the leftist deification of individual desires: rather, it is to commit to social identities fixed in their mutuality and reciprocity, to accept their transcending nature, and to refuse to vandalise them in the name of individual 'liberty'. In short, the left needs to embrace a communitarian conservatism founded on the notion of a good life contested by the virtuous. As such this conservatism would not be the static imposition of a vested group or interest; it would instead be the old and antique ideal of a commitment to the good life and debate around what such a thing might constitute.

In essence, the left needs a conservative account of society in order to create the vibrant civic space through which its goals can be most ably achieved. At the same time, true conservatism needs to recognise crushing economic inequality and its harmful effects on precisely those institutions which conservatives instinctively cherish. This requires dedication to equity and fairness, to distributed wealth and asset ownership, as much as to inherited culture and ethical traditions. Social harmony does not flow from centrally enforced unity, and social justice does not spring unaided from libertarian indifference. If the health of society is the common goal, then society itself must be valued higher than both state and market.

Is David Cameron's conservatism a real alternative?

The Hugo Young Memorial Lecture in November 2009 was not only one of the best speeches David Cameron has ever made, it was also one of the most important speeches made by a Conservative Party leader in decades. In fact you have to go back to Mrs Thatcher's 'the lady's not for turning' speech in 1981 for an oration that so explicitly outlines conservative ideology and a leader's personal commitment to it. But there the similarity ends. If Thatcherism – however inaccurately – became identified with 'there is no such thing as society', Cameron's speech privileged society above everything else. This volte-face by modern conservatism speaks not only to a truer and more radical Toryism of the past (the campaign against slavery, the factory acts and the extension of the electoral franchise) but it envisages a future that most people want – human association, stable communities, well-being, financial security and the genuine extension of social responsibility and economic opportunity. What does this mean? It means that Cameron is trying to chart the values of the future and is re-mapping the centre ground of British politics accordingly.

If one places this 'big society' speech alongside the one made at Davos in April 2009, you have the essence of Cameron's civic conservatism. Cameron has called for a recovery of society and the refashioning of the state to facilitate human relationships and the building of real communities, and a new capitalism that works for society rather than against it. These two intellectual interventions mark the birth of a genuinely new civic conservatism that privileges human association above the state and market ideologies that have for the last thirty years constituted the governing consensus. If we are to escape the miserable failed fusion/confusion of New Labour's market state where too few of us are really entrepreneurial and far too many are trapped in welfare dependency, then we have to come up with a new ordering of our society and our economy. And Cameron is beginning to offer a vision of the type of country we can become: an associative society that is based on human relationships.

Governance through human association avoids the costs of financing the on-going failure of state bureaucracy, just as it avoids bailing out the rampant self-interest of banking speculation. Why? Because it is the extreme collectivisation of the state that helped engender the new individualism of the society-hating libertarian. As Cameron pointed out, 'The paradox at the heart of big government is that by taking power and responsibility away from the individual, it has only served to individuate them.' We have underwritten the costs of both extremes in our society and both approaches have failed us. In the face of both state and market failure, we need something else, and that is the economy of groups and the ethos and values that inform them. It is not accidental that this year's Nobel Prize in economics went to Elinor Ostrom who analysed how group activity, formation and ethos help to create sustainable and successful economic practices.

A cogent critique of Cameron's position has always been that all this society stuff is all well and good, but how can we get there from here? Surely our culture is too far gone – we have been made entirely passive and redundant by state activity and wholly self-advancing and individualist through the market. But if the state is to be remade – if it is to retreat from direct provision to the enabling of association – that is surely going to be, in the initial stages, always more expensive. Though this civic approach will reduce expenditure in the medium term, how can we have the rhetoric of immediate cuts and urgent austerity alongside the more optimistic role cast for the state? There is still a real tension between the appearance of economic Thatcherism and the beginnings of a new Tory political economy. Moreover, some argue that Cameron's approach mirrors the disastrous 'compassionate conservatism' pursued by Bush – where an expropriating political economy condemned ordinary people to wage slavery and depressed and undermined the wages of working people whose jobs and incomes were exported and who gradually slid back down the economic ladder to income levels last seen in the 1970s. After all, it was an alliance between the blue-collar workers who lost out under Bush and the appalled middle classes that drove out Bush and elected Obama. If Cameron is to succeed over the longer term he must drive his economic vision way beyond the Thatcherite 1980s hinterland that too many still inhabit, into a genuine alternative: a new economic model that really distributes wealth and power.

But the radical new conservatism recognises this – it understands that to re-orientate the state from direct provision to facilitation for others requires that the market will also be ordered to associative ends. All of this could leave the Labour Party beached on a statist and individualist shore as the retreating tide of political opinion flows away to something more mutual and reciprocal. Cameron is crafting a politics of meaning that speaks to something more wanted and more needed than welfarism or speculative enrichment: it is the common project that the state has destroyed – nothing less than the recovery of the society we have lost and creation of the society we want. This is the true spirit of a renewed conservatism, and a radical one-nation Toryism, and this is the ideal by which we must judge a future Conservative settlement and the merit of what was done in the light of what was promised.

Notes

Introduction

1 As a concept 'liberal capitalism' doesn't really capture the
extraordinary nature of this alliance between political and financial
power. Nor does the expression laissez-faire capture the current
phenomenon, since in the case of both terms there is nothing liberal
or free about what is going on. Better I think to try to capture the
element of drive and compulsion that is at work in this process.
To that end I shall call Britain and America market states, as
this seems to encapsulate better the current coercive nature of
the relationship between society, the state and the market. See
Philip Bobbitt, *The Shield of Achilles: War Peace and the Course of
History*, Alfred A. Knopf, 2002. I do not, however, endorse all of
Bobbitt's analyses.

2 Simon Jenkins, *Guardian*, 22 Feb. 2006.

3 Mark Mazower, *The Dark Continent: Europe's Twentieth
Century*, Penguin, 2008.

4 John Carey, *The Intellectuals and the Masses*, Faber and Faber,
1992, p. 5.

5 See Graham Turner, *The Credit Crunch*, Pluto Press, 2008, p 26.

6 Linda Colley, *In Defiance of Oligarchy: The Tory Party 1714–60*,
CUP, 1985. See, for example, p. 162: 'In keeping with their dislike
of socially regressive taxation, many tories – such as John Wesley
– urged that road maintenance should be the responsibility of a
county's affluent inhabitants, rather than "saddling the poor people
with the vile impositions of turnpikes for ever" ... tory gentry in
both Gloucestershire and Herefordshire demonstrated a reluctance
to prosecute turnpike rioters. After the Ledbury riots of 1735 some
of the culprits had to be transferred to Whig-dominated Worcester
to ensure their rigorous trial.' Likewise the Whig Mortmain Act
of 1736 tried to restrict Tory–Anglican influence by inhibiting
'corporate Anglican philanthropy' to charity schools. It must be
remembered that the Tory/Whig contrast predates, and does not

Notes

exactly correspond to, the post-French Revolutionary one of right/
left. I am indebted here to Rob Mackey of Emmanuel College
Cambridge.

7 Hilaire Belloc, *The Servile State*, Cosimo Classics, 2007.

PART I: The Mess We're in and How We Got There

1 The Economic Crisis

1 See *Financial Times*, 7 Nov. 2009, p. 1.

2 See http://www.statistics.gov.uk/pdfdir/qnq0908.pdf.

3 ONS, Social Trends', No. 39, 2009, p. 65.

4 See http://www.creditaction.org.uk/debt-statistics/2010/
february-2010.html.

5 FSA, 'Financial capability in the UK: establishing a baseline',
available at http://www.fsa.gov.uk/pubs/other/fincapbaseline.pdf.

6 ONS, 'Wealth and Asset Survey', 2009, p. 90.

7 ABI, 'The State of the Nation', 2008, p. 2.

8 See http://www.mckinsey.com/locations/swiss/news_publications/
pdf.mgidebt_deleveraging_briefing_note.pdf.

9 See for example p. 165 of http://www.iea.org.uk/files/upld-
book307pdf.pdf, or the following quoted from D. B. Smith,
*Living with Leviathan: Public Spending, Taxes and Economic
Performance*, Institute of Economic Affairs, 'The US Congressional
Budget Office has reported that the "typical estimates of the
economic cost of a dollar of tax revenue range from 20 cents to 60
cents over and above the revenue raised".'

10 See N. Bosanquet *et al.*, *The Road to Recovery*, Reform, Oct.
2009, p. 5.

11 Ibid.

12 See http://www.cebr.com/Resources/CEBR/Public%20sector%
20costs.pdf.

13 See Giles Wilkes, *A Balancing Act: Fair solutions to a modern debt
crisis*, Centre Forum, 2009, pp. 30–1.

14 See Paul Lewis, in N. F. B. Allington & J. S. L. McCombie (eds),
The Cambridge Student Handbook in Economics, Cambridge
University Press, forthcoming. For the NHS reference, see
B. Harris, *The Origins of the British Welfare State: Society, State
and Social Welfare in England 1800–1945*, Palgrave, 2004, p 304.

15 Luigi Bruni and Stefano Zamagni, *Civil Economy: Efficiency, Equity, Public Happiness*, Peter Lang, 2007.

2 The Democratic Crisis

1 Hansard Society, 'Audit of Political Engagement 6', Hansard Society, 2009.
2 Ipsos-MORI (Oct. 2009) 'Trust in Professionals'. Available at: http://www.ipsos-mori.com/researchpublications/researcharchive/poll.aspx?oItemId=15&view=wide.
3 Hansard Society, 'Audit of Political Engagement 6', p. 64.
4 Ibid.
5 Ibid., p. 28.
6 Hansard Society, 'Audit of Political Engagement 6', p. 66.
7 Electoral Reform Society, 'The UK general election of 5 May 2005: Report and analysis', ERS, 2005, p. 5.
8 Lewis Baston & Ken Ritchie, 'Turning out or turning off?', ERS, 2004, p. 6.
9 Electoral Reform Society, 'The UK general election of 5 May 2005', p. 7.
10 Ibid., p. 3.
11 Ibid., p. 10.
12 Ibid.
13 Tom Baldwin, 'The hidden election: Parties spend millions on new techniques to target just 800,000 key voters', *The Times*, 6 Apr. 2005.
14 Electoral Reform Society, 'The UK general election of 5 May 2005', p. 10.
15 Electoral Reform Society, 'The UK general election of 5 May 2005', p. 16.

3 The Social Crisis

1 R. D. Putnam, *Bowling Alone*, Simon & Schuster, 2000, pp. 18–19.
2 David Halpern, *RSA Journal*, available at http:// www.thersa.org/fellowship/journal/features/features/capital-gains.
3 'Trade Union Membership 2008', BERR, 2009, p. 21.
4 British Election Studies, in *British Social Attitudes 2006/2007*, National Centre for Social Research, p. 9.

Notes

5 Library of the House of Commons, 'Membership of Political Parties', Aug. 2009.

6 Home Office, *Citizenship 2003*, Home Office Research Studies, 2004, p. 144.

7 ONS, 'Social Trends', 2008, p. 16.

8 ONS, 'Marriages in England and Wales', 2007, available at http://www.statistics.gov.uk/cci/nugget.asp?id=322.

9 ONS, 'Divorces in England and Wales', 2008, available at http://www.statistics.gov.uk/cci/nugget.asp?id=322.

10 ONS, 'Social Trends'.

11 Cabinet Office, 'Alcohol Harm Reduction Strategy for England', Cabinet Office, 2004, p. 4; 'Breakdown Britain: Addiction', Centre for Social Justice, 2006, p. 53.

12 J. H. Liu, A. Raine, P. H. Venables & S. A. Mednick, 'Malnutrition at age 3 years and externalizing behavior problems at ages 8, 11 and 17 years', *American Journal of Psychiatry* 161 (2004).

13 Social Exclusion Unit, 'Reducing re-offending by ex-prisoners', Social Exclusion Unit, 2002, p. 18.

14 Ministry of Justice, 'Population in Custody Monthly Tables 2009 England and Wales', Ministry of Justice, 2009, Table 1.

15 Home Affairs Select Committee, 'Policing in the 21st Century', Home Affairs Select Committee, 2008, p. 34, available at http://www.publications.parliament.uk/pa/cm200708/cmselect/cmhaff/364/36402.htm; C. Kershaw, S. Nicholas & A. Walker, 'Crime in England and Wales 2007/08', Home Office, 2008, p. 76, available at http://www.homeoffice.gov.uk/rds/pdfs08/hosb0708.pdf.

16 Mayor of London, 'Alcohol use and alcohol related harm in London', GLADA, 2003, p. 9.

17 J. Shaw, *et al.*, 'The role of alcohol and drugs in homicides in England and Wales', *Addiction* 101, 2006, pp. 1117–24.

18 Strategy Unit, 'Strategy Unit Drugs Report: Phase One – Understanding The Issues', Cabinet Office, 2003, p. 22.

19 Home Office, 'Unique Scheme To Crack Drug Crime Expands', available at http://press.homeoffice.gov.uk/press-releases/Unique_Scheme_To_ Crack_Drug_Crim?version=1.

20 Children's Commissioner for England, Professor Sir Al Aynsley Green, said, 'The most important cause of unhappiness in children is the threat of family breakdown.'

21 Provisional figures for 2007, published Feb. 2009 by the ONS. Some figures are for England and Wales only, others for UK; see text.

22 Civitas, 'Second thoughts on the family', based on IpsosMori poll, 2008, p. 147.

23 Kay Hymowitz, *Marriage and Caste in America*, Manhattan Institute, 2006.

24 J. Ermisch & M. Murphy, 'Changing household and family structures and complex living arrangements', ESRC Seminar Series, 2005.

25 See Peter Laslett, 'The European Family and Early Industrialization', in J. Baeckler *et al*, eds., *Europe and the Rise of Capitalism*, Basil Blackwell, 1988.

26 See Adam Kuper, *The Reinvention of Primitive Society*, Routledge, 2005.

27 Lawrence Stone, 'The Road to Polygamy', *New York Review of Books*, vol. 36, no. 3, 1989, pp. 12–15.

28 Tristram Hunt, 'Divorced From Reality' *Guardian*, 8 Jan. 2010.

4 The Errors of the Right

1 Barry Eichengreen, *The European Economy since 1945: Co-ordinated Capitalism and Beyond*, Princeton UP, 2007, p 4.

2 See table 2.2, Eichengreen, p. 17.

3 Table 2.3, Eichengreen, p. 18

4 Table 2.5, Eichengreen, p. 25

5 Geoffrey Owen, *From Empire to Europe: The Decline and Revival of British Industry since the Second World War*, Harper Collins, 2000, p 227.

6 In this paragraph I paraphrase Geoffrey Owen's analysis, see p. 208 of *From Empire to Europe*.

7 See for example the conclusion to Dominic Sandbrook's deeply felt and moving history of the swinging sixties *White Heat* (Abacus 2006). He writes in the epilogue quite rightly of the popularity that *Dad's Army* enjoyed from its first broadcast on 31 July 1968 to its final programme in 1977 as an example of social and cultural continuity. Yet it was the very nostalgia of this series, with its deep yearning for social connectedness and stability, that tells you society was undergoing profound and systemic change that the majority did not necessarily want to embrace or even acknowledge. And though history, being a story of progression, always underestimates inertia and continuity – it surely and evidently is not and was not the case that 'Britain in 1970 was still

fundamentally the same country it had been twenty, thirty or a hundred years before' (*White Heat*, p. 794).

8 See Simon Heffer, *Like The Roman: The Life of Enoch Powell*, Weidenfeld & Nicolson, 1998, p. 568. Interestingly, and bizarrely for such a brilliant classical scholar, Enoch Powell seemed to ignore the Roman legacy that the British took most to heart – a civic rather than a racial constitution of Britishness. Powell, who was right on so much, was wrong on race. He was far too negative about the power of Britain to assimilate and persuade new arrivals to adopt and inculcate British values. One would have thought he would have learnt more from the legacy of Rome – that racial visions are always limited in their scope and impact and that only a civic vision can persuade others to adopt your values and extend your remit. Perhaps this was because Powell had the object of his first love, the British Empire, taken away from him. Powell was such a romantic imperialist that the post-empire world of the 1950s, and what he viewed as the betrayal of empire by the Attlee government, turned him into an inward isolationist who as a result underestimated the attraction and global reach of a British civic culture. Enoch Powell was too cynical about what he believed in the most.

9 The figures for long-term interest rates are adjusted for the change in consumer prices in eight European countries, see Eichengreen, p. 278.

10 John Campbell, *Margaret Thatcher*, Vintage, 2008, vol. 2, p. 222.

11 Ibid., p. 208.

12 The economic crisis of the late 1970s was exacerbated when the production of oil from the North Sea turned sterling into a petro-currency. Exchange controls led the pound to rise sharply, from the equivalent of $1.5 to $2.5, which adversely affected Britain's export and manufacturing sector. Geoffrey Howe quickly lifted these exchange controls in 1979, aiming to stop the exchange rate from rising excessively. This would also turn London into an international financial centre by making sterling available to support international lending and investment. Soon after these controls were lifted, the City began to lobby for credit controls to be lifted – which of course they were. It was argued that if sterling could be moved freely offshore, British and foreign banks would be able to use their offshore subsidiaries to lend to the British public. This was – and still is – a massive enabling factor in the resulting credit boom.

13 See the 'Pride and Fall' quartet: *The Collapse of British Power*, 1972; *The Audit of War*, 1986; *The Lost Victory*, 1995; and *The Verdict of Peace*, 2001. All published by Pan Macmillan.

14 See Simon Jenkins, *Thatcher and Sons*, Allen Lane, 2006, p. 148.

15 In the business sector as a whole the increase in labour productivity in the period 1979–88 rose to 2.6% from 1.5% in the period 1973–9, see Eichengreen, p. 282. O'Mahony and Wagner conclude that about 50% of this gain was due to the elimination of inefficient plants and workers from the economy and half was a genuine productivity gain. See Mary O'Mahoney & Karin Wagner, *Changing Fortunes: An Industry Study of British and German Productivity Growth over Three Decades*, NIESR, 1994.

16 W. Hutton, *The State We're In*, Vintage, 1996, p. 67.

17 E. J. Evans, *Thatcher and Thatcherism*, Routledge, 2004 (2nd edn), p. 139.

18 This is visible from Gordon Brown's refusal to increase direct taxation to pay for various social policies, instead introducing the now infamous 'stealth taxes' of not letting allowances rise in line with inflation and making various raids on pension contributions.

19 P. Hetherington, 'Challenging Thatcher's legacy', *Guardian*, 19 Nov. 2003, available at: http://www.guardian.co.uk/society/2003/nov/19/guardiansocietysupplement.politics3 (accessed: 15 Jan. 2010).

20 Evans, *Thatcher and Thatcherism*, p. 139.

21 Hutton, *The State We're In*, p. 71.

22 Ibid.

23 Ibid.

24 Ibid, p. 1.

25 Ibid, pp. 3 & 5.

26 F. A. Hayek, *Law Legislation and Liberty*, University of Chicago Press, 1973–9, p. 534.

27 See Maurice Glasmann, *Unnecessary Suffering*, Verso, 1996.

28 John Gray, *Gray's Anatomy: Selected Writings*, Allen Lane, 2009, p. 131

5 Errors of the Left

1 The Convention on Modern Liberty lists some fifty individual restrictions on, or removals of, traditional rights, liberties and freedoms since 1997. See http://www.henry-porter.com/Legislation/What-We-ve-Lost.html.

Notes

2 My objection to the invasion of Iraq is not on the basis of illegality as I think that this debate is beside the point. If the US and the UK had wished to intervene in Rwanda (and tragically they did not) and sought the approval of the UN Security Council, and if for reasons of geopolitics the Chinese had not sanctioned it by virtue of their burgeoning interests in Africa, would we still argue that any such intervention in Rwanda would be illegal and therefore wrong? National interest is expressed just as easily through a UN veto as it can be through unilateral action, and in this respect voting at the UN should not constitute an ultimate barrier to the moral and political demands for military action. Legality in this regard is a formality that can either serve or frustrate the good and the good ultimately should decide in matters of state action whether military intervention was right or not. International law in this respect is no guarantor of morality or rightness – hence to focus on it as if it were is to get the world wrong. There is no avoiding the responsibility to do the right thing whether it is sanctioned by other nations or not.

3 Will Hutton, *The State We're In*, passim.

4 See Anthony Giddens, *The Third Way: The Renewal of Social Democracy*, Polity Press, 1998.

5 Ibid., p. 53.

6 Ibid., p. 100.

7 Ibid., p. 63.

8 Ibid., p. 15

9 Gordon Brown budget speech 1997, as quoted in the *Financial Times*, 2 December 2009.

10 Chris Giles, 'Lofty ideals give way to thwarted hopes', *Financial Times*, 2 December 2009.

11 John Hills, 'An Anatomy of Economic Inequality in the UK', National Equality Panel Report, 2010, p. 60.

12 Ibid., p. 62

13 Ibid, p. 212.

14 Ibid.

15 Ibid.

16 Ibid.

17 See David Willetts, *The Pinch: How the Baby-Boomers Took Their Children's Future – And Why They Should Give It Back*, Atlantic, 2010.

6 The Illiberal Legacy of Liberalism

1 See John Stuart Mill and Jeremy Bentham, *Utilitarianism and Other Essays*, Penguin, 1987.
2 J. S. Mill, *On Liberty and Other Writings*, CUP, 2003.
3 See Maurice Cowling, *Mill and Liberalism*, CUP, 2005.
4 John Rawls, *A Theory of Social Justice*, Harvard UP, 1999.
5 See Michael J. Sandel, *Liberalism and the Limits of Justice*, CUP 1983.
6 Jean-Jacques Rousseau (trans. Maurice Cranston), *The Social Contract*, Penguin Books, 1968. p. 50. See also Jean-Jacques Rousseau (trans. R. D. and J. R. Masters), *The First and Second Discourses*, St Martin's, 1964.
7 Rousseau, *The Social Contract*, pp. 149–51.
8 Rousseau, *The Social Contract*.
9 See F. W. Maitland, *State, Trust and Corporation*, CUP 2003; J. N. Figgis, *Churches in the Modern State*, Longmans, Green, 1913.

PART II: Alternatives

7 The Restoration of Ethos

1 See Alasdair Macintyre, *After Virtue*, Duckworth, 1981, pp. 6–21.
2 Lytton Strachey, *Eminent Victorians*, Penguin, 1989.
3 I owe this point to Alison Milbank.
4 Mervyn Peake, *The Gormenghast Trilogy*, Vintage, 2000.
5 See Ivan Illich, *De-Schooling Society*, Open Forum, 1995.
6 Jean-Jacques Rousseau (trans. Alan Bloom), *Emile*, Basic Books, 2009.
7 See Luigi Giussani, *The Risk of Education*, Crossroads, 2007.
8 John Rawls, *A Theory of Social Justice*, *passim*.

8 Moralising the Market

1 See Michael Perelman, *The Invention of Capitalism*, Duke, 2000.
2 See Karl Polonyi, *The Great Transformation*, Beacon, 2002.
3 See Luigino Bruni and Stefano Zamagni, *Civil Economy*, OUP, 2001.
4 Ibid.

Notes

5 See Ernesto Screponti and Stefano Zamagni, *An Outline of the History of Economic Thought*, OUP, 2005.
6 See: Screponti and Zamagni, *loc. cit.*; Hannah Arendt, *Imperialism*, Harvest, 1976; Robert Brenner, *The Boom and the Bubble*, Norton, 2002. Though Brenner's overall analysis is questionable, he is good on the issue of unrealisable capital.
7 Bruni and Zamagni, *Civil Economy*, pp. 239–45.

9 Creating Popular Prosperity

1 *Hansard*, 8 October 2008.
2 See, for example, 'Businesses forced to resort to credit cards, says IoD', *Guardian*, 16 February 2010.
3 Bank of England, *Trends in Lending*, February 2010; 'Lending to Businesses Falls at Record Pace', *New York Times*, 18 February 2009; Bank of England, *Trends in Lending*, February 2010.
4 *Hansard*, 13 October 2009.
5 ONS, *Company liquidations in England and Wales 1960 to present*, 2010.
6 'Businesses forced to resort to credit cards, says IoD', *Guardian*, 16 February 2010.
7 Bank of England, *Inflation Report*, November 2009.
8 Bank of England, *Trends in Lending*, May 2009.
9 Fraser, S., *Finance for Small and Medium-Sized Enterprises: A Report on the 2004 UK Survey of SME Finances*, Centre for Small and Medium-Sized Enterprises, Warwick Business School, available at http://www.berr.gov.uk/files/file39407.pdf.
10 Ibid.
11 Bank of Italy, *Annual Regional Reports: Lombardy*, 2005. Available at: http://www.bancaditalia.it/pubblicazioni/econo/ecore/note/ecore05/lombardia;internal&action=_setlanguage.action?LANGUAGE=en.
12 G. Vulpes, *Multiple bank lending relationships in Italy: their determinants and the role of firms' governance features*, 2005, available at http://ideas.repec.org/e/pvu2.html.
13 Instituto Regionale di Ricerca della Lombardi, *Lombardy Region 2009*, 2009.
14 Ibid.
15 Ibid.

16 Financial institutions are required to ensure their services are equally available to all communities and groups. Banks can meet their responsibilities either directly, for example opening a branch or banking facilities in a deprived area, or through an intermediary, by investing in a community development finance institution or a local credit union.

17 Jed Emerson & Sheila Bonini, *The Blended Value Map: Tracking the Intersects and Opportunities of Economic, Social and Environmental Value Creation*, 2003, available at http://www.blendedvalue.org/media/pdf-bv-map.pdf, accessed 20 August 2009, p. 107.

18 'FSA tightens mortgage lending rules', *Guardian*, 19 October 2009, available at http://www.guardian.co.uk/business/2009/oct/19/fsa-tough-new-mortgage-rules.

19 Traiger Law, 'The Community Reinvestment Act: A Welcome Anomaly in the Foreclosure Crisis', available at http://www.traigerlaw.com/publications/traiger_hinckley_llp_cra_foreclosure_study_1-7-08.pdf.

20 Renate Finke, 'An International Comparison of household assets, Special Focus, Economy & Markets, 09/2007', available at http://www.group-economics.allianz.com/images_englisch/pdf_downloads/economy_and_markets/financial_markets/sep07_e_haushaltsvermoegen.pdf (accessed 2 July 2009).

21 Richard Barwell of the Bank of England's Inflation Report and Bulletin Division and Orla May and Silvia Pezzini of the Bank's Systemic Risk Assessment Division, 'The distribution of assets, income and liabilities across UK households: results from the 2005 NMG Research survey', *Bank of England Quarterly Bulletin*, Spring 2006, p. 6, available at http://www.bankofengland.co.uk/publications/quarterlybulletin/qb060102.pdf (accessed 10 July 2009).

22 The Poverty Site, 'UK Incomes: Inequality', available at http://www.poverty.org.uk/09/index.shtml?2 (accessed 15 Sept. 2009).

23 Chris Leslie and Alex Hood, 'Circling the loan sharks: Predatory lending in the recession and the emerging role for local government', NLGN, 2009, p. 8.

24 Centre for Cities, 'Cities Outlook 2010', p. 7; available at http://www.centreforcities.org/assets/files/10-01-15%20Cities%20Outlook%202010.pdf (accessed 5 Feb. 2010).

Notes

25 Heather Stewart, 'Recession widens gap between strong and weak regions, report finds', *Guardian*, 18 Jan. 2010, available at http://www.guardian.co.uk/business/2010/jan/18/recession-widens-gap-regions (accessed 4 Feb. 2010).

26 Ibid.

27 According to the government, in 2006–7 there were 3 million adults (13% of the adult population) without a bank account, and this rises to 35% in deprived areas. It had increased by 100,000 on the previous year, and many predict this rise will continue.

28 See the authors' briefing on this report at http://www.savethechildren.org.uk/en/docs/poverty_briefing.pdf.

29 ONS Website, pub. 2004, sources quoted:Citizenship Survey, Home Office British Household Panel Survey, Institute for Social and Economic Research, http://www.statistics.gov.uk/cci/nugget.asp?id=1008 (accessed 10 July 2009)

30 See for example, Richard Wilkinson & Kate Pickett, *The Spirit Level: Why More Equal Societies Almost Always Do Better*, Allen Lane, 2009.

31 Trade Union Congress, 'Decent Pensions for All', 2009, available at http://www.tuc.org.uk/extras/decentpensionsforall.pdf.

32 Association of British Insurers, 'Q3 2009 ABI Savings and Protection survey', ABI Research Brief, October 2009.

33 In an effort to compensate for this, the 2009 Finance Act introduced measures to restrict this relief to 20% beginning in 2011.

34 Audit Commission, 'Room for Improvement, Strategic Asset Management in Local Government', June 2009, p. 6.

35 Ibid.

36 BBC News, 'Community Hospital Site is Sold', 12 Apr. 2006, available at http://news.bbc.co.uk/1/hi/england/gloucestershire/4902052.stm.

37 Audit Commission, 'Room for Improvement, p. 10.

38 The Asset Transfer Unit was set up to provide advice/materials to local authorities and organisations interested in asset transfers; see www.atu.org.uk.

39 See http://www.stroudcommunityagriculture.org/.

40 Chris Hill, 'Community Share and Bond Issues: The sharpest tool in the box', Development Trust Association, 2007, p. 7.

41 See http://www.slaithwaite.coop/.

42 DTA, 'Community Allowance Briefing', Sept. 2008.

43 See George Kelling & James Wilson, 'Broken Windows', *The Atlantic*, Mar. 1982, available at http://www.theatlantic.com/doc/198203/broken-windows.

44 Associated Press, 'Buildings levelled to avoid rates', 22 Apr. 2009, available at http://www.directlineforbusiness.co.uk/news/2009/april/buildings-levelled-to-avoid-rates.htm (accessed 7 July 2009).

45 Calculated 18 Sept. 2009 using www.lloydstsb.com.

46 Calculated 18 Sept. 2009 using www.halifax.co.uk.

47 Calculated 18 Sept. 2009 using www.lenderscompared.org.uk.

48 Financial Inclusion Taskforce Working Group estimate, 'Towards a step-change in 3rd sector lending coverage and capacity', 2008, p. 6.

49 Bernie Morgan, 'Hidden Lenders to the rescue', *Guardian Comment is Free*, 11 Mar. 2009, available at http://www.guardian.co.uk/commentisfree/2009/mar/10/banks-lending-finance (accessed 25 July 2009).

50 D. Black, M. Berger & J. Barron, 'Job Training Approaches and Costs in Small and Large Firms', 1993, [electronic version] from http://www.sba.gov/advo/research/rs135.html; D. Phillips, 'Generalists vs. Specialists: Do Small Firms Produce Better Entrepreneurs?', 2005, [electronic version] Capital Ideas from http://www.chicagogsb.edu/capideas/dec05/3.aspx.

51 Research from The Children's Mutual.

52 TISA statistics covering approx. 70% of CTF providers.

53 Low-income families at 1.4% of disposable income save double that of the most affluent group at 0.7%.

54 John Davis, 'The diverse role of financial capability in building future economic stability', 23 Oct. 2009, available at http://mybnk.wordpress.com/.

55 Centre for Social Justice & Local Government Association, 'Hidden Talents: re-engaging young people', July 2009, p. 4, available at http://www.lga.gov.uk/lga/aio/2164402.

56 Quoted in Heidi Blake, 'LGA says schemes to pay students are waste of money', *Daily Telegraph*, 22 Oct. 2009, available at http://www.telegraph.co.uk/education/educationnews/6397646/LGA-says-schemes-to-pay-students-are-waste-of-money.html.

57 Expenditure for the Education Maintenance Allowance (EMA) totalled £600m in 2007/08, available at http://image.guardian.co.uk/sys-files/Guardian/documents/2008/09/12/13.09.08.Public.spending.pdf (accessed 18 Sept. 2009).

Notes

58 David Ainsworth, 'Disagreement over role of social investment bank', Third Sector, 13 Oct. 2009, available at http://www.thirdsector.co.uk/News/FinanceBulletin/944774/Disagreement-role-social-investment-bank/98802E2BC62559A2350431A7D26AAFB0/?DCMP=EMC-FinanceBulletin (accessed 18 Oct. 2009).

59 'Statistical Bulletin: Public sector finances', ONS, July 2009, p. 5, available at http://www.statistics.gov.uk/pdfdir/psf0809.pdf (accessed 18 Sept. 2009).

60 'From Crisis to Confidence: Plan for Sound Banking', Conservative Party Policy White Paper, p. 49.

61 Quoted in 'Money talks when building a bank', Daily Telegraph, 30 Aug. 2009, Business p. 6.

62 British Bankers Association Annual Abstract 2008; figures based on 2007 financial structure, CML Statistics, Table MM10. Figure based on total mortgage balances outstanding, end year 2007.

63 George Osborne, speech, 'Policy making after the crash', 8 Apr. 2009.

64 'Tilting at windmills', Financial Times, 10 Oct. 2009, p. 4.

65 'Households in fuel poverty to hit 4.6m', Guardian, 21 Oct. 2009, http://www.guardian.co.uk/money/2009/oct/21/households-fuel-poverty (accessed 21 Oct. 2009).

66 Federation of Small Businesses, 'Keep Trade Local: Manifesto', p. 4, available at http://www.fsb.org.uk/keeptradelocal/images/ktl%20manifesto.pdf (accessed 18 Sept. 2009).

67 For more information see P. Blond, The Ownership State, NESTA & ResPublica, 2009.

68 House of Commons All-Party Parliamentary Small Shops Group, 'High Street Britain: 2015', p. 30.

69 See http://www.localfoodworks.org/.

70 'Village Fuel Pumps are Dying Out', The Sun, 24 Sept. 2009, available at http://www.thesun.co.uk/sol/homepage/news/2652023/Village-fuel-pumps-closing-at-rate-of-600-a-year.html.

71 Limiting how much banks can lend from a given amount of capital. 'From Crisis to Confidence: Plan for Sound Banking', Conservative Party Policy White Paper, p. 6.

72 Bank of England, Financial Stability Report, June 2009, p. 27.

73 http://www.nlgn.org.uk/public/articles/secure-reserves-in-a-new-councils-bank/ (accessed 10 Aug. 2009).

74 'Inside Out 2008: The State of Community Development Finance', CDFA, May 2009, p. 2.

75 Quoted by Local Government Association, http://www.lga.gov.uk/
    lga/core/page.do?pageId=1739811 (accessed 13 Aug. 09).

76 As of 7 Oct. 2008.

77 http://www.nlgn.org.uk/public/articles/secure-reserves-in-a-new-
    councils-bank/ (accessed 10 Aug. 2009).

78 World Economic Forum, 'Blended Value Investing: Capital
    Opportunities for Social and Environmental Impact', Mar. 2006,
    p. 20, available at http://www.weforum.org/pdf/Initiatives/
    Blended_ Value_Report_2006.pdf (accessed 01 Aug. 2009).

79 Ibid., p. 66.

80 Kate Burgess, 'Pension funds turn to low-risk microfinance',
    Financial Times, 8 October 2009, available at http://www.ft.com/
    cms/s/0/2bcd04a4-b429-11de-bec8-00144feab49a.html.

10 The Civil State

The original version of this chapter was published as 'The Ownership
State', by ResPublica and NESTA in September 2009.

1 John Seddon, *Systems Thinking in the Public Sector*, Triarchy
   Press, 2008, p. 198.

2 J. K. Galbraith, *The New Industrial State*, Princeton UP, 2007.

3 Douglas McWilliams, 'The UK's public sector productivity
   shortfall is costing taxpayers £58.4 billion a year – in other words,
   not far short of half our income tax is paying for public sector
   inefficiency.' Policy Briefing, CEBR, 23 Aug. 2009, available at:
   http://www. cebr.com/Resources/CEBR/Public%20sector%20
   costs.pdf (accessed 10 Sept. 2009).

4 Michael Barber, *Instruction to Deliver: Tony Blair, the Public
   Services and the Challenge of Achieving Targets*, Politico's
   Publishing, 2007.

5 Care Quality Commission, 'NHS Staff Survey 2008', available at
   http://www.cqc.org.uk/_db/_documents/NHSStaffSurvey_Nat_
   briefing_final_200904233323.pdf (accessed 5 Sept. 2009).

6 Seddon, *Systems Thinking in the Public Sector*, p. 53.

7 Ibid., pp. 198–9.

8 Jo Ellins & Chris Ham, 'NHS Mutual: Engaging staff and aligning
   incentives to achieve higher levels of performance', Nuffield Trust,
   2009, available at http://www.nuffieldtrust.org.uk/members/

download.aspx?f=/ecomm/files/NHS_Mutual_01JUL09.pdf
(accessed 15 July 2009).

9   Ibid., pp. 58–60.

10   http://business.timesonline.co.uk/tol/business/industry_sectors/
retailing/article6976118.ece.

11   'Annual Survey of Hours and Earnings', ONS, 2008, Analysis by
Public and Private Sector, Table 13.7, available at http://www.
statistics.gov.uk/StatBase/Product.asp?vlnk=15187.

12   'Labour Force Survey March 2009', ONS, available at: http://
www. poverty.orh.uk/52/index.html.

13   Ben Page, Helen Rice & Patrick Fraser, 'CPA and employee
attitudes: the impact of motivation on organisational success',
IPSOS Mori/Improvement and Development Agency, 2005, p. 4,
available at http://www.idea.gov.uk/idk/aio/708802 (accessed 17
Sept. 2009).

14   Ibid.

15   'Employee Outlook: Job Seeking in a Recession', CIPD Quarterly
Survey Report, Summer 2009, p. 10, Fig. 4.

16   Marc Thompson, 'High Performance Workplace Organisation
in UK Aerospace', SBAC, 2002, p. 5, available at http://www.
templeton. ox.ac.uk/pdf/researchpapers/sbac.pdf.

17   Douglas L. Kruse, Richard B. Freeman & Joseph R. Blasi (eds),
'Shared Capitalism at Work: Employee Ownership, Profit and Gain
Sharing, and Broadbased Stock Options', NBER, p. 7, available
at http://www.nber.org/books/krus08-1/ (preliminary drafts,
accessed 27 July 2009).

18   Ernst Fehr & Simon Gaechter, 'Cooperation and Punishment in
Public Goods Experiments', *American Economic Review*, Vol 90
(4), pp. 980–94.

19   See for example Grameen Bank, http://www.grameen-info.org/.

20   Kruse, Freeman & Blasi, 'Shared Capitalism at Work', p. 274.

21   Adalbert Evers, 'Consumers, Citizens and Coproducers: A
Pluralistic Perspective on Democracy in Social Services', in Gaby
Flösser and Otto Hans-Uwe (eds.), *Towards More Democracy in
Social Services: Models and Culture of Welfare*, Walter de Gruyter,
1998, pp 43–51.

22   Rajendra Sisodia, David B. Wolfe & Jagdish N. Sheth, *Firms of
Endearment*, Wharton, 2007, p. 16.

23   Home Affairs Select Committee, 'Policing in the 21st Century',
Home Affairs Select Committee, 2008, p 3, available at: http://

www.publications.parliament.uk/pa/cm200708/cmselect/cmhaff/364/36402.htm.

24 Mark Sproule-Jones, *Co-production: a different approach to public sector efficiency*, McMaster University Press, 1983.

25 Lisa Buckner & Sue Yeandle, 'Valuing Carers: calculating the value of unpaid care', Carers UK and University of Leeds, 2007.

26 http://www.diabetes.org.uk/Get_involved/Volunteer/User-involvement/Effective-user-involvement-in-local-diabetes-care/ (accessed 29 Sept. 2009).

27 'Excellence and fairness: Achieving world class public services', Cabinet Office, 2008, p. 41.

28 Department of Health, 'High Quality Care For All: NHS Next Stage Review Final Report', June 2008, p. 14.

29 http://www.monitor-nhsft.gov.uk/home/developing-nhs-foundation-trusts/service-line-management-0.

30 http://www.designcouncil.org.uk/Case-Studies/All-Case-Studies/Design-for-public-services/.

31 See http://www.patientopinion.org.uk/blog/post/2009/06/Voice-outside-the-NHS-box.aspx.

32 A community interest company is a new type of company introduced in 2005 under the Companies (Audit, Investigations and Community Enterprise) Act 2004. It was designed to create a new commercial company structure for social enterprise that would not have the constrictions and limitations of a charity but would have an asset lock to prevent any extraction of value or selling of the company's asset base. See also http://www.cicregulator. gov.uk/.

33 See again William Davies's compelling report, 'Reinventing The Firm', Demos, 2009, p. 70; and also A. Bryson & R. Freeman, 'How does shared capitalism affect economic performance in the UK', NBER, 2007.